DAN **PANOSIAN**   MARIANNA **IGNAZZI**   FABIANA **MASCOLO**

An UnKindness of Ravens ™

Published by

BOOM!
STUDIOS

Series Designer
SCOTT NEWMAN

Collection Designer
CHELSEA ROBERTS

Editors
AMANDA LAFRANCO
& MATTHEW LEVINE

Senior Editor
ERIC HARBURN

AN UNKINDNESS OF RAVENS, June 2021. Published by BOOM! Studios, a division of Boom Entertainment, Inc. An Unkindness of Ravens is ™ & © 2021 Daniel Panosian. Originally published in single magazine form as AN UNKINDNESS OF RAVENS No. 1-5. ™ & © 2020, 2021 Daniel Panosian. All rights reserved. BOOM! Studios™ and the BOOM! Studios logo are trademarks of Boom Entertainment, Inc., registered in various countries and categories. All characters, events, and institutions depicted herein are fictional. Any similarity between any of the names, characters, persons, events, and/or institutions in this publication to actual names, characters, and persons, whether living or dead, events, and/or institutions is unintended and purely coincidental. BOOM! Studios does not read or accept unsolicited submissions of ideas, stories, or artwork.

BOOM! Studios, 5670 Wilshire Boulevard, Suite 400, Los Angeles, CA, 90036-5679. Printed in China. First Printing.

ISBN: 978-1-68415-708-2, eISBN: 978-1-64668-252-2

An Unkindness of Ravens ™

Created by **DAN PANOSIAN**

Written by
DAN PANOSIAN

Illustrated by
MARIANNA IGNAZZI

Colored by
FABIANA MASCOLO

Lettered by
MIKE FIORENTINO

With excerpts from the Abigail House
Illustrated by
DAN PANOSIAN

Cover by
DAN PANOSIAN

Chapter Break Illustrations by
DAN PANOSIAN

CHAPTER ONE

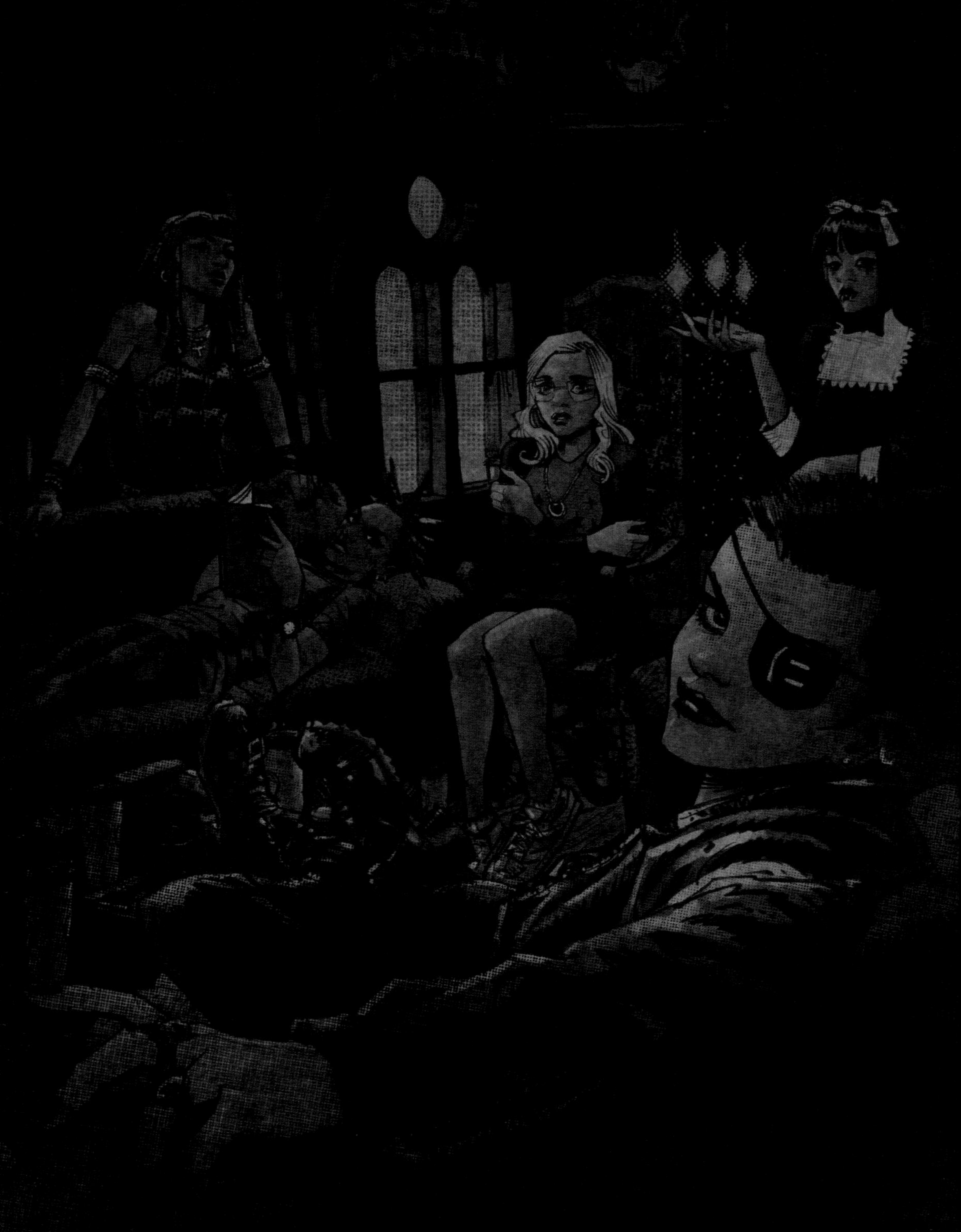

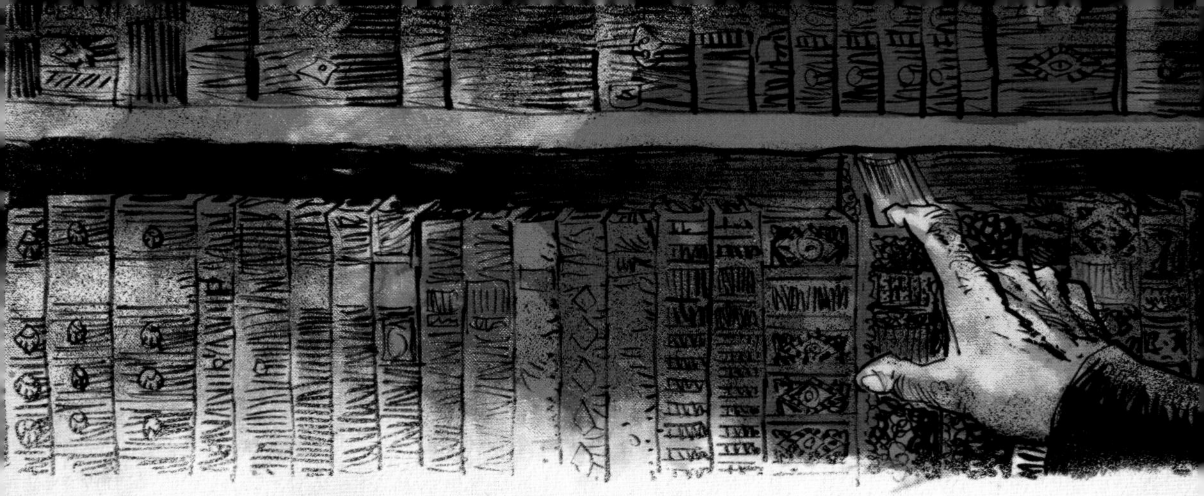

There it is. So many collected journals. Records. Notes. Tomes, some call them. I collect them here in the library of The Abigail House.

These books hold accounts of our history here in Crab's Eye. The ledgers of the past that can reveal secrets about us today. They can shed light on what transpired in the darkness centuries ago.

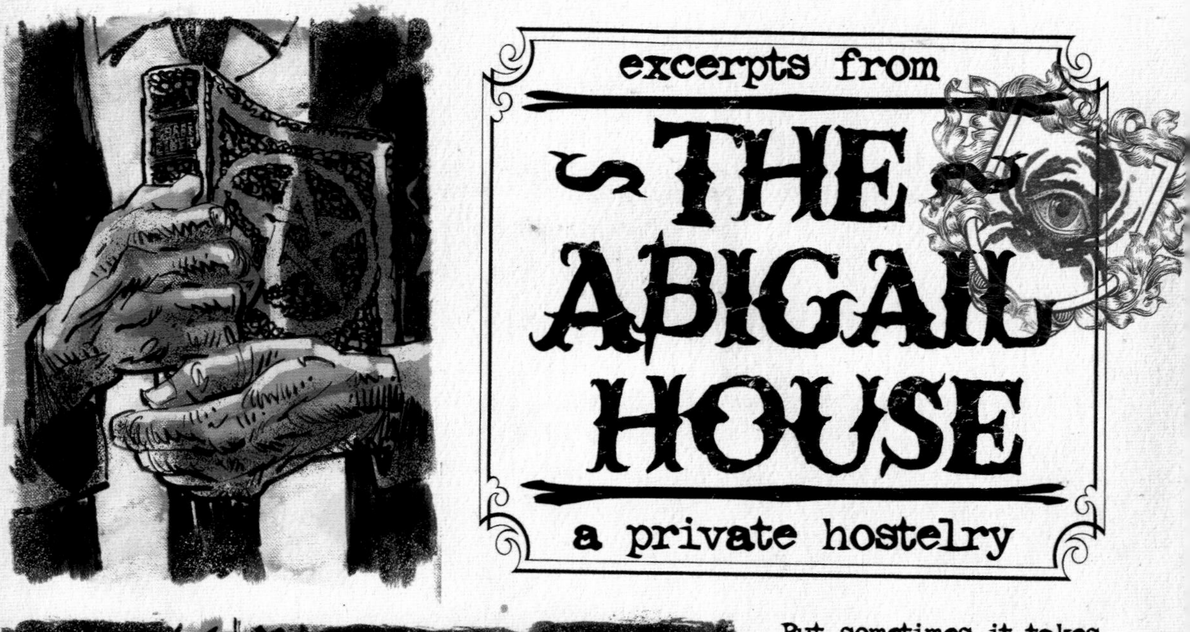

excerpts from

THE ABIGAIL HOUSE

a private hostelry

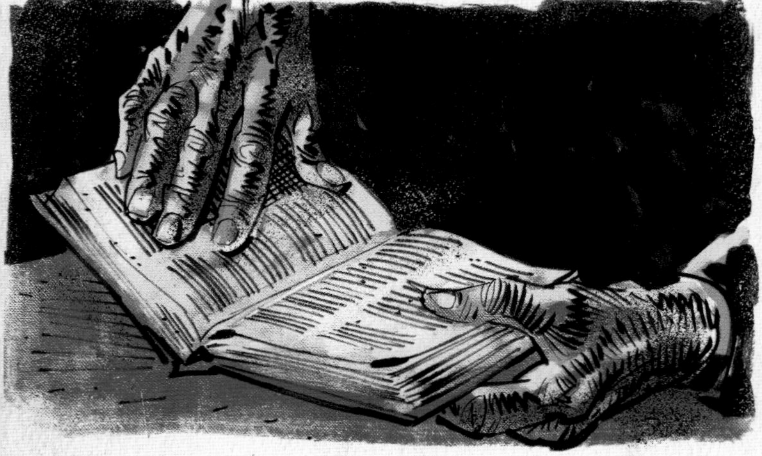

But sometimes it takes more than historical accounts to gain insight about our past. You may need to read between the lines of history to truly understand it. A book can tell you the when and where.

I can tell you the how and why...

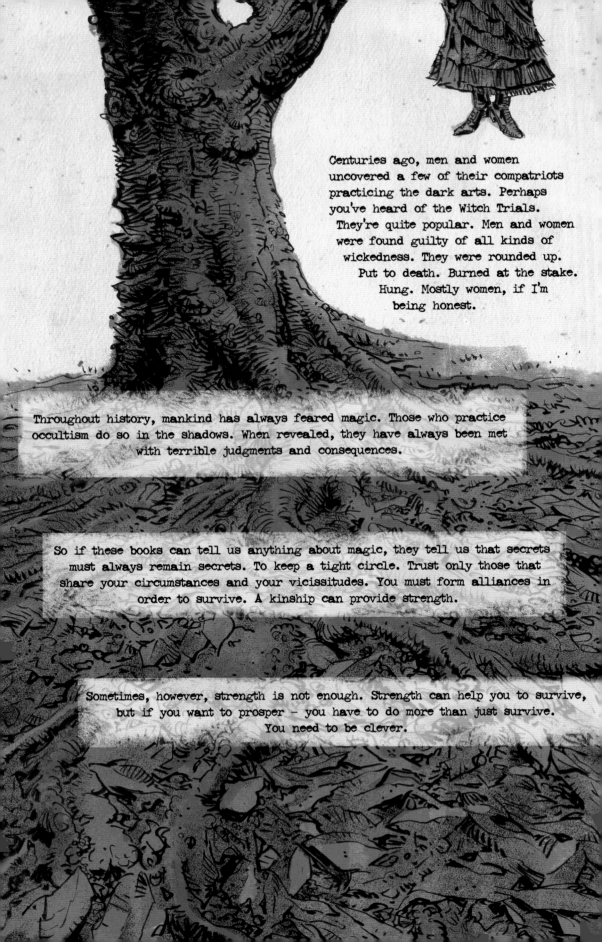

Centuries ago, men and women
uncovered a few of their compatriots
practicing the dark arts. Perhaps
you've heard of the Witch Trials.
They're quite popular. Men and women
were found guilty of all kinds of
wickedness. They were rounded up.
Put to death. Burned at the stake.
Hung. Mostly women, if I'm
being honest.

Throughout history, mankind has always feared magic. Those who practice
occultism do so in the shadows. When revealed, they have always been met
with terrible judgments and consequences.

So if these books can tell us anything about magic, they tell us that secrets
must always remain secrets. To keep a tight circle. Trust only those that
share your circumstances and your vicissitudes. You must form alliances in
order to survive. A kinship can provide strength.

Sometimes, however, strength is not enough. Strength can help you to survive,
but if you want to prosper — you have to do more than just survive.
You need to be clever.

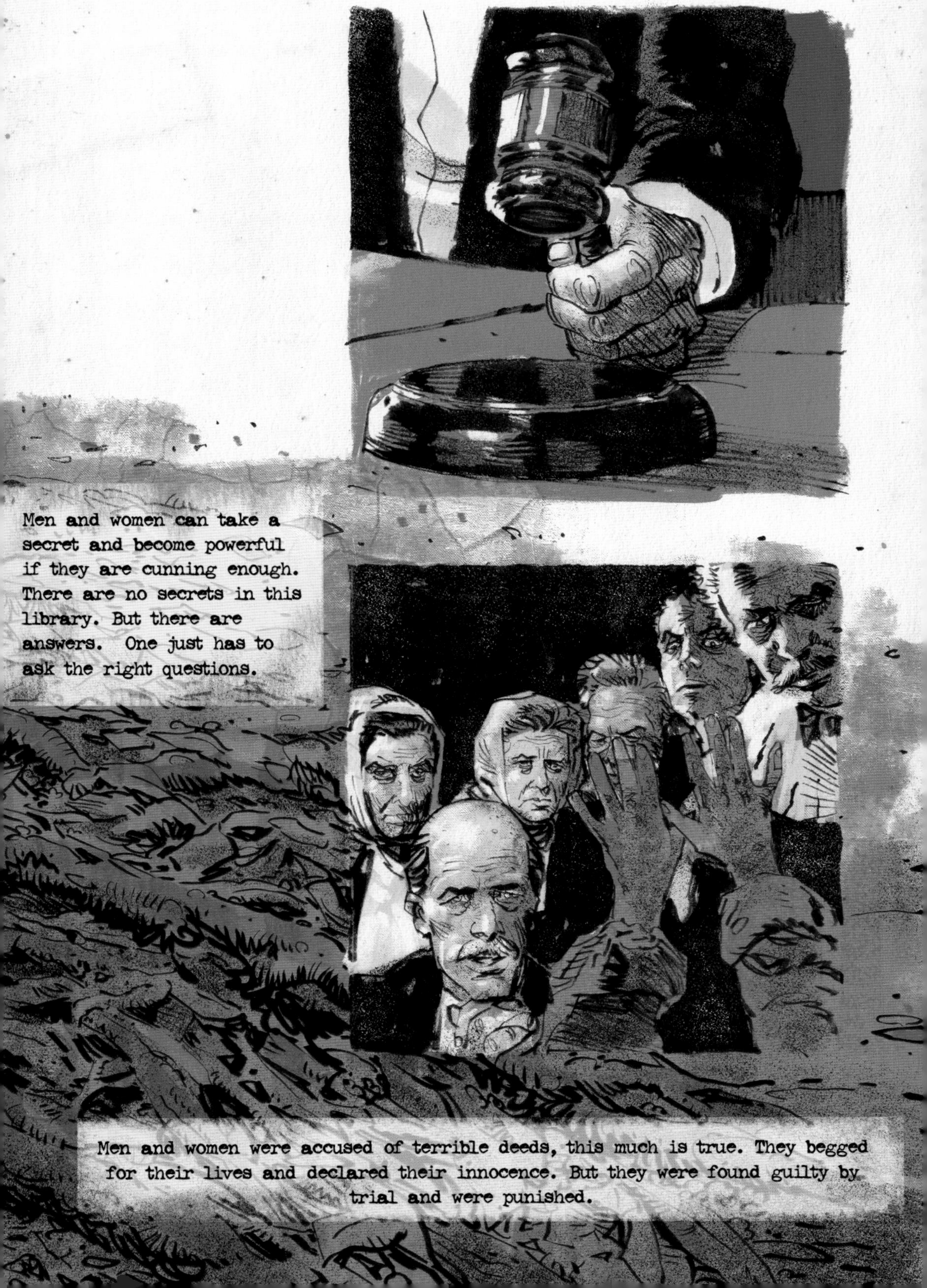
Men and women can take a secret and become powerful if they are cunning enough. There are no secrets in this library. But there are answers. One just has to ask the right questions.
Men and women were accused of terrible deeds, this much is true. They begged for their lives and declared their innocence. But they were found guilty by trial and were punished.

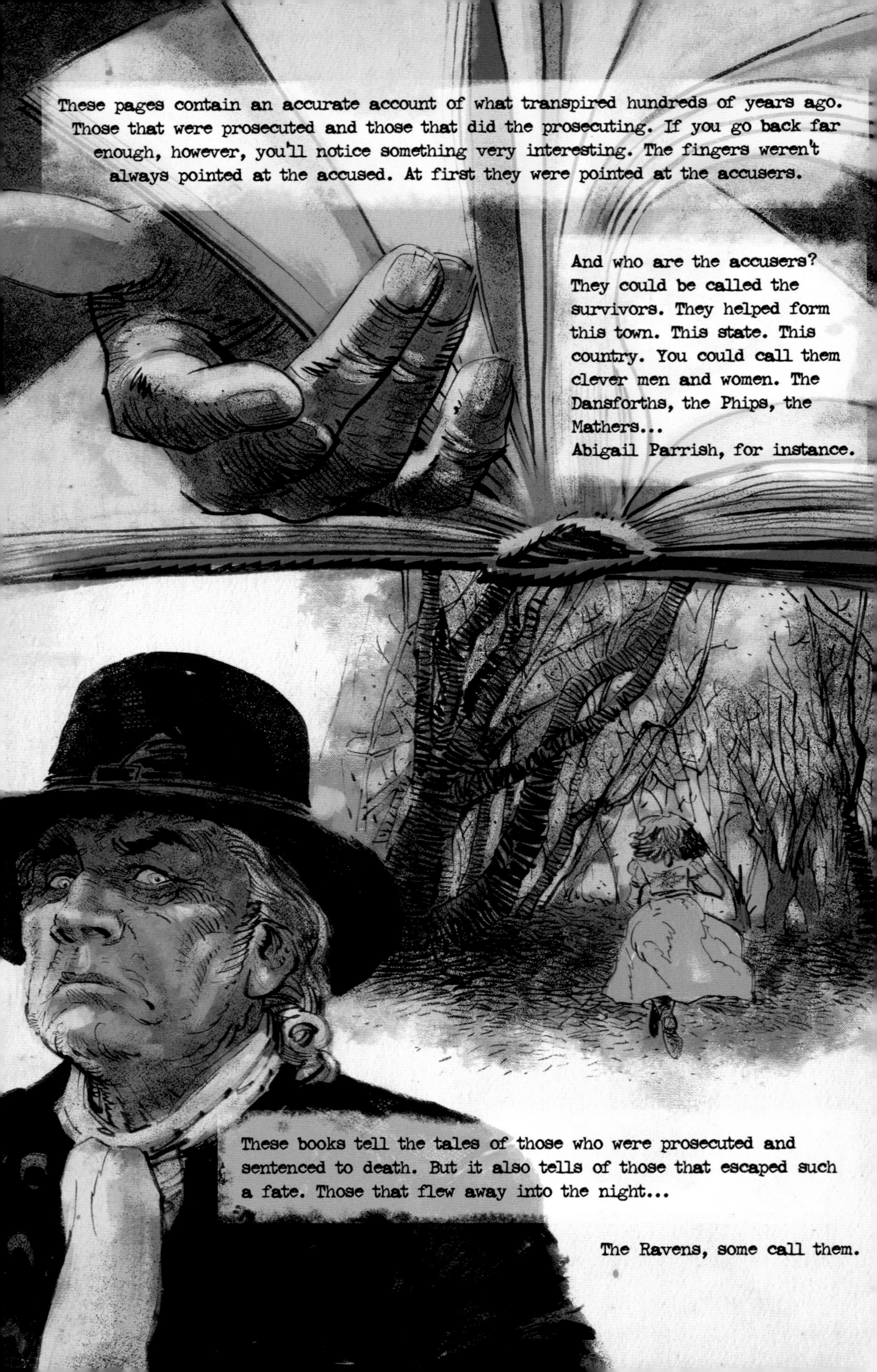
These pages contain an accurate account of what transpired hundreds of years ago. Those that were prosecuted and those that did the prosecuting. If you go back far enough, however, you'll notice something very interesting. The fingers weren't always pointed at the accused. At first they were pointed at the accusers.
And who are the accusers? They could be called the survivors. They helped form this town. This state. This country. You could call them clever men and women. The Dansforths, the Phips, the Mathers...
Abigail Parrish, for instance.
These books tell the tales of those who were prosecuted and sentenced to death. But it also tells of those that escaped such a fate. Those that flew away into the night...
The Ravens, some call them.

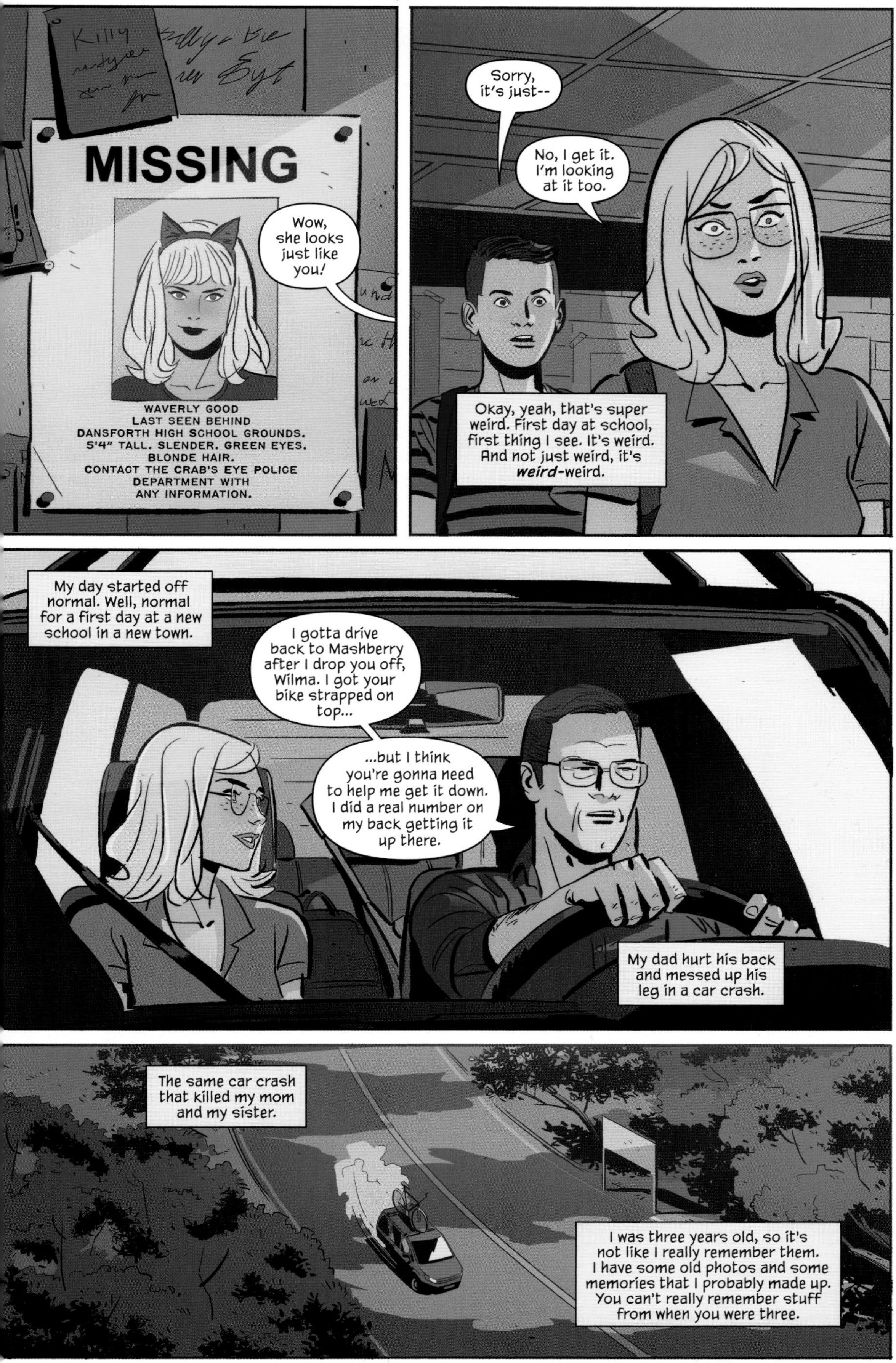

MISSING
WAVERLY GOOD
LAST SEEN BEHIND
DANSFORTH HIGH SCHOOL GROUNDS.
5'4" TALL. SLENDER. GREEN EYES.
BLONDE HAIR.
CONTACT THE CRAB'S EYE POLICE DEPARTMENT WITH ANY INFORMATION.
Wow, she looks just like you!
Sorry, it's just--
No, I get it. I'm looking at it too.
Okay, yeah, that's super weird. First day at school, first thing I see. It's weird. And not just weird, it's *weird*-weird.
My day started off normal. Well, normal for a first day at a new school in a new town.
I gotta drive back to Mashberry after I drop you off, Wilma. I got your bike strapped on top...
...but I think you're gonna need to help me get it down. I did a real number on my back getting it up there.
My dad hurt his back and messed up his leg in a car crash.
The same car crash that killed my mom and my sister.
I was three years old, so it's not like I really remember them. I have some old photos and some memories that I probably made up. You can't really remember stuff from when you were three.

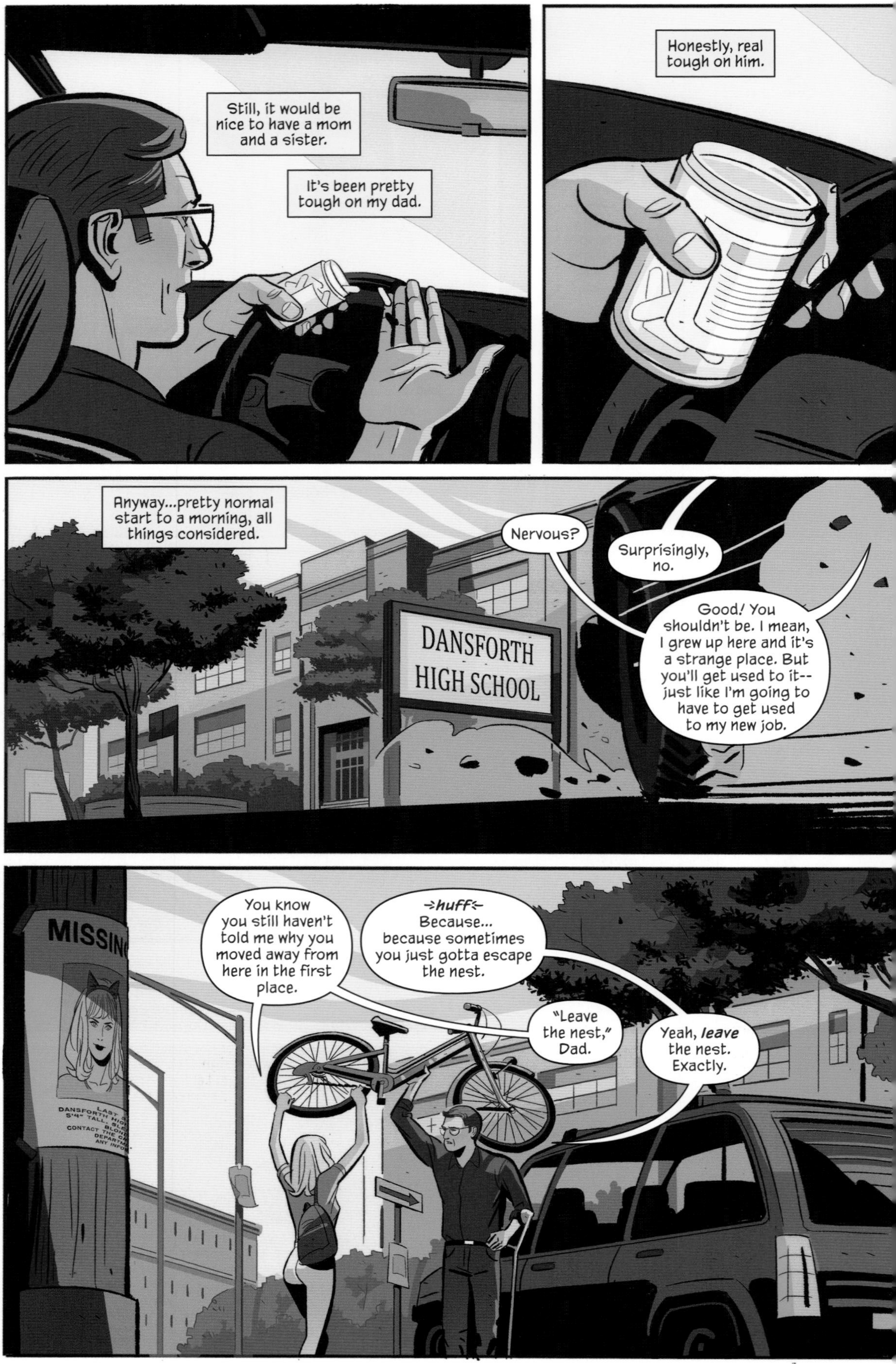

Still, it would be nice to have a mom and a sister.
It's been pretty tough on my dad.
Honestly, real tough on him.
Anyway...pretty normal start to a morning, all things considered.
DANSFORTH HIGH SCHOOL
Nervous?
Surprisingly, no.
Good! You shouldn't be. I mean, I grew up here and it's a strange place. But you'll get used to it-- just like I'm going to have to get used to my new job.
MISSING
You know you still haven't told me why you moved away from here in the first place.
huff
Because... because sometimes you just gotta escape the nest.
"Leave the nest," Dad.
Yeah, leave the nest. Exactly.

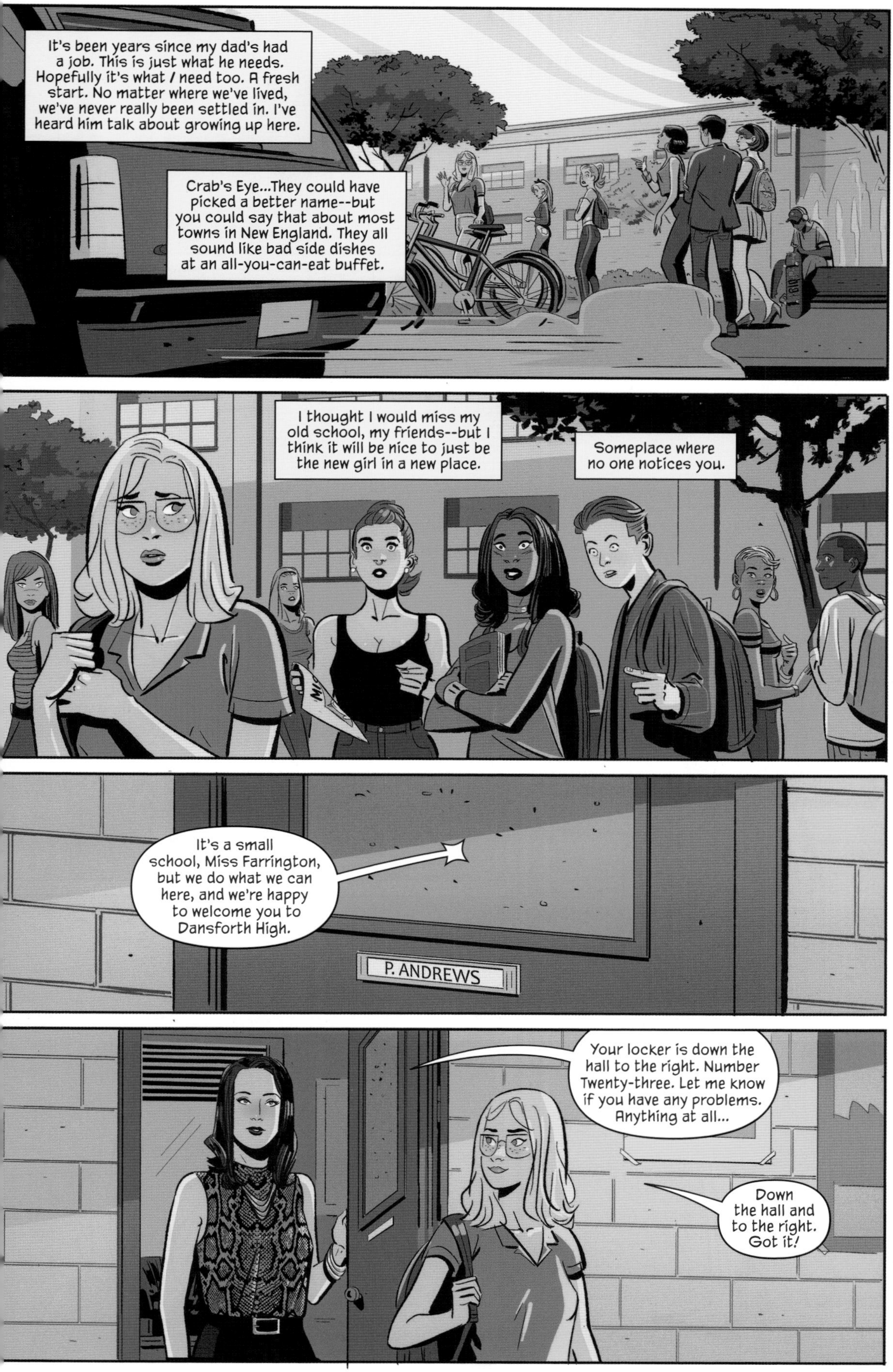
It's been years since my dad's had a job. This is just what he needs. Hopefully it's what I need too. A fresh start. No matter where we've lived, we've never really been settled in. I've heard him talk about growing up here.
Crab's Eye...They could have picked a better name--but you could say that about most towns in New England. They all sound like bad side dishes at an all-you-can-eat buffet.
I thought I would miss my old school, my friends--but I think it will be nice to just be the new girl in a new place.
Someplace where no one notices you.
It's a small school, Miss Farrington, but we do what we can here, and we're happy to welcome you to Dansforth High.
P. ANDREWS
Your locker is down the hall to the right. Number Twenty-three. Let me know if you have any problems. Anything at all...
Down the hall and to the right. Got it!

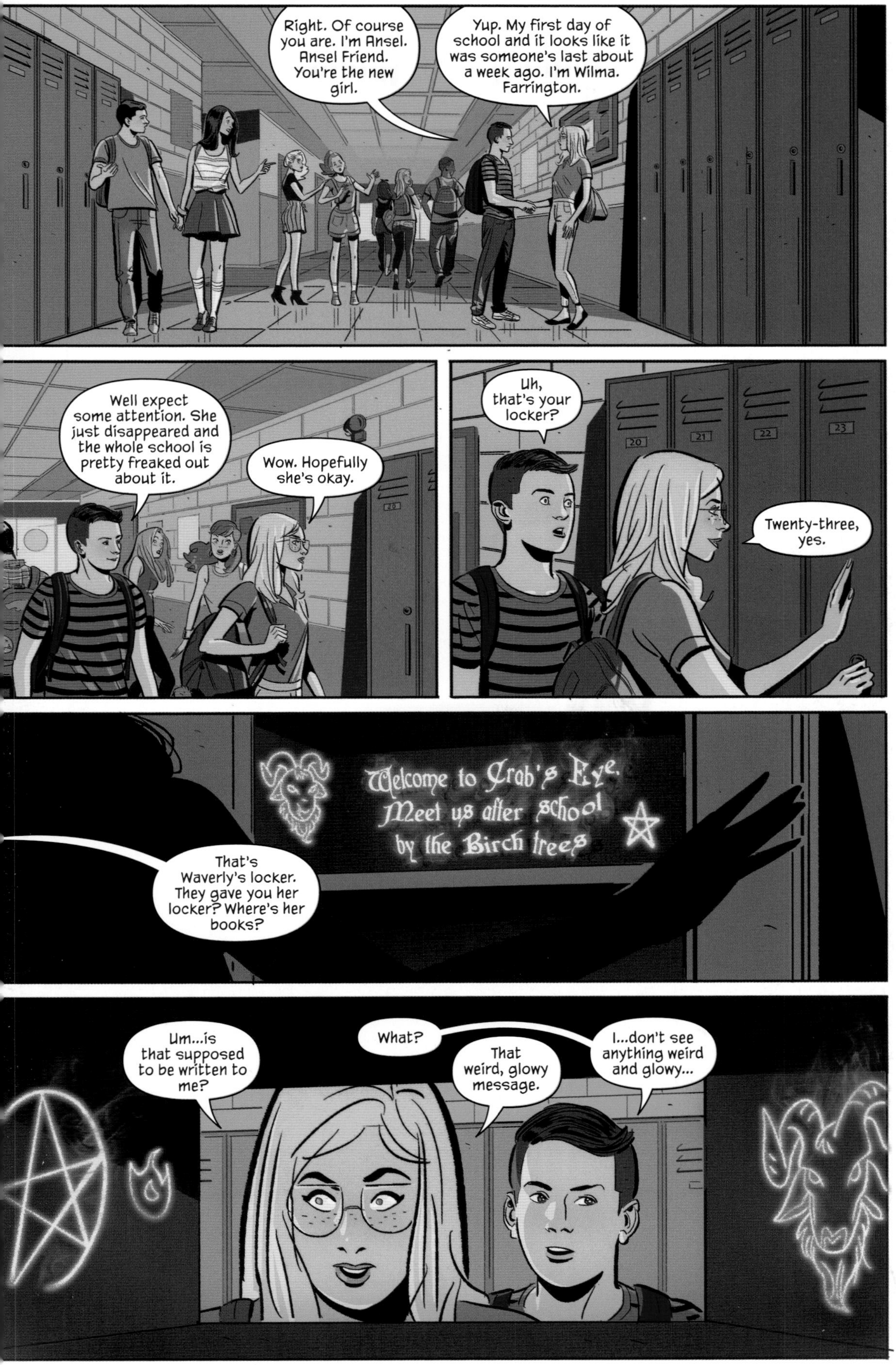

Right. Of course you are. I'm Ansel. Ansel Friend. You're the new girl.
Yup. My first day of school and it looks like it was someone's last about a week ago. I'm Wilma. Farrington.
Well expect some attention. She just disappeared and the whole school is pretty freaked out about it.
Wow. Hopefully she's okay.
Uh, that's your locker?
20
21
22
23
Twenty-three, yes.
Welcome to Crab's Eye. Meet us after school by the Birch trees
That's Waverly's locker. They gave you her locker? Where's her books?
Um...is that supposed to be written to me?
What?
That weird, glowy message.
I...don't see anything weird and glowy...

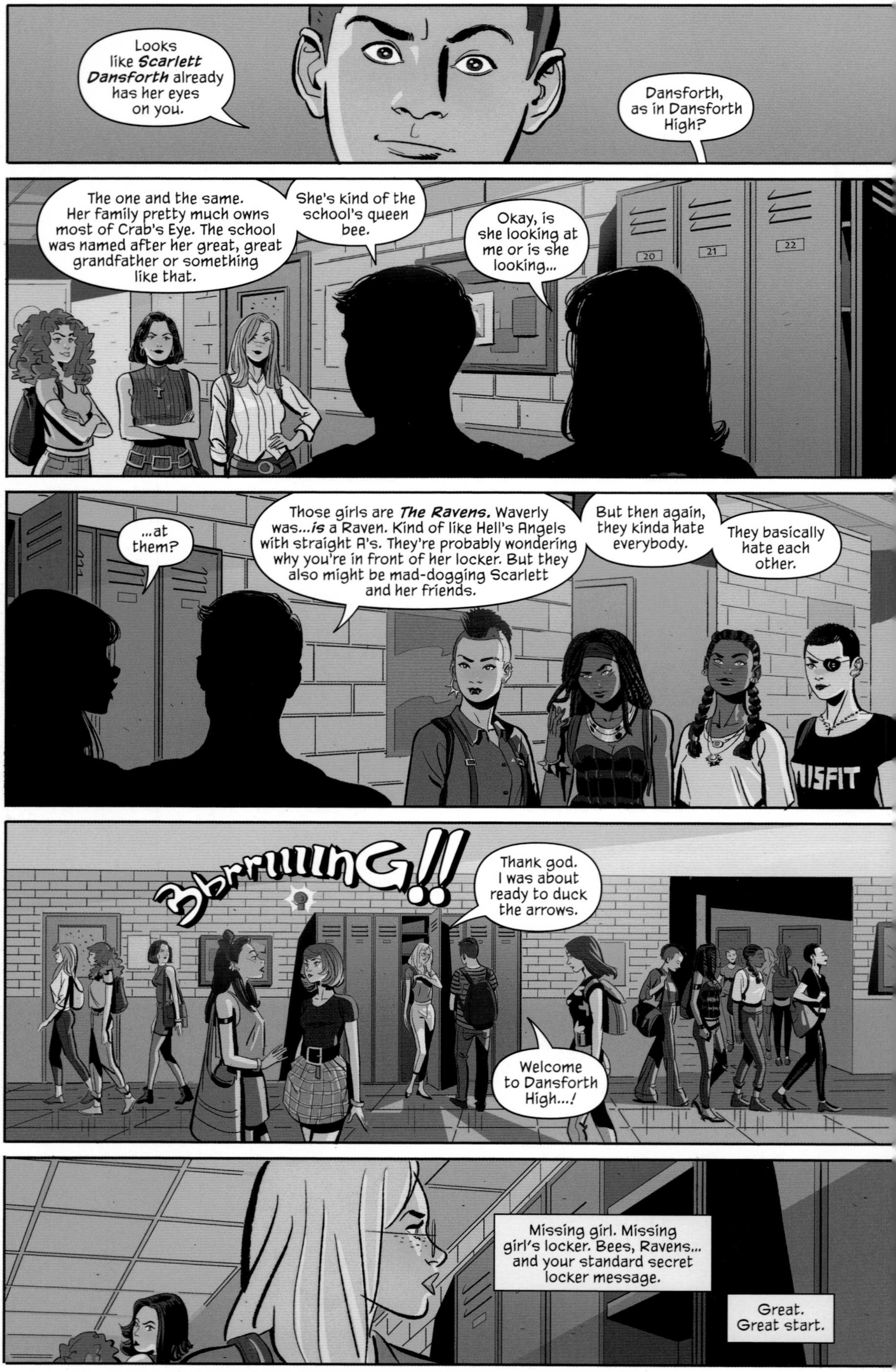
Looks like Scarlett Dansforth already has her eyes on you.
Dansforth, as in Dansforth High?
The one and the same. Her family pretty much owns most of Crab's Eye. The school was named after her great, great grandfather or something like that.
She's kind of the school's queen bee.
Okay, is she looking at me or is she looking...
20
21
22
...at them?
Those girls are The Ravens. Waverly was...is a Raven. Kind of like Hell's Angels with straight A's. They're probably wondering why you're in front of her locker. But they also might be mad-dogging Scarlett and her friends.
But then again, they kinda hate everybody.
They basically hate each other.
ISFIT
BRRRIIIING!!
Thank god. I was about ready to duck the arrows.
Welcome to Dansforth High...!
Missing girl. Missing girl's locker. Bees, Ravens... and your standard secret locker message.
Great. Great start.

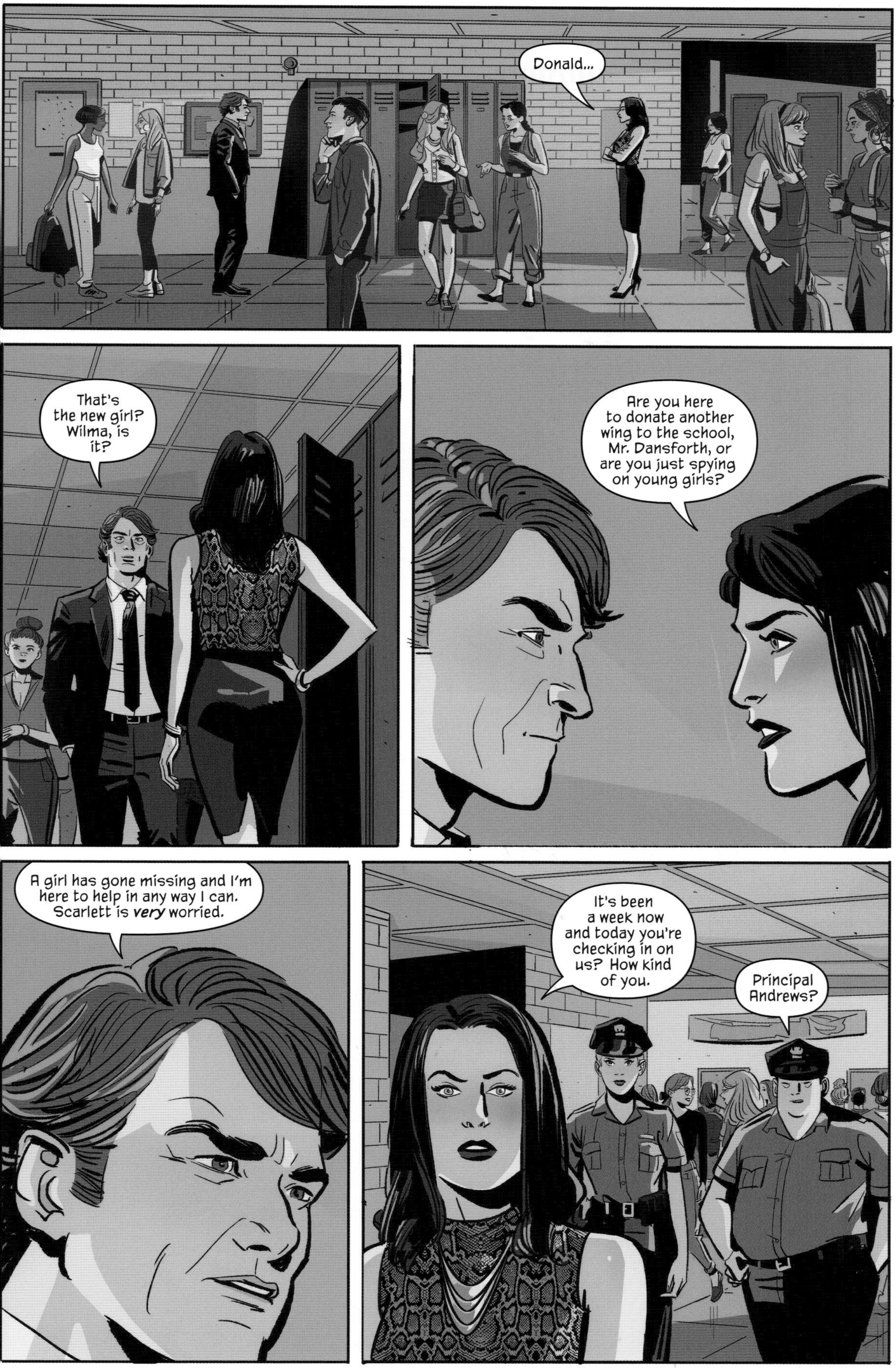
Donald...
That's the new girl? Wilma, is it?
Are you here to donate another wing to the school, Mr. Dansforth, or are you just spying on young girls?
A girl has gone missing and I'm here to help in any way I can. Scarlett is *very* worried.
It's been a week now and today you're checking in on us? How kind of you.
Principal Andrews?

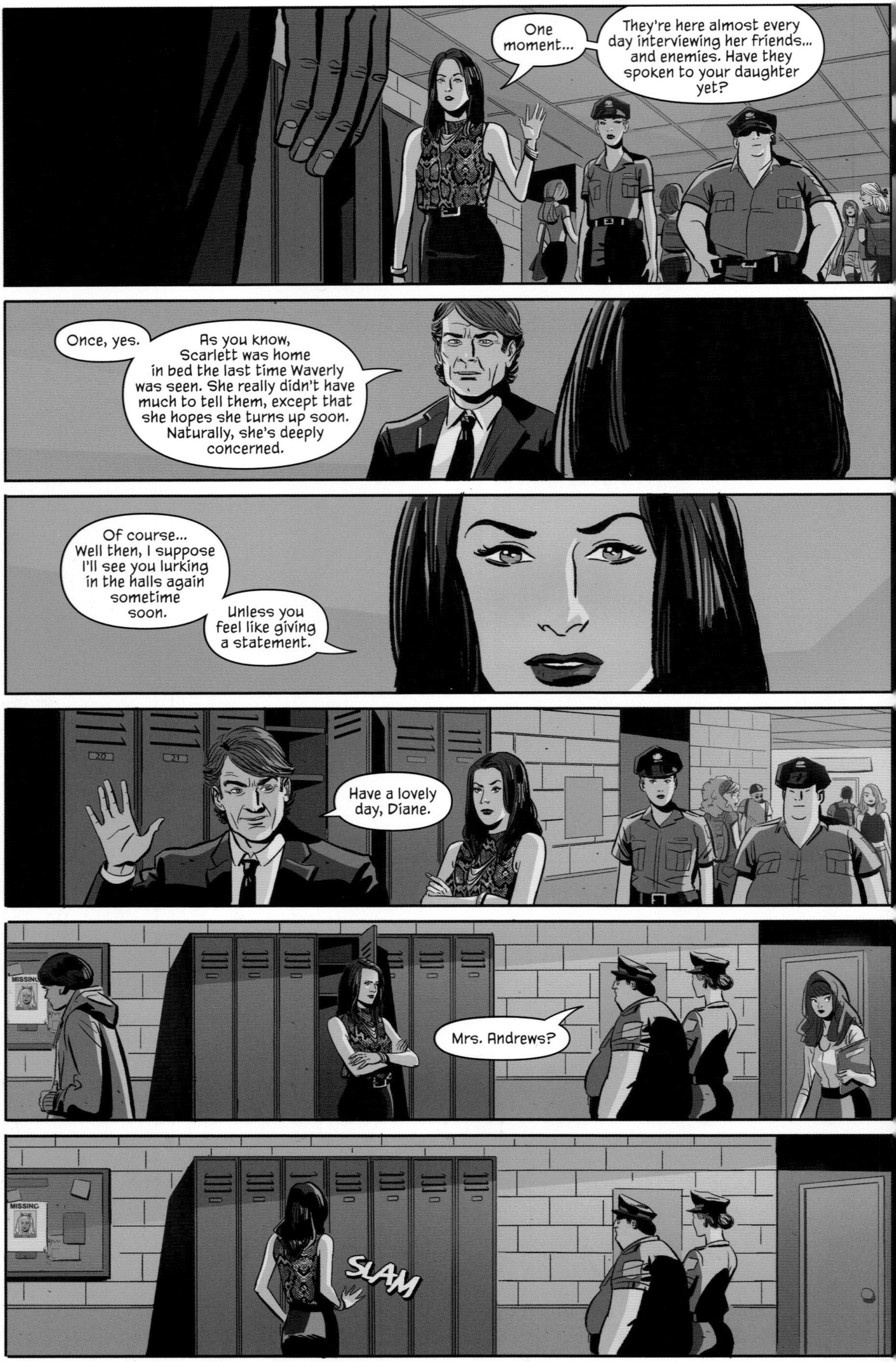

One moment...
They're here almost every day interviewing her friends... and enemies. Have they spoken to your daughter yet?
Once, yes.
As you know, Scarlett was home in bed the last time Waverly was seen. She really didn't have much to tell them, except that she hopes she turns up soon. Naturally, she's deeply concerned.
Of course... Well then, I suppose I'll see you lurking in the halls again sometime soon.
Unless you feel like giving a statement.
Have a lovely day, Diane.
MISSING
Mrs. Andrews?
MISSING
SLAM

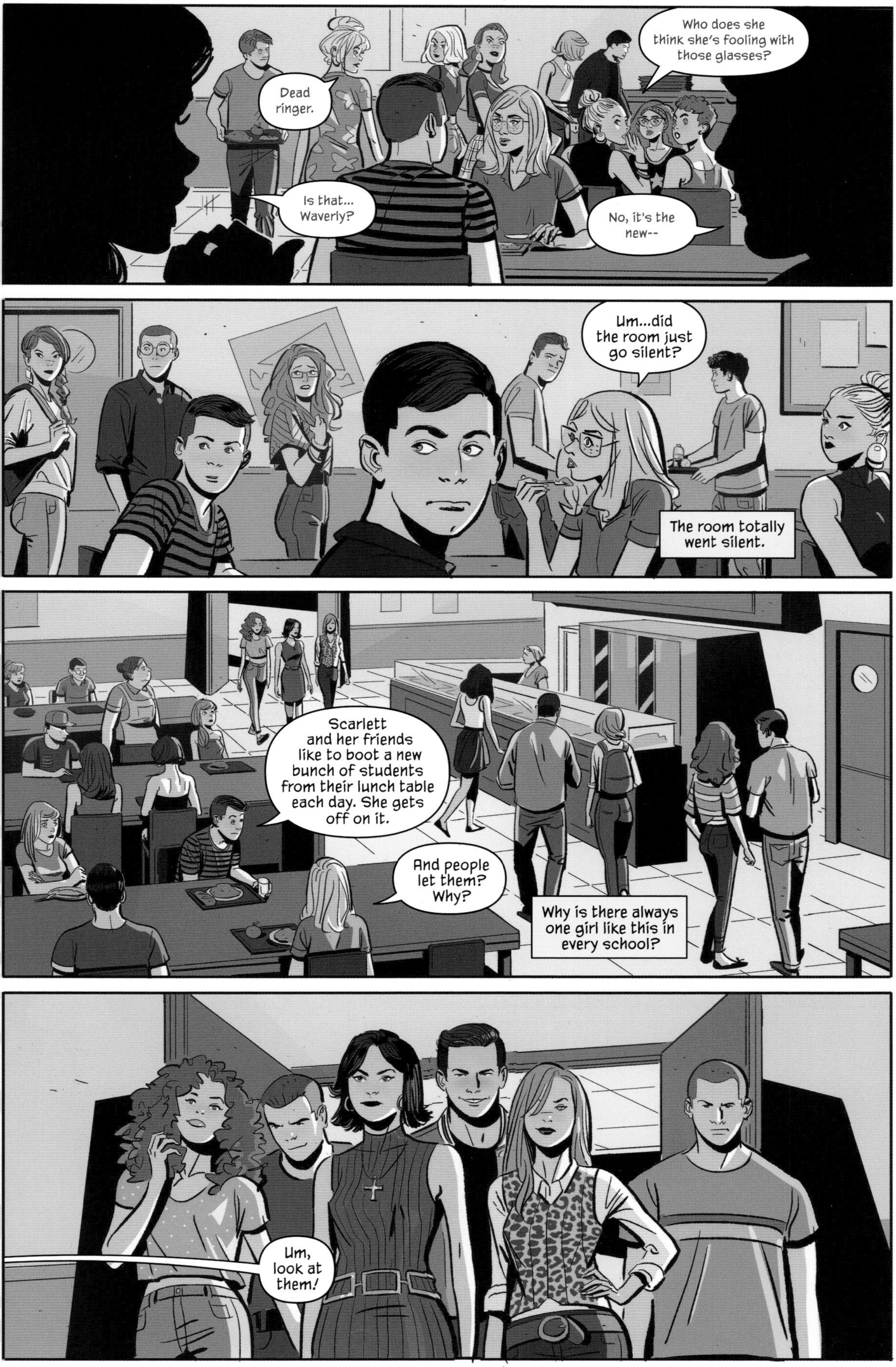
Who does she think she's fooling with those glasses?
Dead ringer.
Is that... Waverly?
No, it's the new--
Um...did the room just go silent?
The room totally went silent.
Scarlett and her friends like to boot a new bunch of students from their lunch table each day. She gets off on it.
And people let them? Why?
Why is there always one girl like this in every school?
Um, look at them!

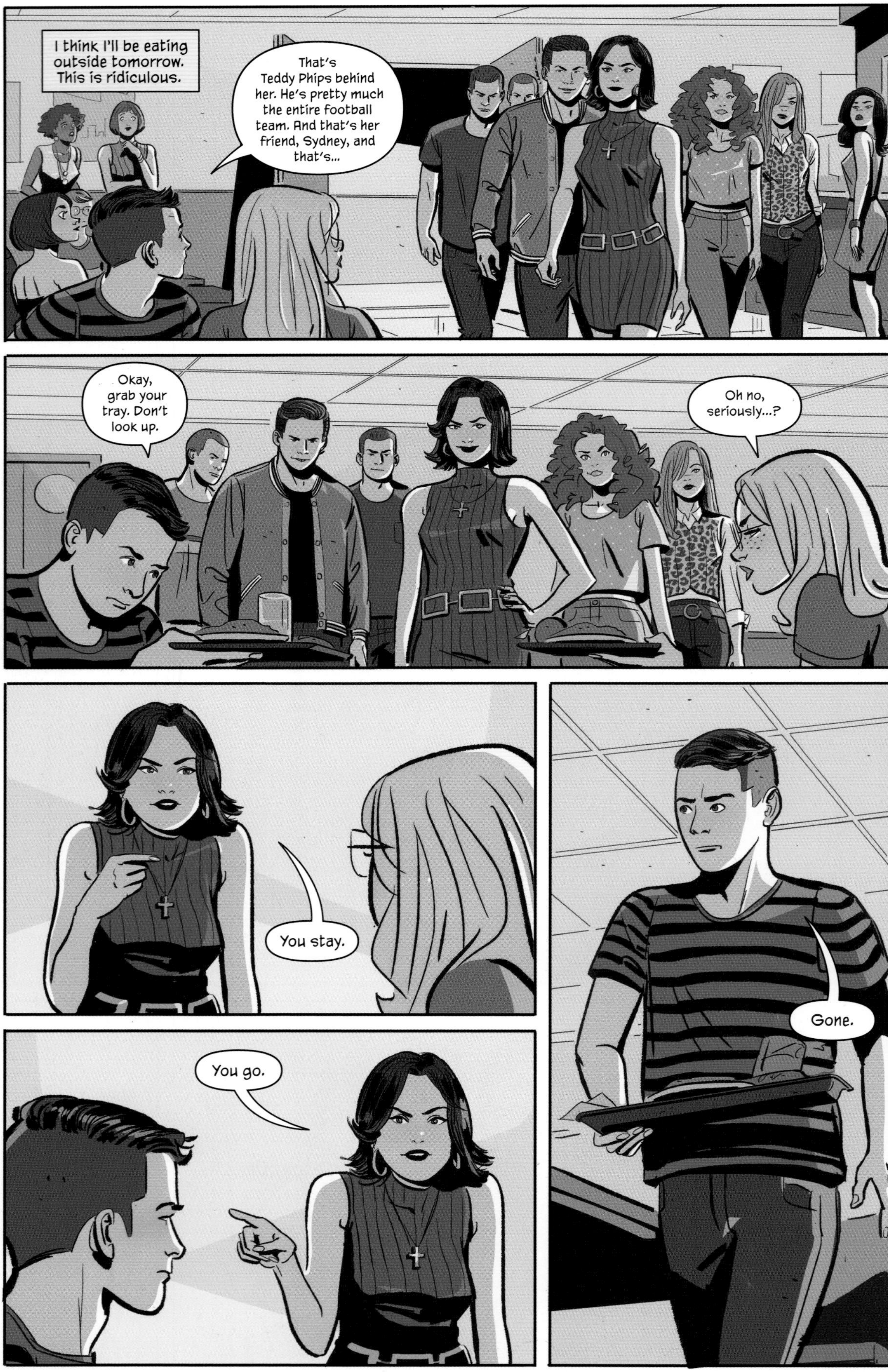
I think I'll be eating outside tomorrow. This is ridiculous.
That's Teddy Phips behind her. He's pretty much the entire football team. And that's her friend, Sydney, and that's...
Okay, grab your tray. Don't look up.
Oh no, seriously...?
You stay.
You go.
Gone.

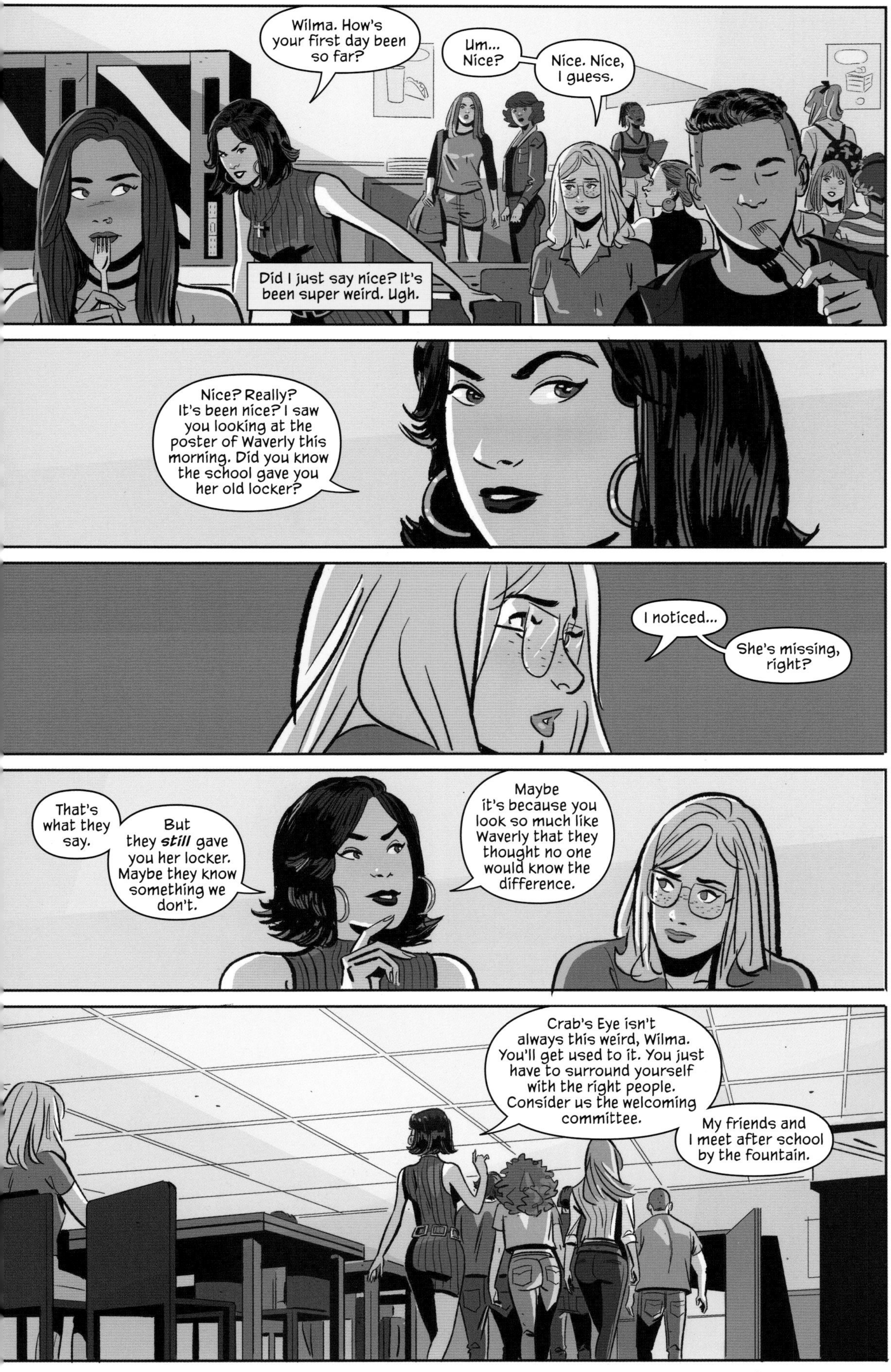
Wilma. How's your first day been so far?
Um... Nice?
Nice. Nice, I guess.
Did I just say nice? It's been super weird. Ugh.
Nice? Really? It's been nice? I saw you looking at the poster of Waverly this morning. Did you know the school gave you her old locker?
I noticed...
She's missing, right?
That's what they say.
But they *still* gave you her locker. Maybe they know something we don't.
Maybe it's because you look so much like Waverly that they thought no one would know the difference.
Crab's Eye isn't always this weird, Wilma. You'll get used to it. You just have to surround yourself with the right people. Consider us the welcoming committee.
My friends and I meet after school by the fountain.

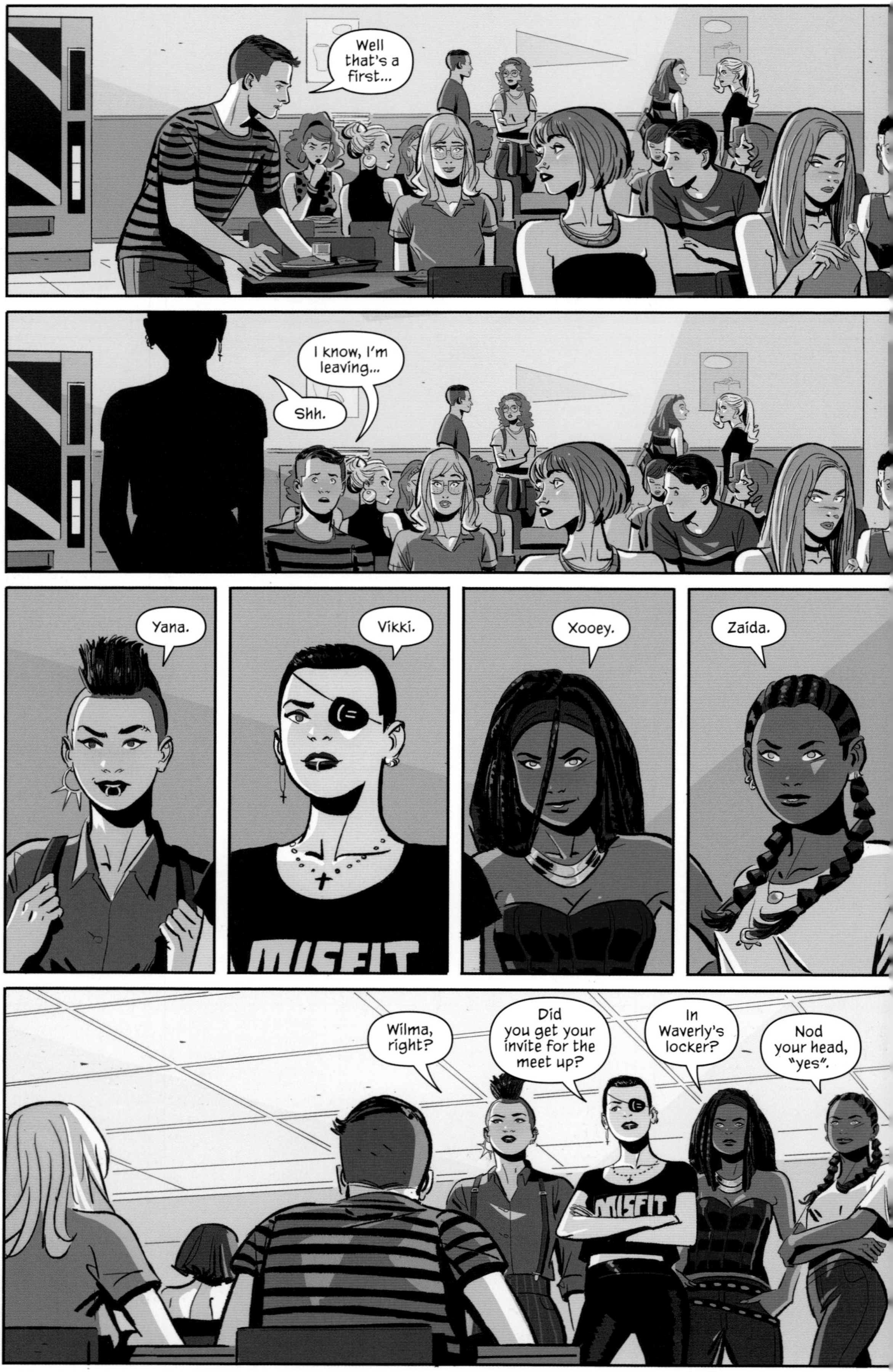

Well that's a first...
I know, I'm leaving...
Shh.
Yana.
Vikki.
MISFIT
Xooey.
Zaida.
Wilma, right?
Did you get your invite for the meet up?
In Waverly's locker?
Nod your head, "yes".
MISFIT

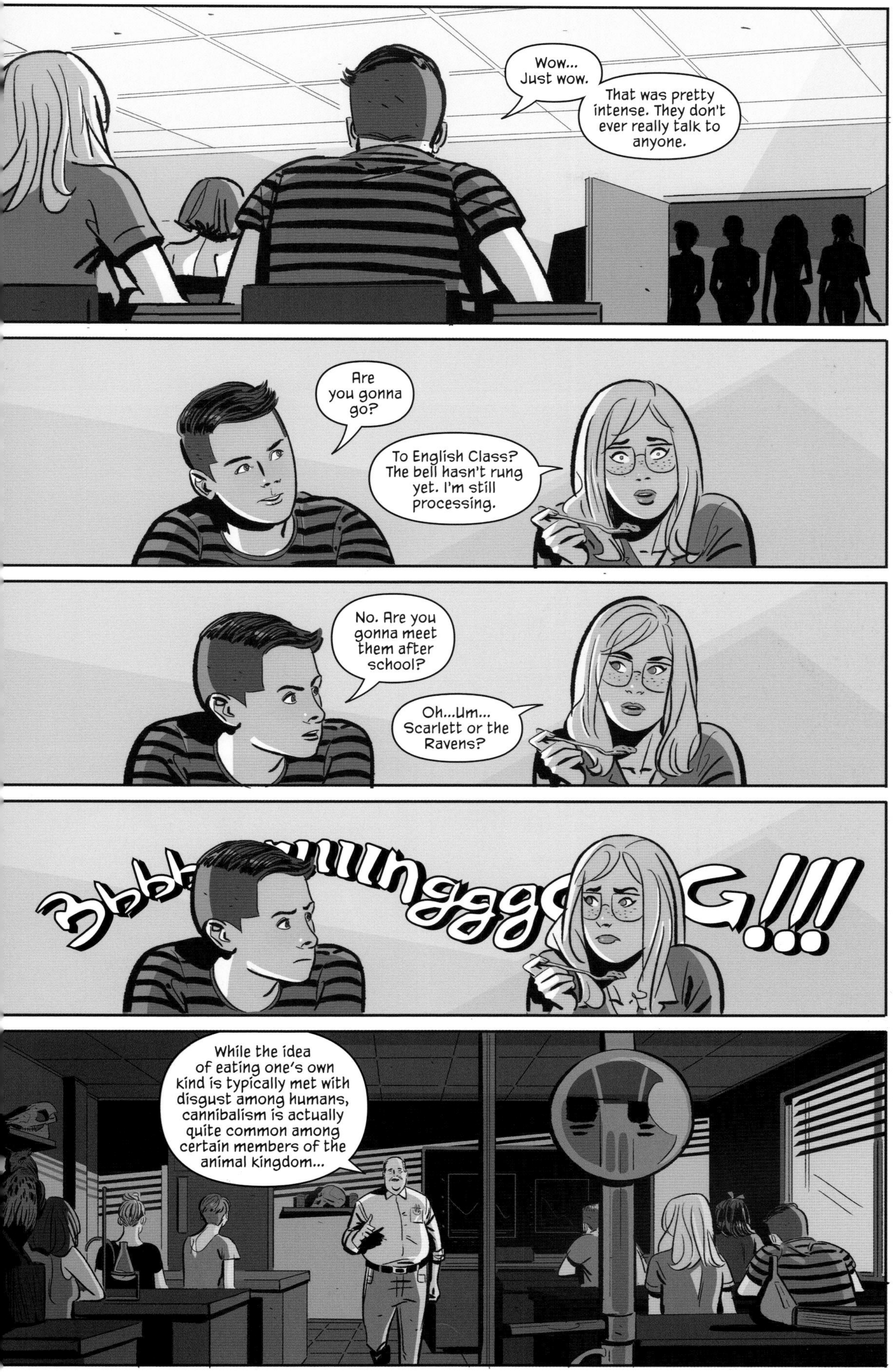
Wow... Just wow.
That was pretty intense. They don't ever really talk to anyone.
Are you gonna go?
To English Class? The bell hasn't rung yet. I'm still processing.
No. Are you gonna meet them after school?
Oh...Um... Scarlett or the Ravens?
G!!!
While the idea of eating one's own kind is typically met with disgust among humans, cannibalism is actually quite common among certain members of the animal kingdom...

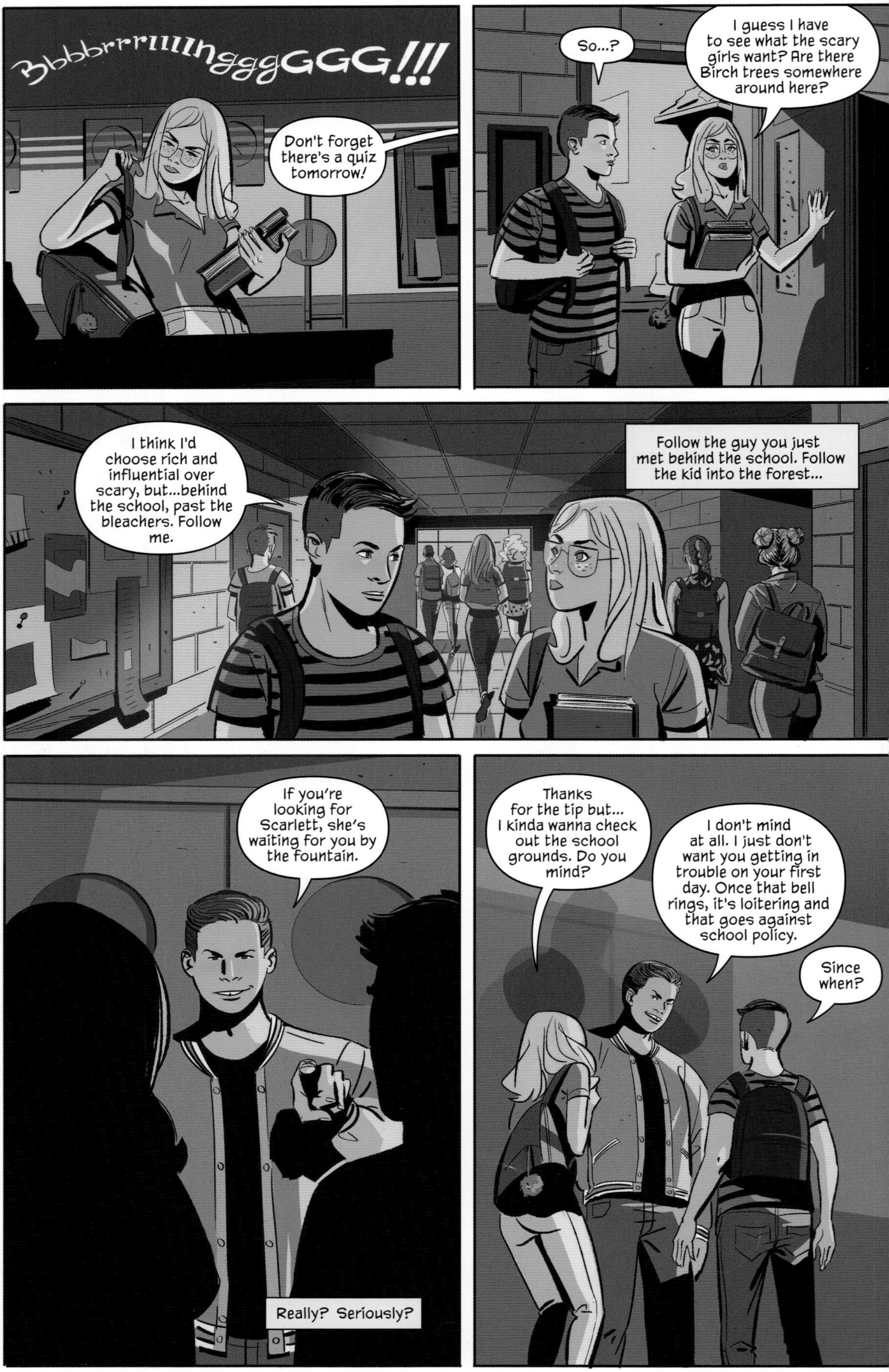
Bbbbrrrriiiilnggg GGG!!!
Don't forget there's a quiz tomorrow!
So...?
I guess I have to see what the scary girls want? Are there Birch trees somewhere around here?
I think I'd choose rich and influential over scary, but...behind the school, past the bleachers. Follow me.
Follow the guy you just met behind the school. Follow the kid into the forest...
If you're looking for Scarlett, she's waiting for you by the fountain.
Really? Seriously?
Thanks for the tip but... I kinda wanna check out the school grounds. Do you mind?
I don't mind at all. I just don't want you getting in trouble on your first day. Once that bell rings, it's loitering and that goes against school policy.
Since when?

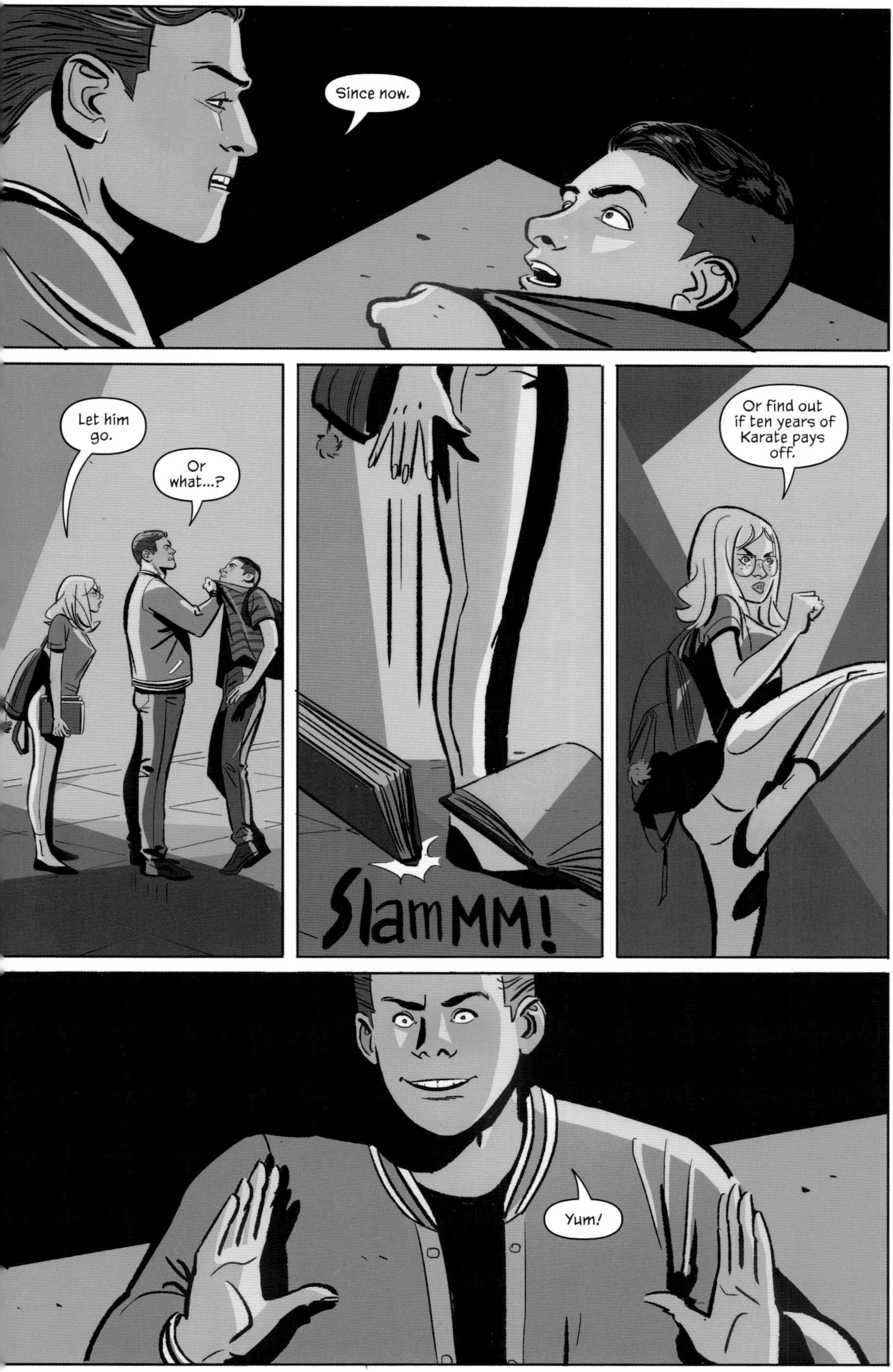
Since now.
Let him go.
Or what...?
SlamMM!
Or find out if ten years of Karate pays off.
Yum!

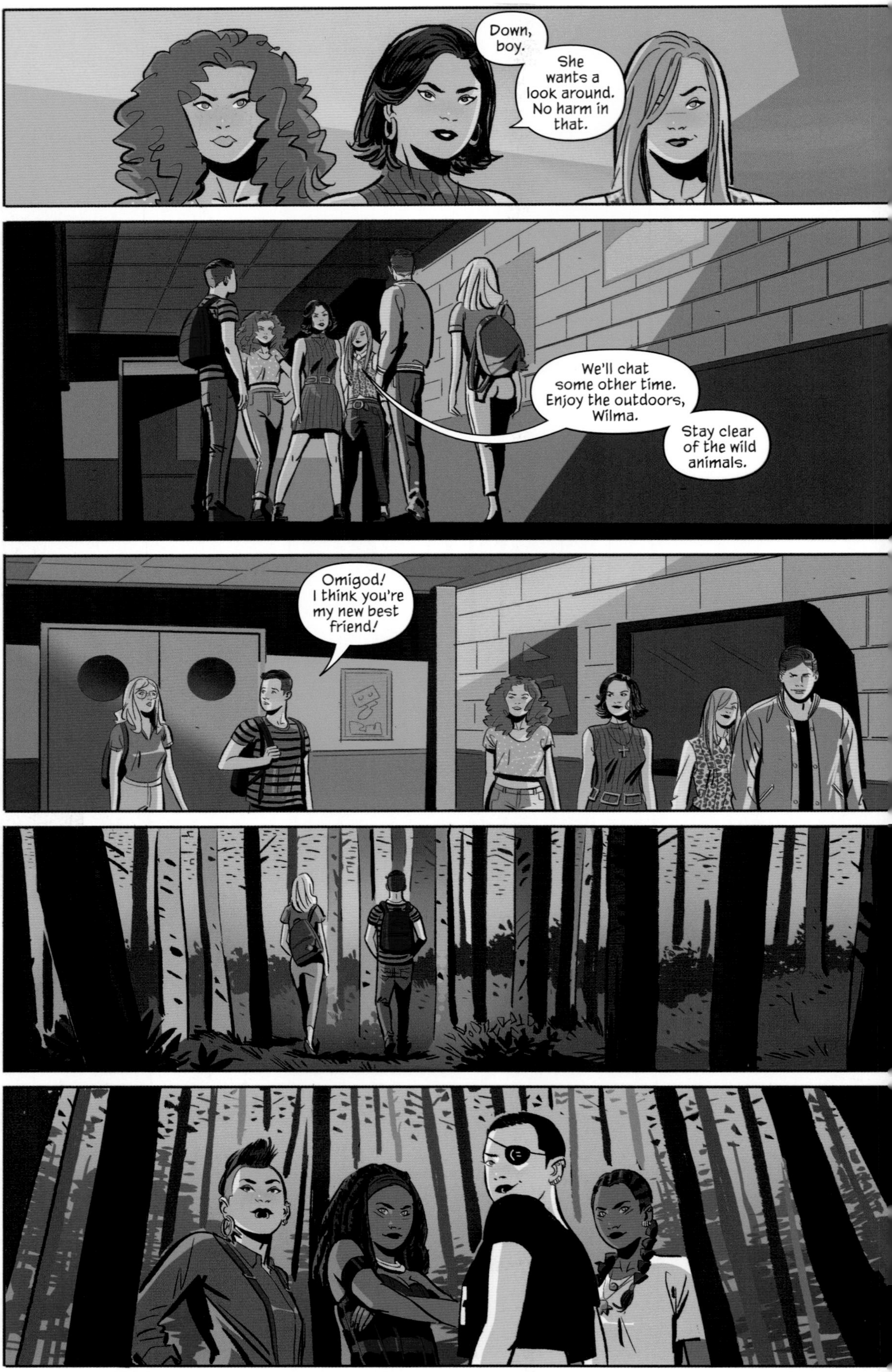
Down, boy.
She wants a look around. No harm in that.
We'll chat some other time. Enjoy the outdoors, Wilma.
Stay clear of the wild animals.
Omigod! I think you're my new best friend!

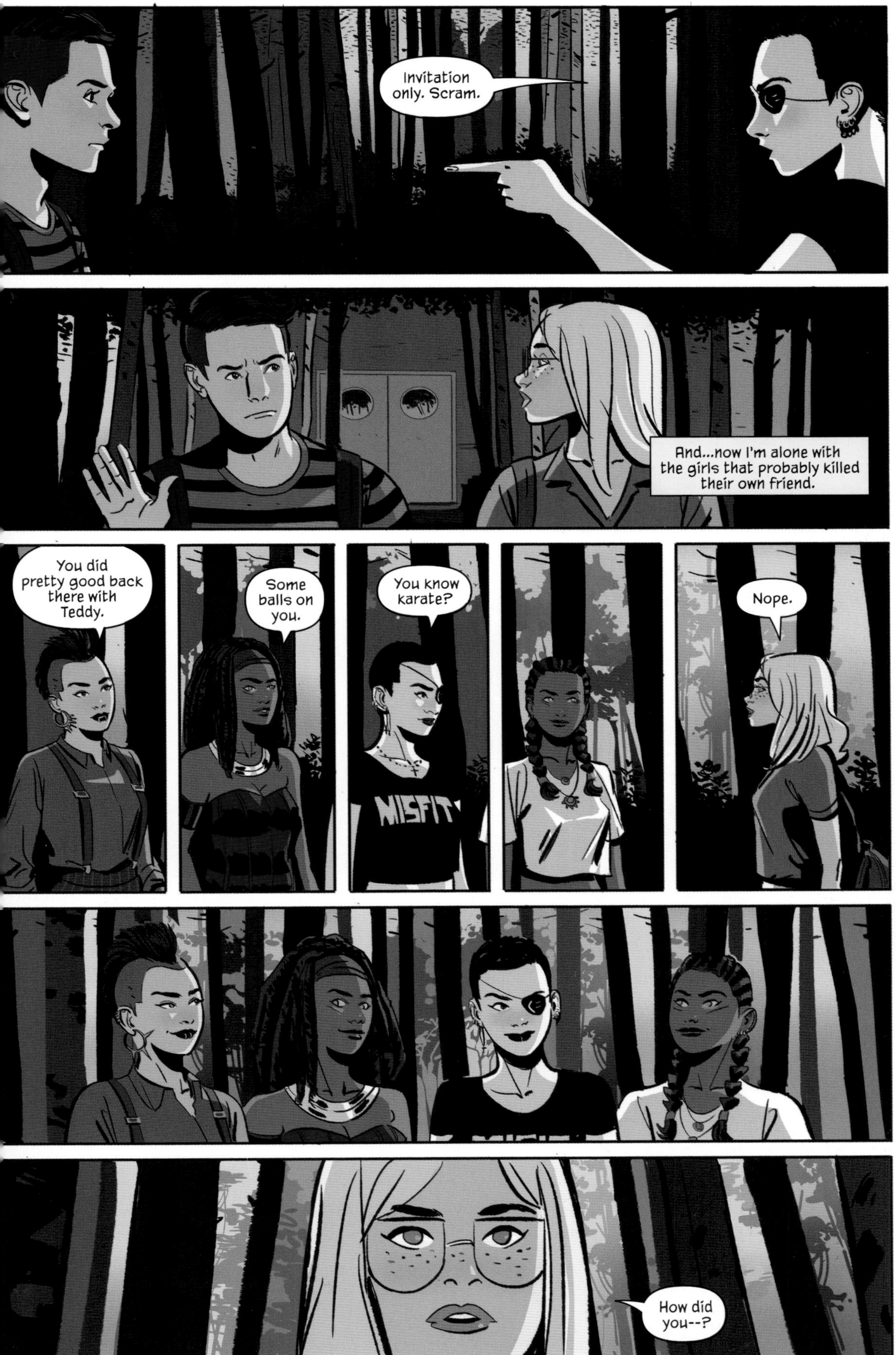
Invitation only. Scram.
And...now I'm alone with the girls that probably killed their own friend.
You did pretty good back there with Teddy.
Some balls on you.
You know karate?
MISFIT
Nope.
How did you--?

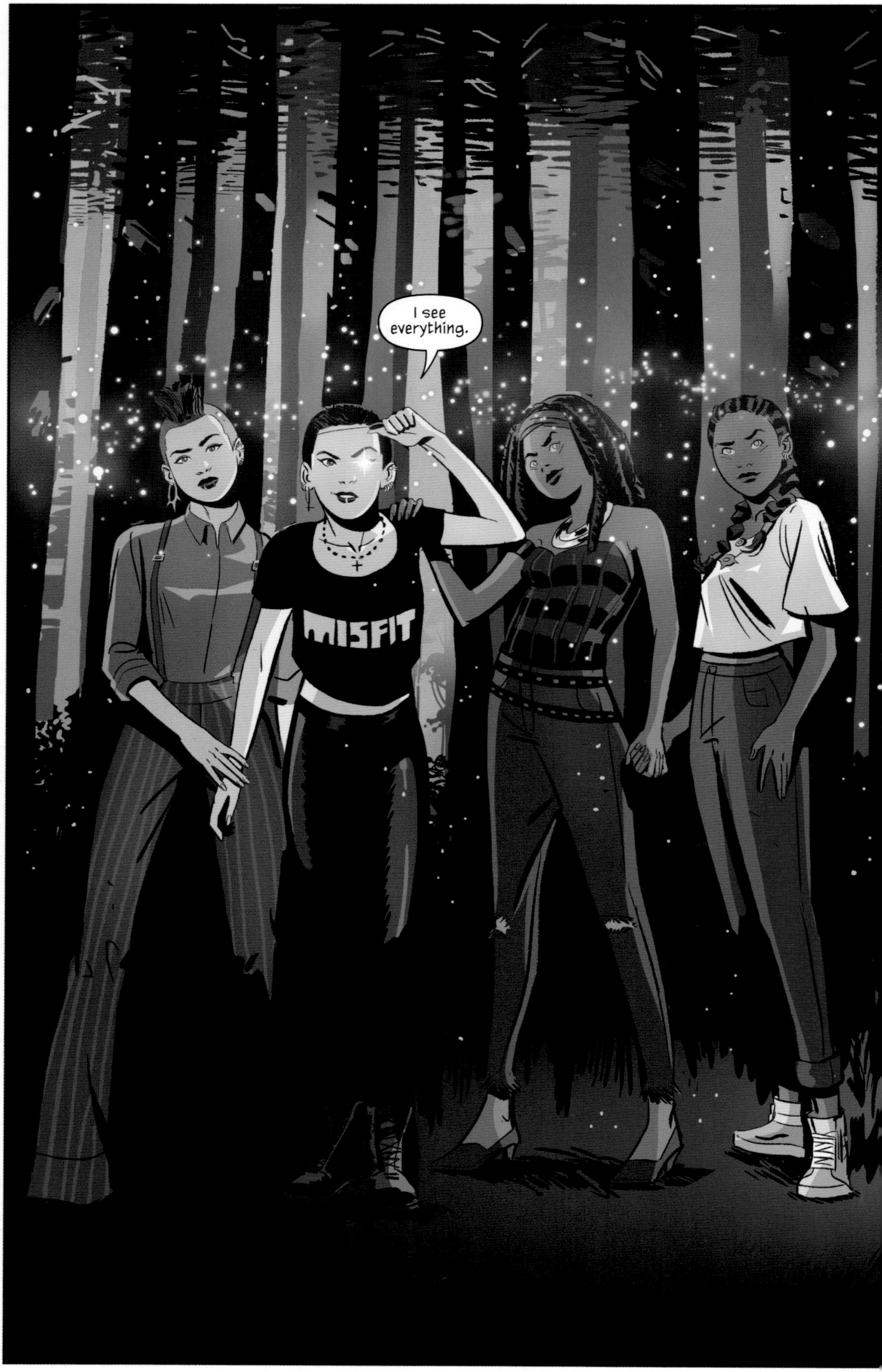
I see everything.
MISFIT

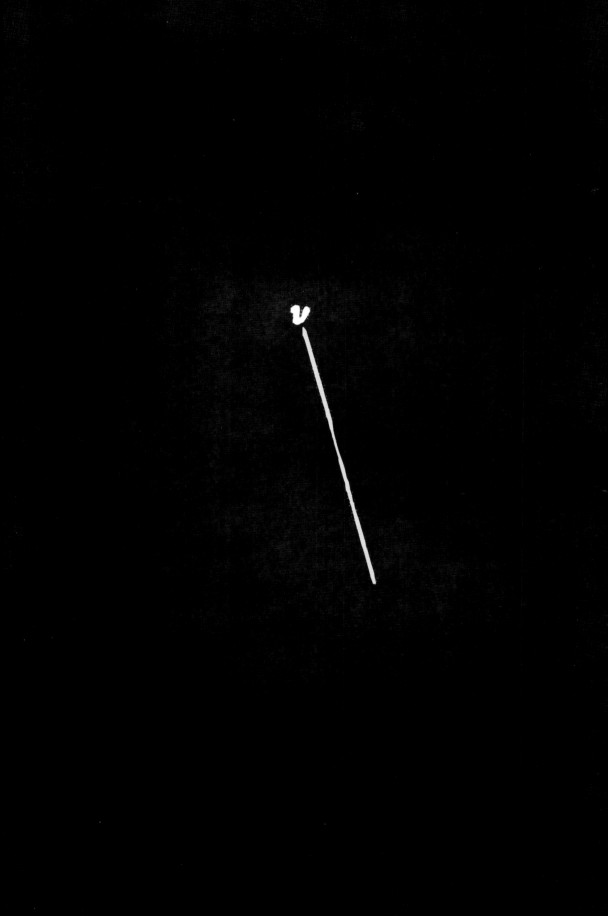

CHAPTER
TWO

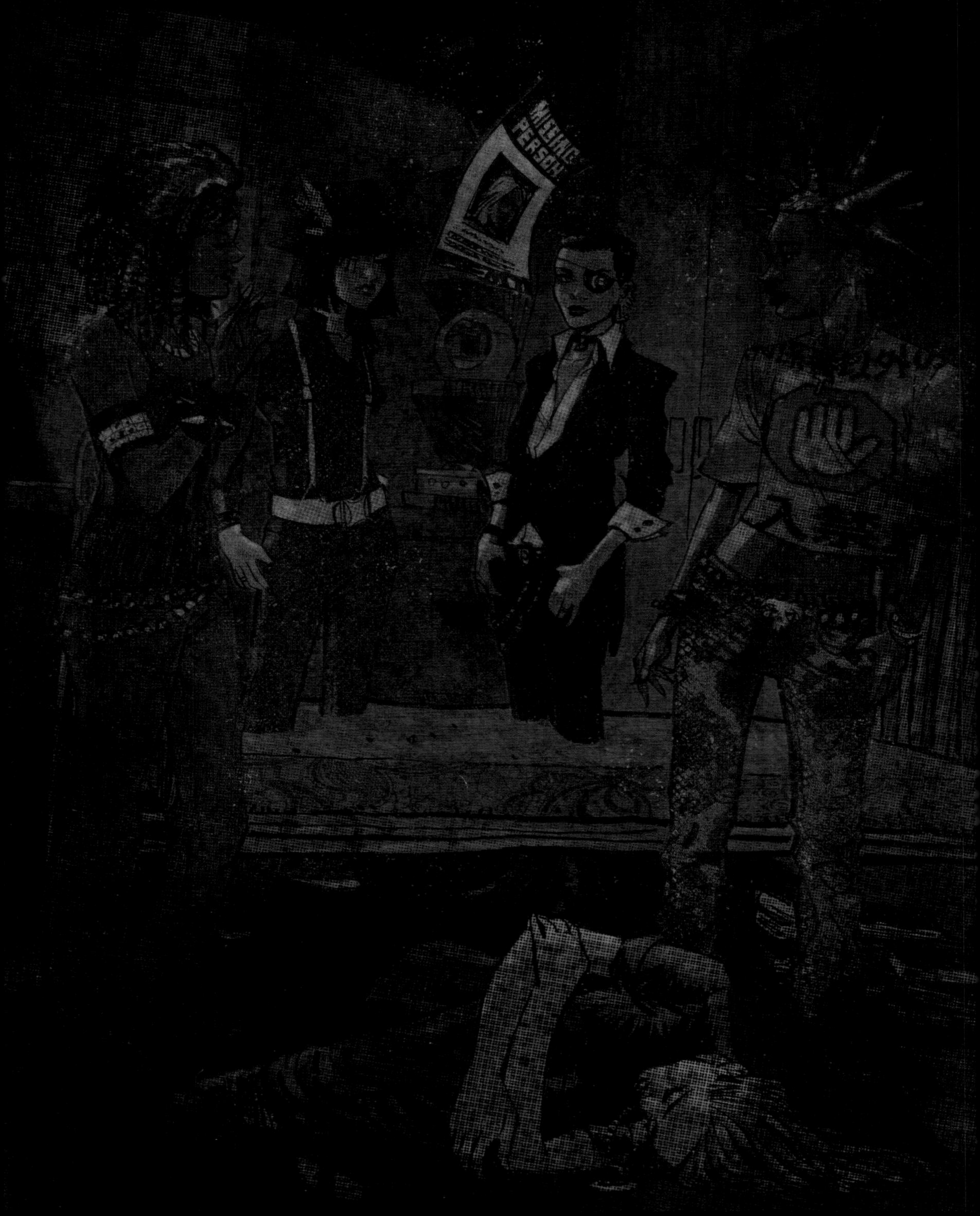

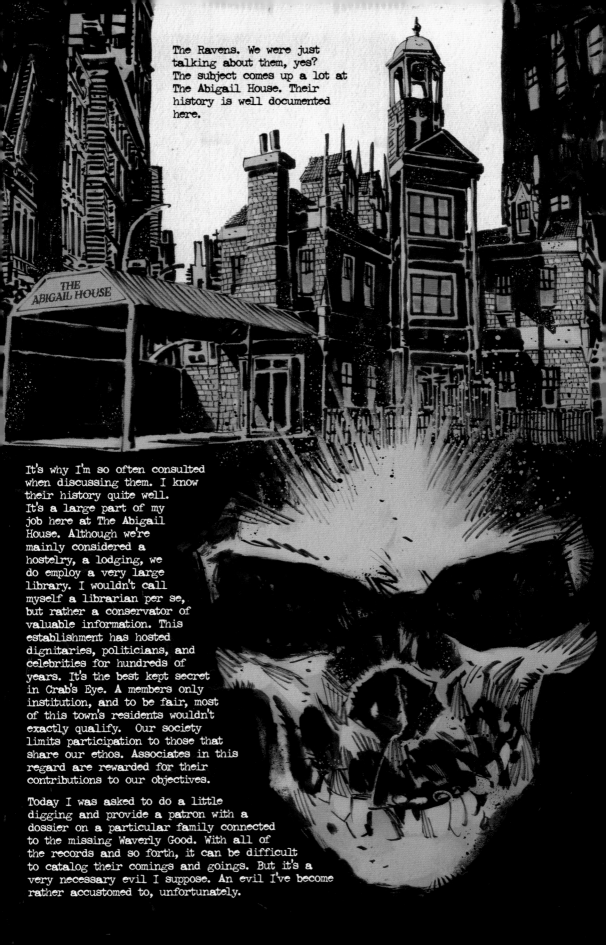

The Ravens. We were just talking about them, yes? The subject comes up a lot at The Abigail House. Their history is well documented here.

It's why I'm so often consulted when discussing them. I know their history quite well. It's a large part of my job here at The Abigail House. Although we're mainly considered a hostelry, a lodging, we do employ a very large library. I wouldn't call myself a librarian per se, but rather a conservator of valuable information. This establishment has hosted dignitaries, politicians, and celebrities for hundreds of years. It's the best kept secret in Crab's Eye. A members only institution, and to be fair, most of this town's residents wouldn't exactly qualify. Our society limits participation to those that share our ethos. Associates in this regard are rewarded for their contributions to our objectives.

Today I was asked to do a little digging and provide a patron with a dossier on a particular family connected to the missing Waverly Good. With all of the records and so forth, it can be difficult to catalog their comings and goings. But it's a very necessary evil I suppose. An evil I've become rather accustomed to, unfortunately.

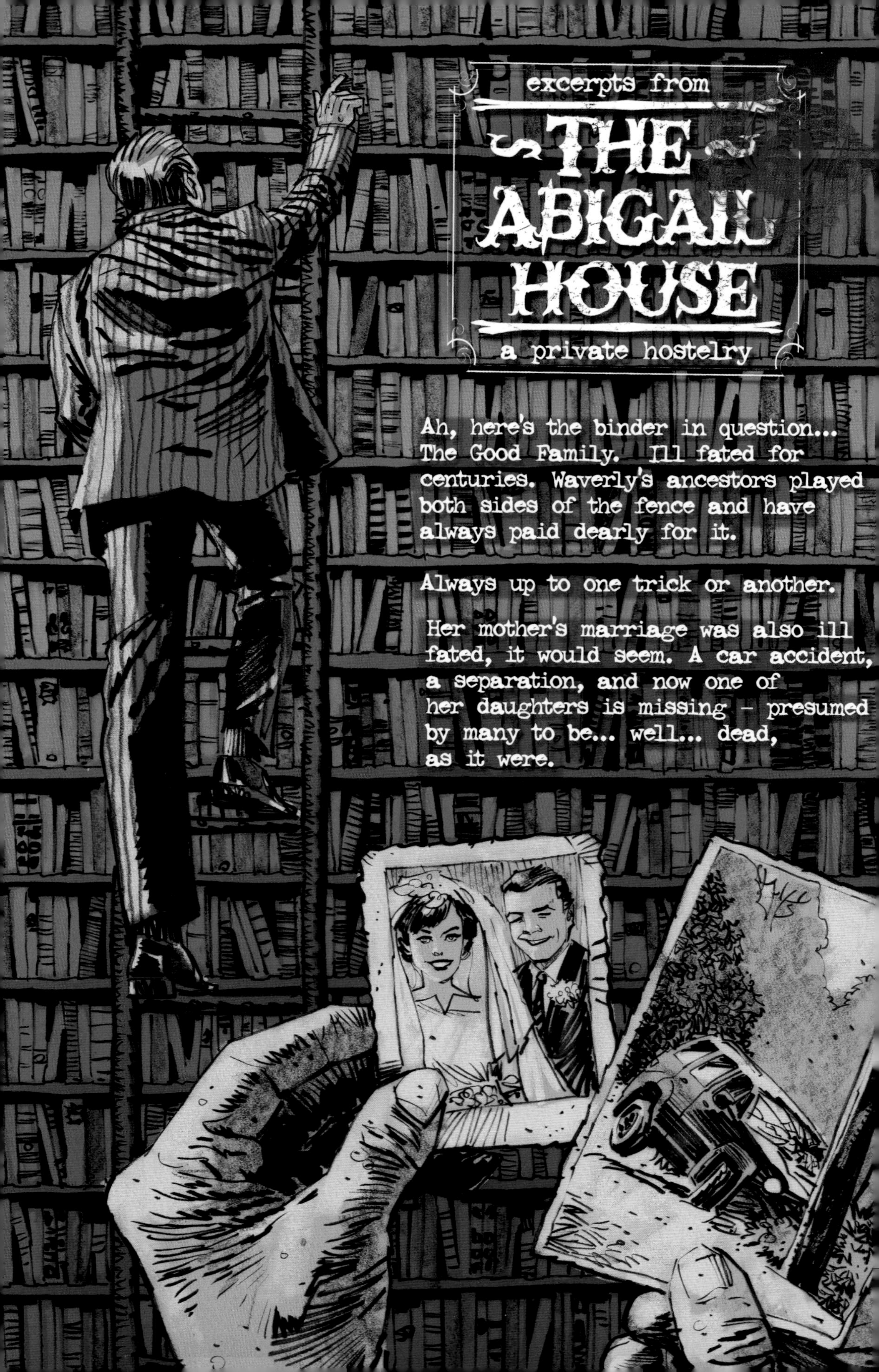
excerpts from
THE ABIGAIL HOUSE
a private hostelry
Ah, here's the binder in question... The Good Family. Ill fated for centuries. Waverly's ancestors played both sides of the fence and have always paid dearly for it.
Always up to one trick or another.
Her mother's marriage was also ill fated, it would seem. A car accident, a separation, and now one of her daughters is missing - presumed by many to be... well... dead, as it were.

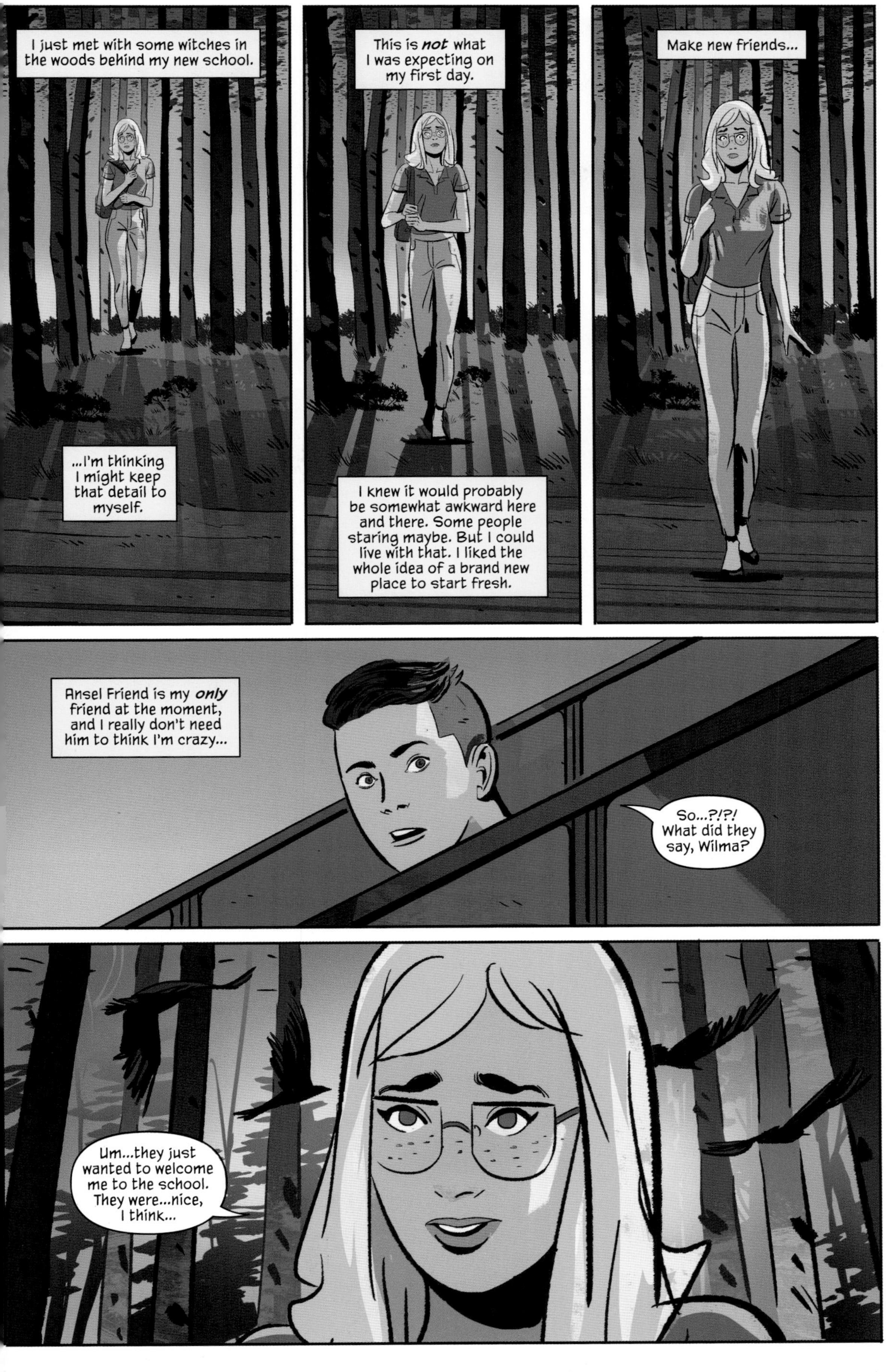
I just met with some witches in the woods behind my new school.
...I'm thinking I might keep that detail to myself.
This is *not* what I was expecting on my first day.
I knew it would probably be somewhat awkward here and there. Some people staring maybe. But I could live with that. I liked the whole idea of a brand new place to start fresh.
Make new friends...
Ansel Friend is my *only* friend at the moment, and I really don't need him to think I'm crazy...
So...?!?! What did they say, Wilma?
Um...they just wanted to welcome me to the school. They were...nice, I think...

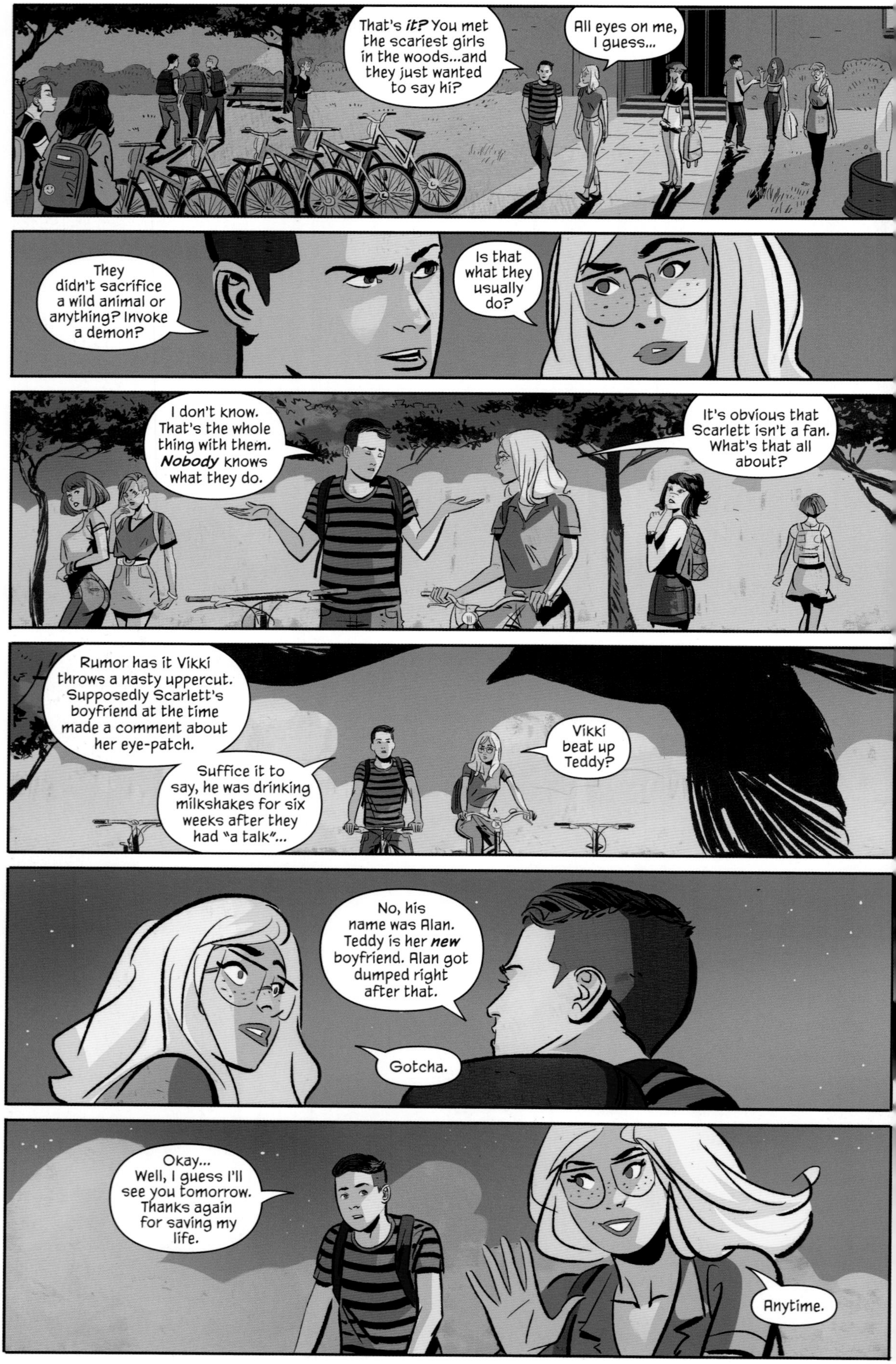
That's *it?* You met the scariest girls in the woods...and they just wanted to say hi?
All eyes on me, I guess...
They didn't sacrifice a wild animal or anything? Invoke a demon?
Is that what they usually do?
I don't know. That's the whole thing with them. *Nobody* knows what they do.
It's obvious that Scarlett isn't a fan. What's that all about?
Rumor has it Vikki throws a nasty uppercut. Supposedly Scarlett's boyfriend at the time made a comment about her eye-patch.
Suffice it to say, he was drinking milkshakes for six weeks after they had "a talk"...
Vikki beat up Teddy?
No, his name was Alan. Teddy is her *new* boyfriend. Alan got dumped right after that.
Gotcha.
Okay... Well, I guess I'll see you tomorrow. Thanks again for saving my life.
Anytime.

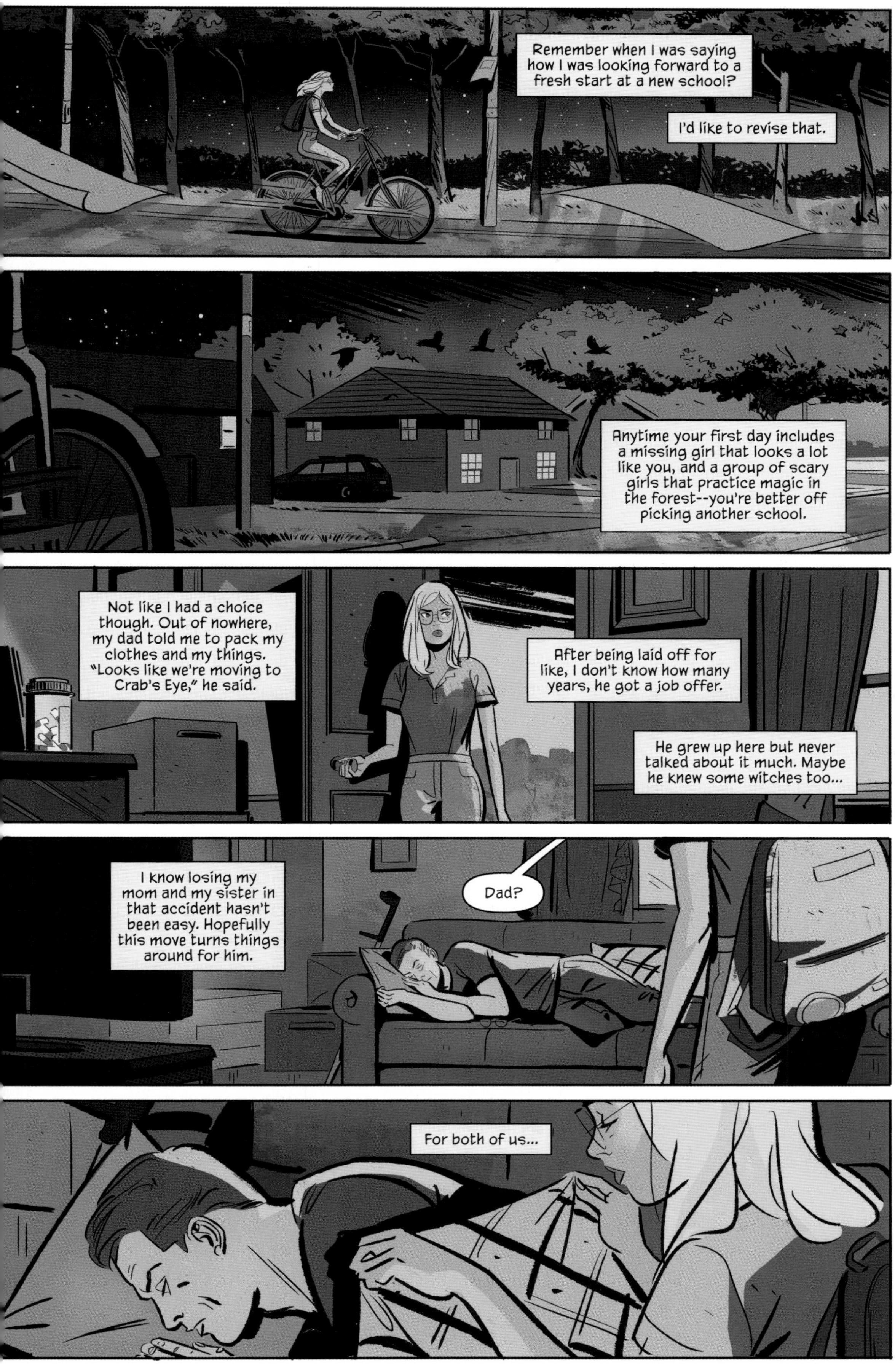
Remember when I was saying how I was looking forward to a fresh start at a new school?
I'd like to revise that.
Anytime your first day includes a missing girl that looks a lot like you, and a group of scary girls that practice magic in the forest--you're better off picking another school.
Not like I had a choice though. Out of nowhere, my dad told me to pack my clothes and my things. "Looks like we're moving to Crab's Eye," he said.
After being laid off for like, I don't know how many years, he got a job offer.
He grew up here but never talked about it much. Maybe he knew some witches too...
I know losing my mom and my sister in that accident hasn't been easy. Hopefully this move turns things around for him.
Dad?
For both of us...

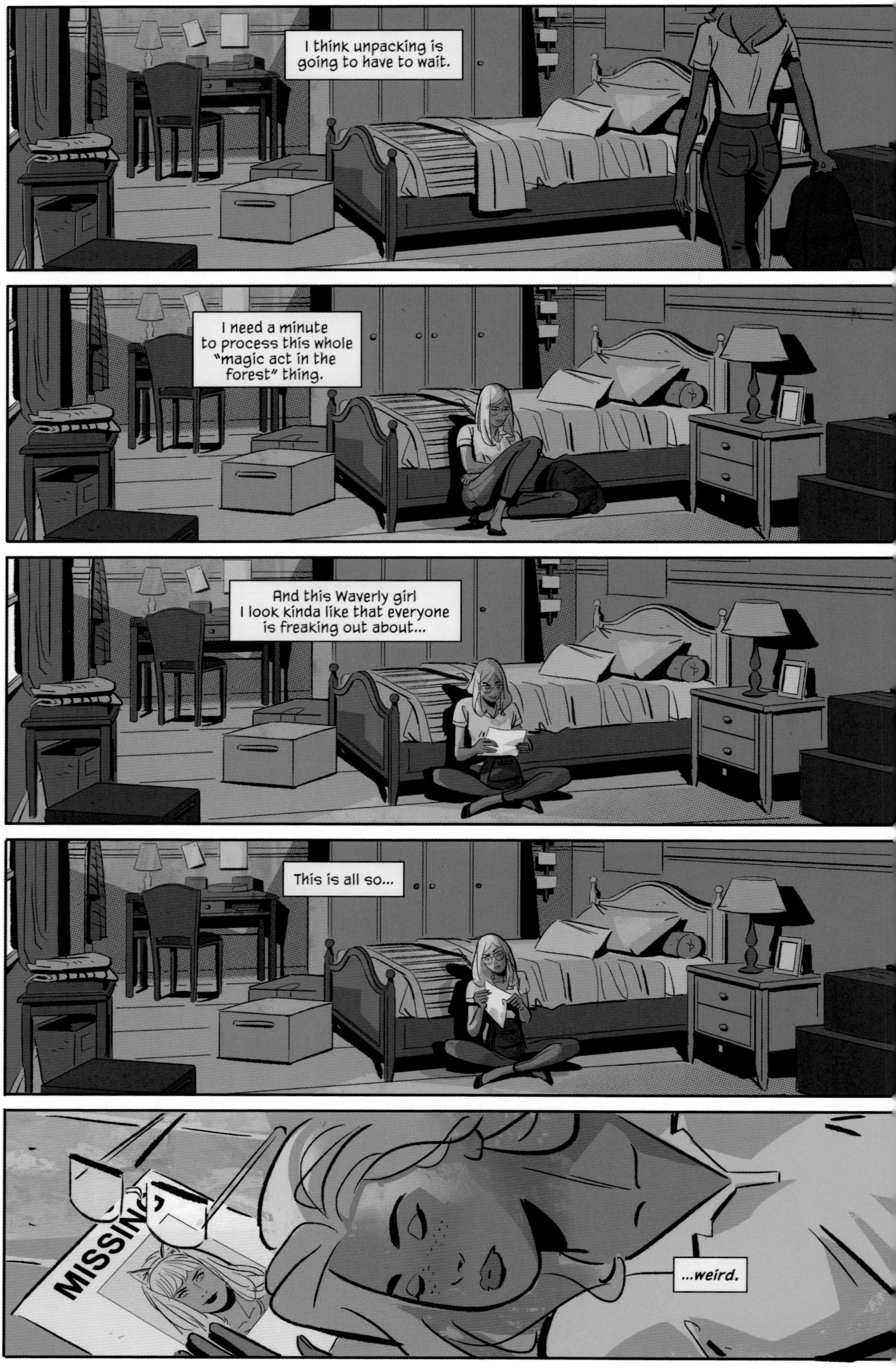
I think unpacking is going to have to wait.
I need a minute to process this whole "magic act in the forest" thing.
And this Waverly girl I look kinda like that everyone is freaking out about...
This is all so...
MISSING
...weird.

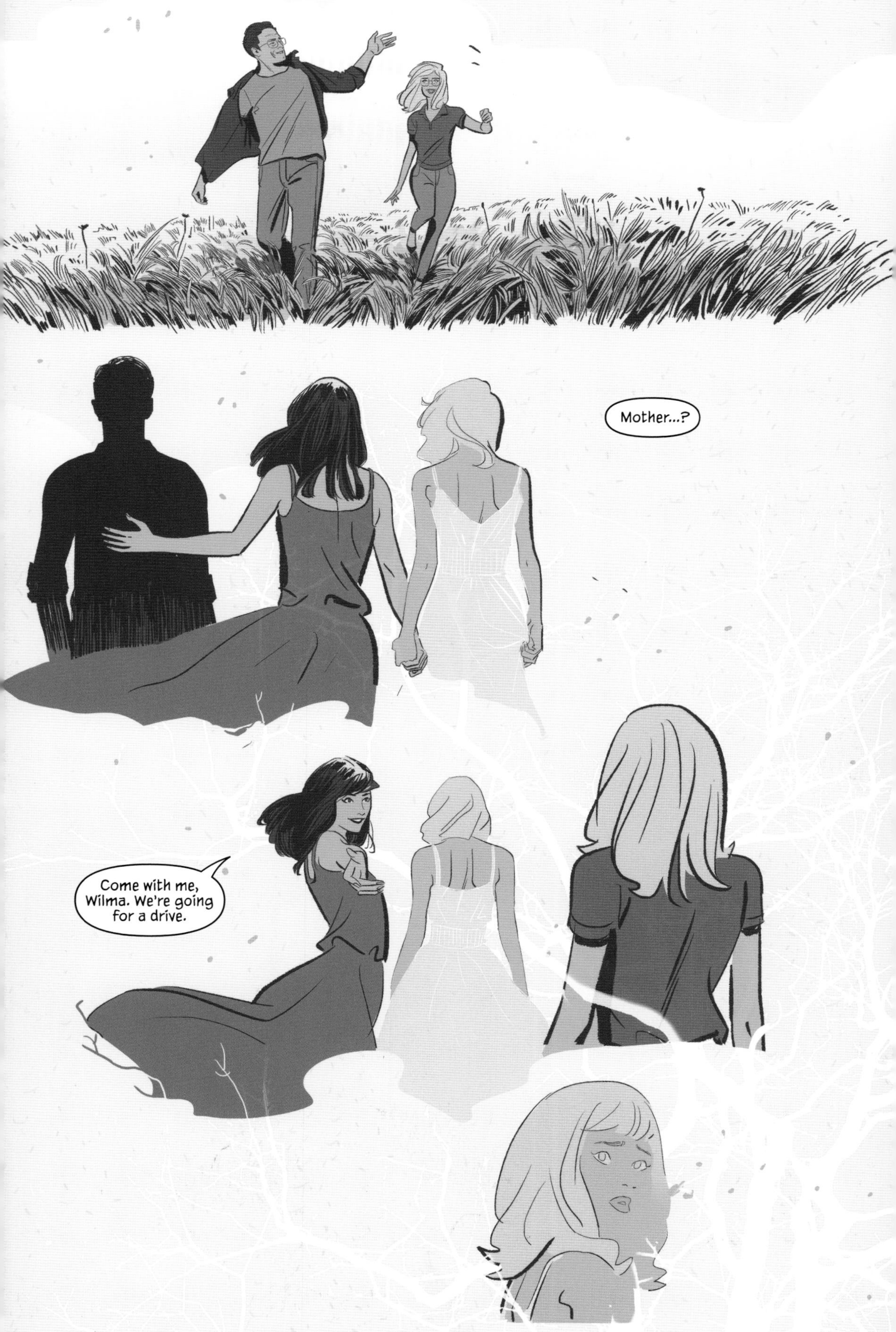
Mother...?
Come with me, Wilma. We're going for a drive.

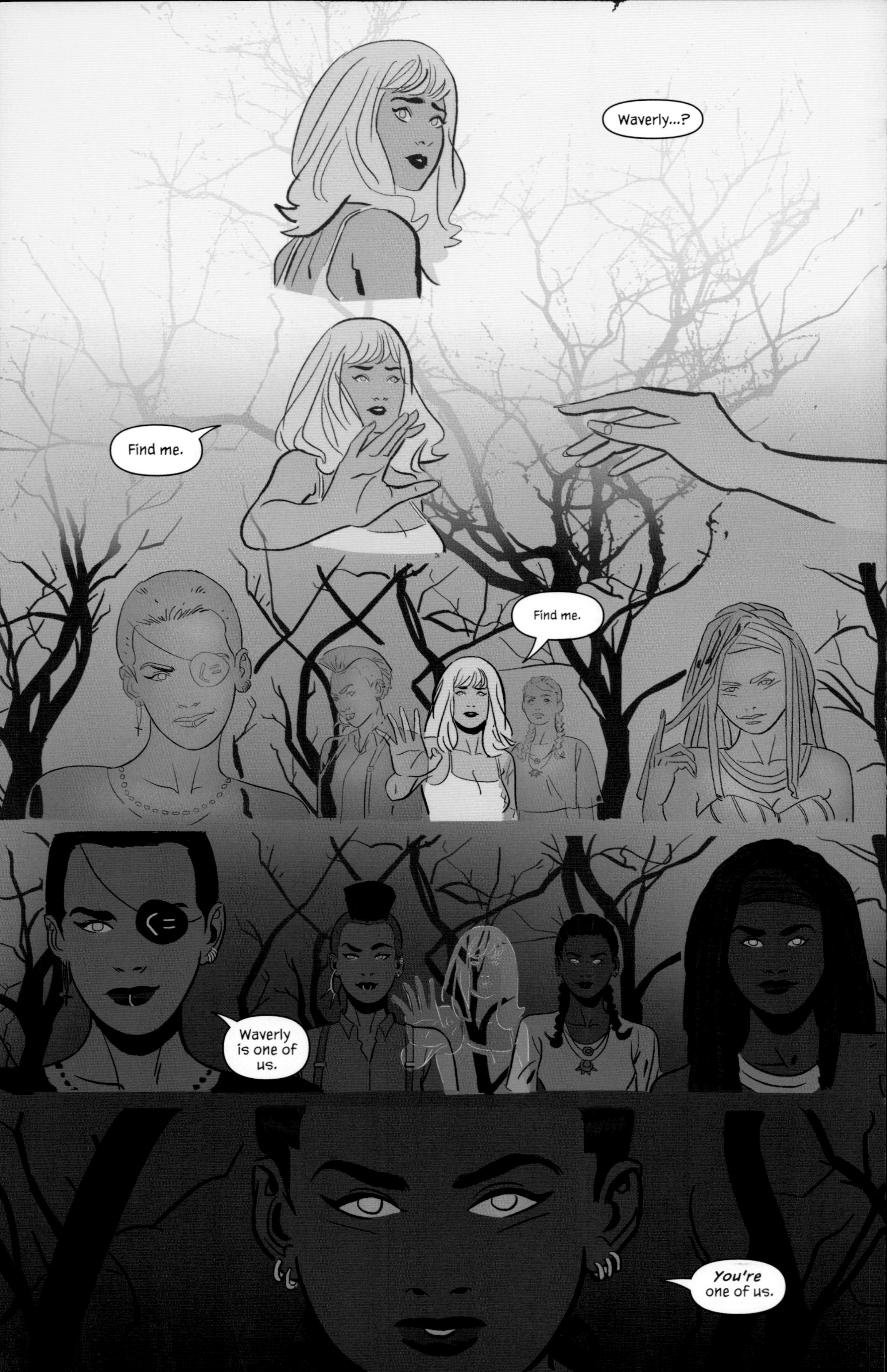
Waverly...?
Find me.
Find me.
Waverly is one of us.
You're one of us.

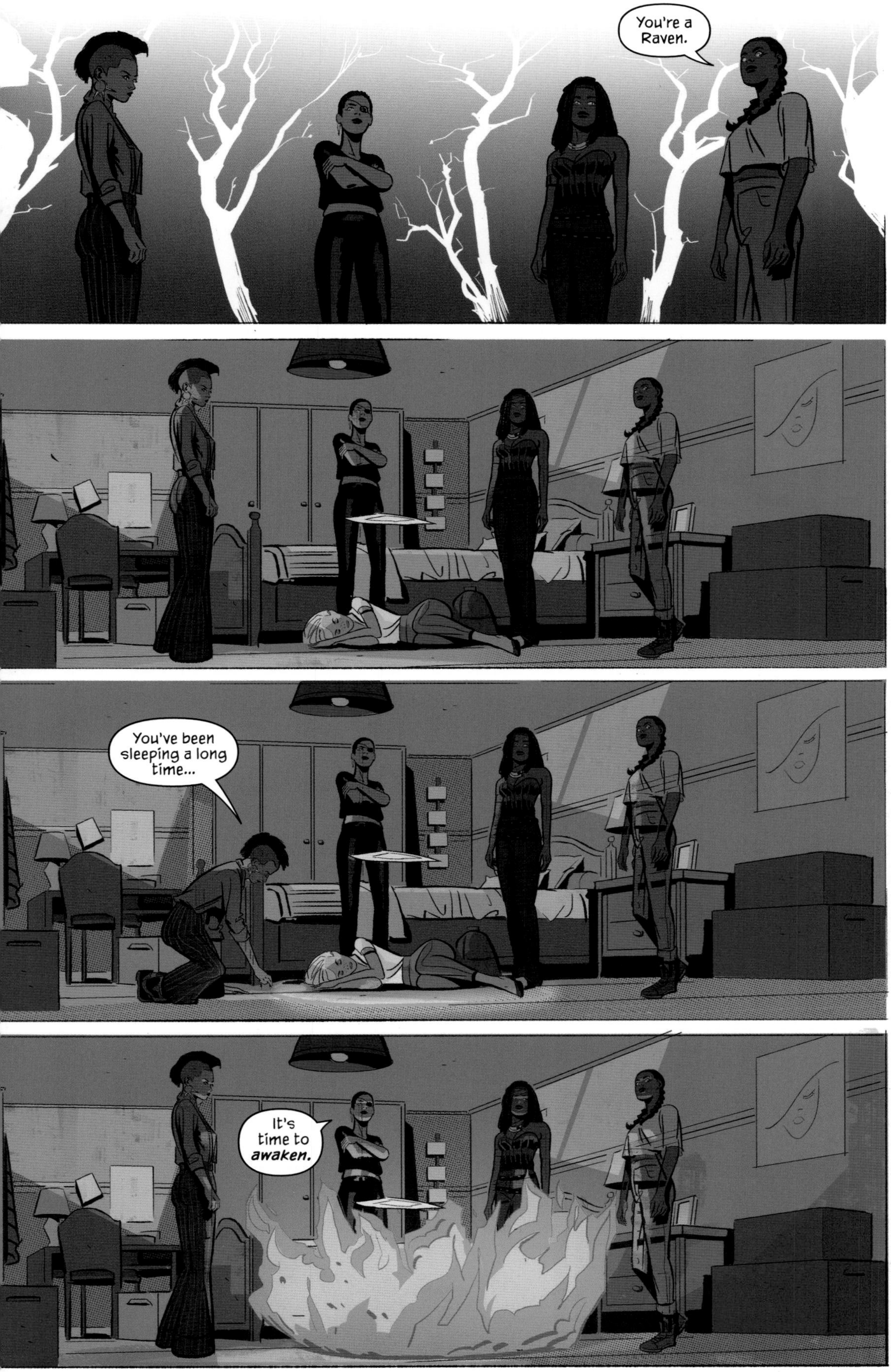
You're a Raven.
You've been sleeping a long time...
It's time to *awaken.*

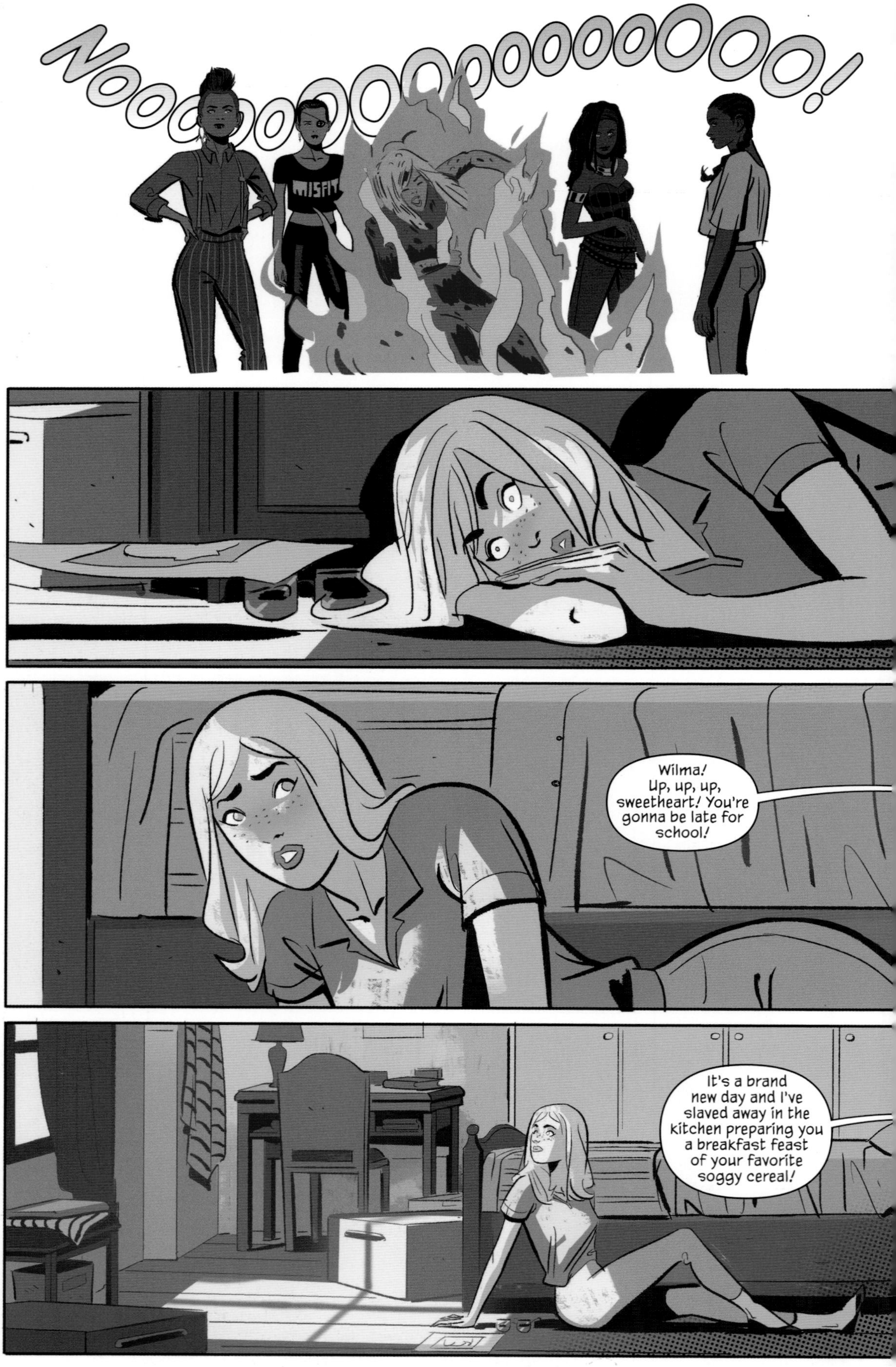
NOOOOOOOOOOOOOOOOOO!
Wilma! Up, up, up, sweetheart! You're gonna be late for school!
It's a brand new day and I've slaved away in the kitchen preparing you a breakfast feast of your favorite soggy cereal!

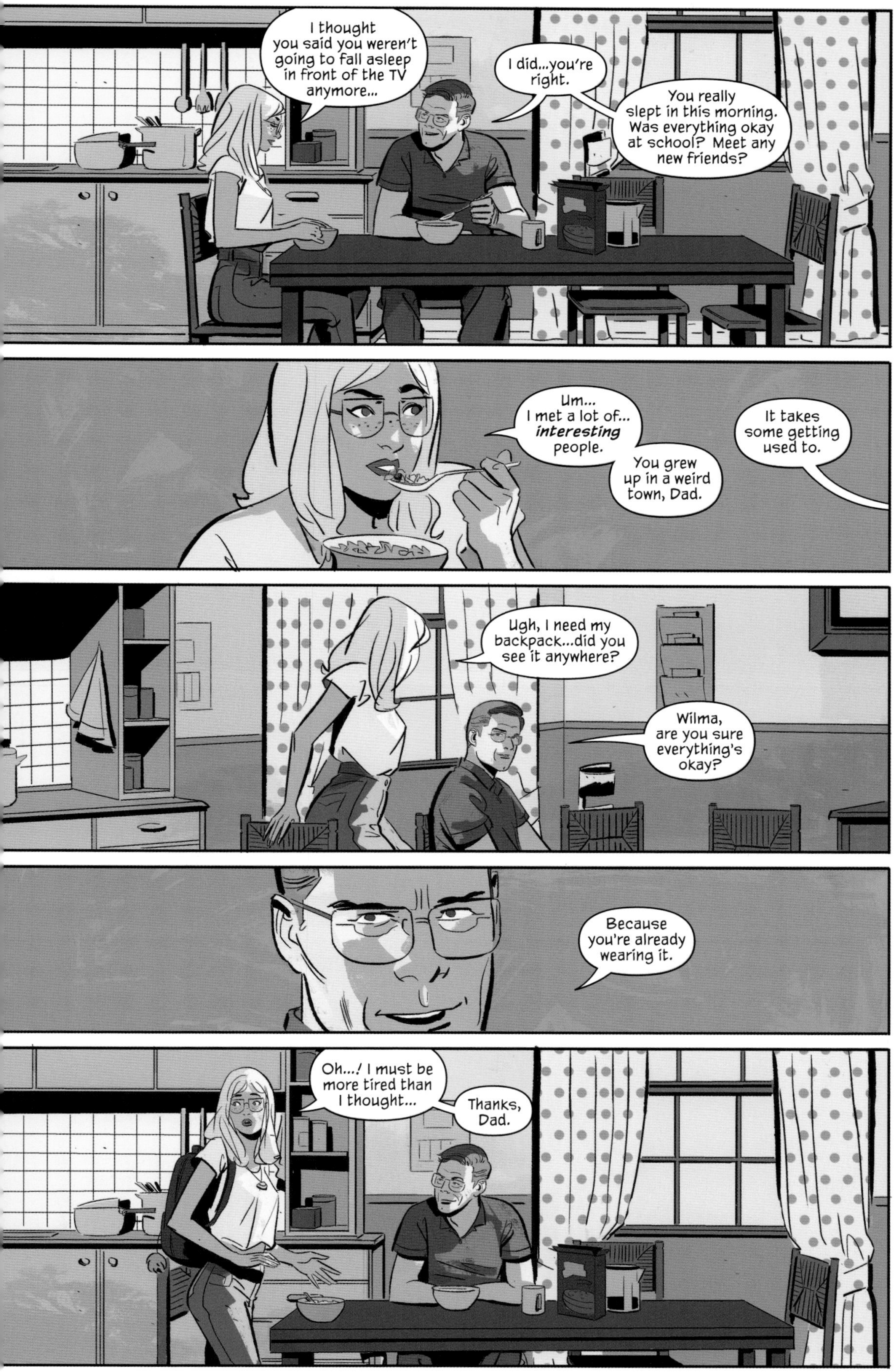
I thought you said you weren't going to fall asleep in front of the TV anymore...
I did...you're right.
You really slept in this morning. Was everything okay at school? Meet any new friends?
Um... I met a lot of... *interesting* people.
You grew up in a weird town, Dad.
It takes some getting used to.
Ugh, I need my backpack...did you see it anywhere?
Wilma, are you sure everything's okay?
Because you're already wearing it.
Oh...! I must be more tired than I thought...
Thanks, Dad.

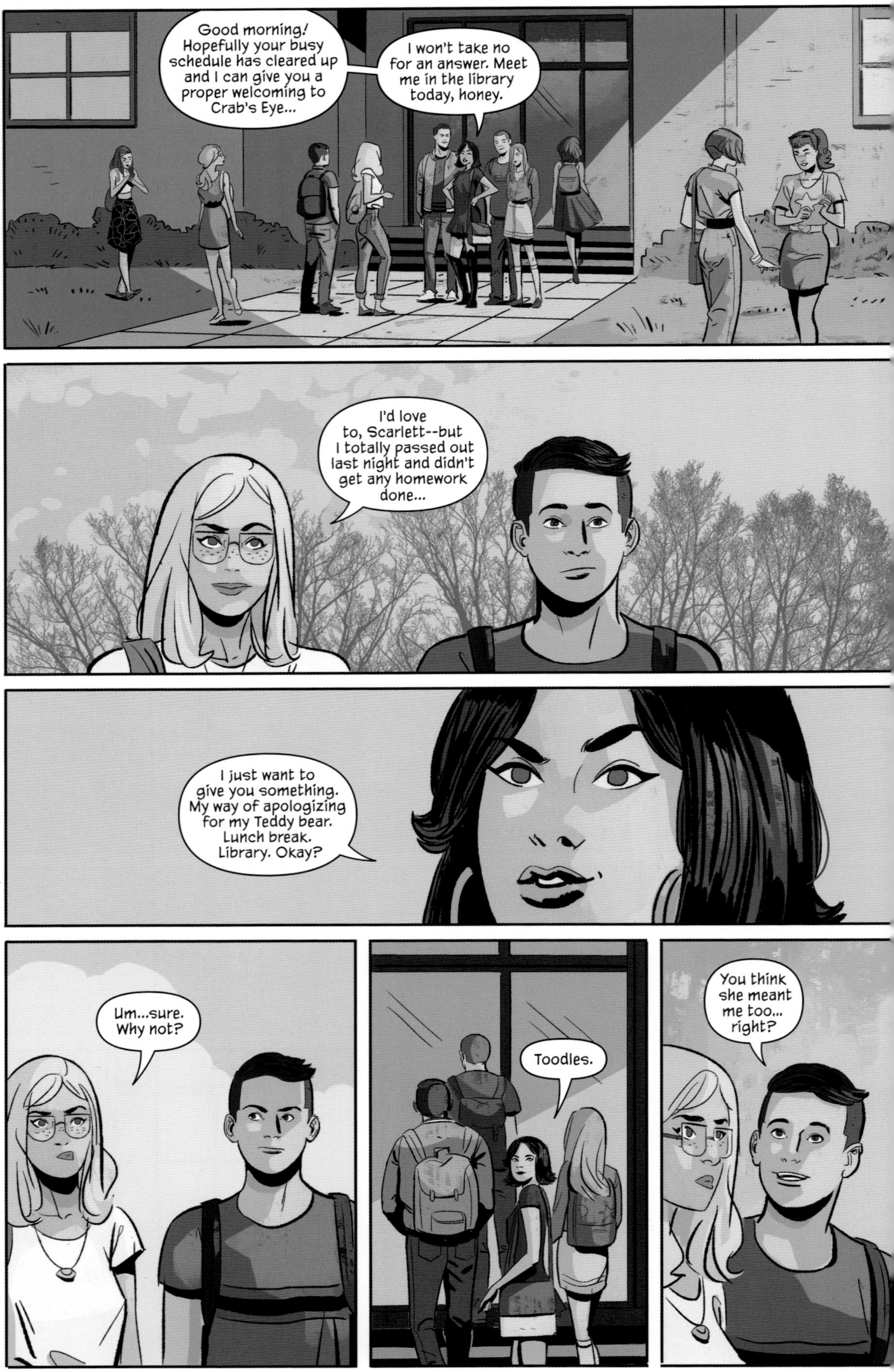

Good morning! Hopefully your busy schedule has cleared up and I can give you a proper welcoming to Crab's Eye...
I won't take no for an answer. Meet me in the library today, honey.
I'd love to, Scarlett--but I totally passed out last night and didn't get any homework done...
I just want to give you something. My way of apologizing for my Teddy bear. Lunch break. Library. Okay?
Um...sure. Why not?
Toodles.
You think she meant me too... right?

MISSING

More fun and surprises and the bell hasn't even rung yet. Alright, let's see what Scarlett has to say...Between her and the Ravens I'm--

Okay...who is *he*, and why are things suddenly looking more interesting?

Who's that...?

Him?

You don't want to know. I'll tell you all about him later.

Let's just enjoy this! I don't think you know how lucky you are. Scarlett doesn't just talk to *anyone.*

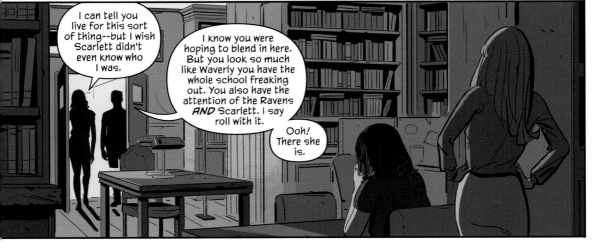

I can tell you live for this sort of thing--but I wish Scarlett didn't even know who I was.

I know you were hoping to blend in here. But you look so much like Waverly you have the whole school freaking out. You also have the attention of the Ravens *AND* Scarlett. I say roll with it.

Ooh! There she is.

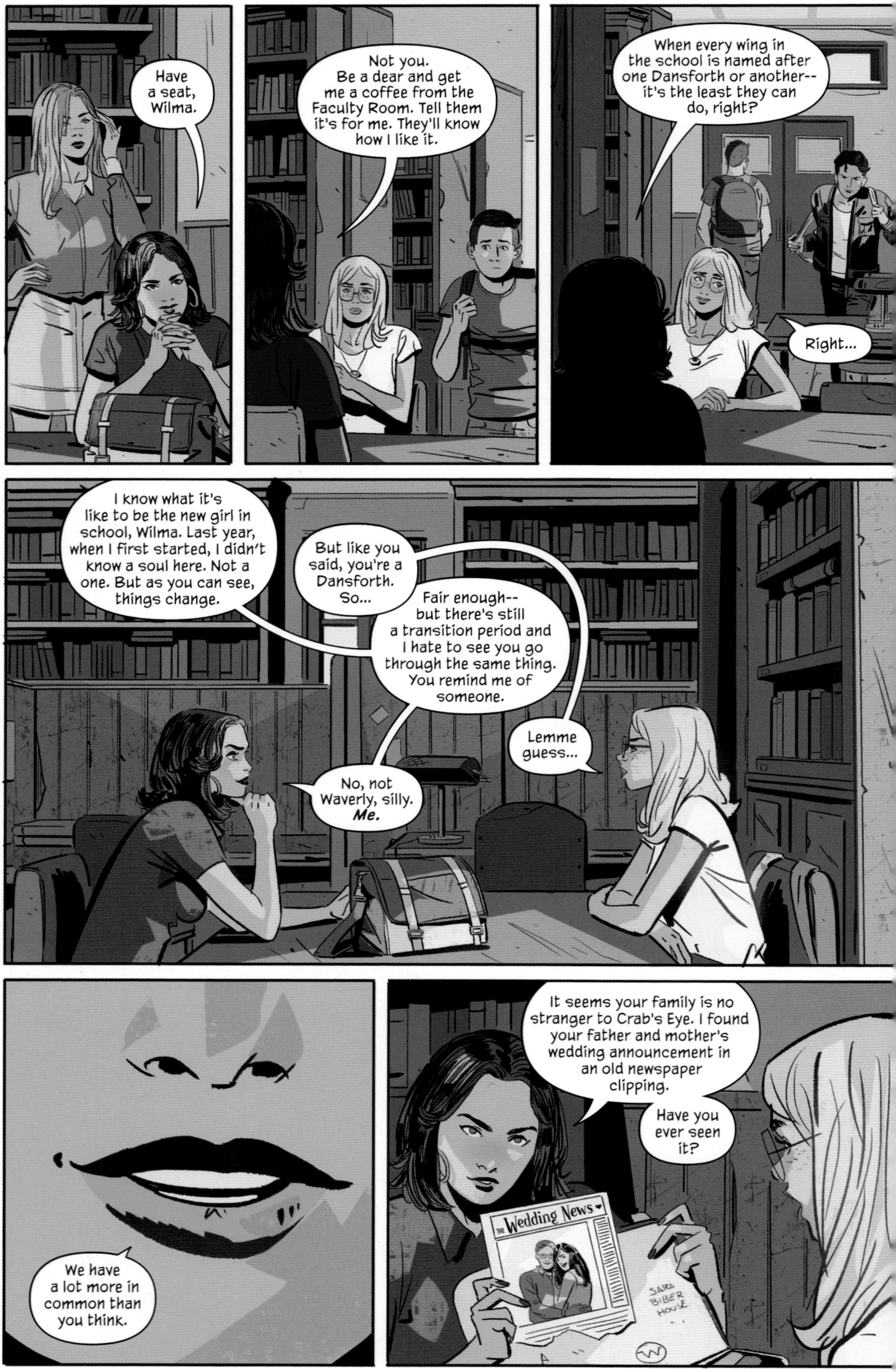

Have a seat, Wilma.
Not you. Be a dear and get me a coffee from the Faculty Room. Tell them it's for me. They'll know how I like it.
When every wing in the school is named after one Dansforth or another-- it's the least they can do, right?
Right...
I know what it's like to be the new girl in school, Wilma. Last year, when I first started, I didn't know a soul here. Not a one. But as you can see, things change.
But like you said, you're a Dansforth. So...
Fair enough-- but there's still a transition period and I hate to see you go through the same thing. You remind me of someone.
Lemme guess...
No, not Waverly, silly. *Me.*
We have a lot more in common than you think.
It seems your family is no stranger to Crab's Eye. I found your father and mother's wedding announcement in an old newspaper clipping.
Have you ever seen it?
THE Wedding News
SARA BIBER HOUSE

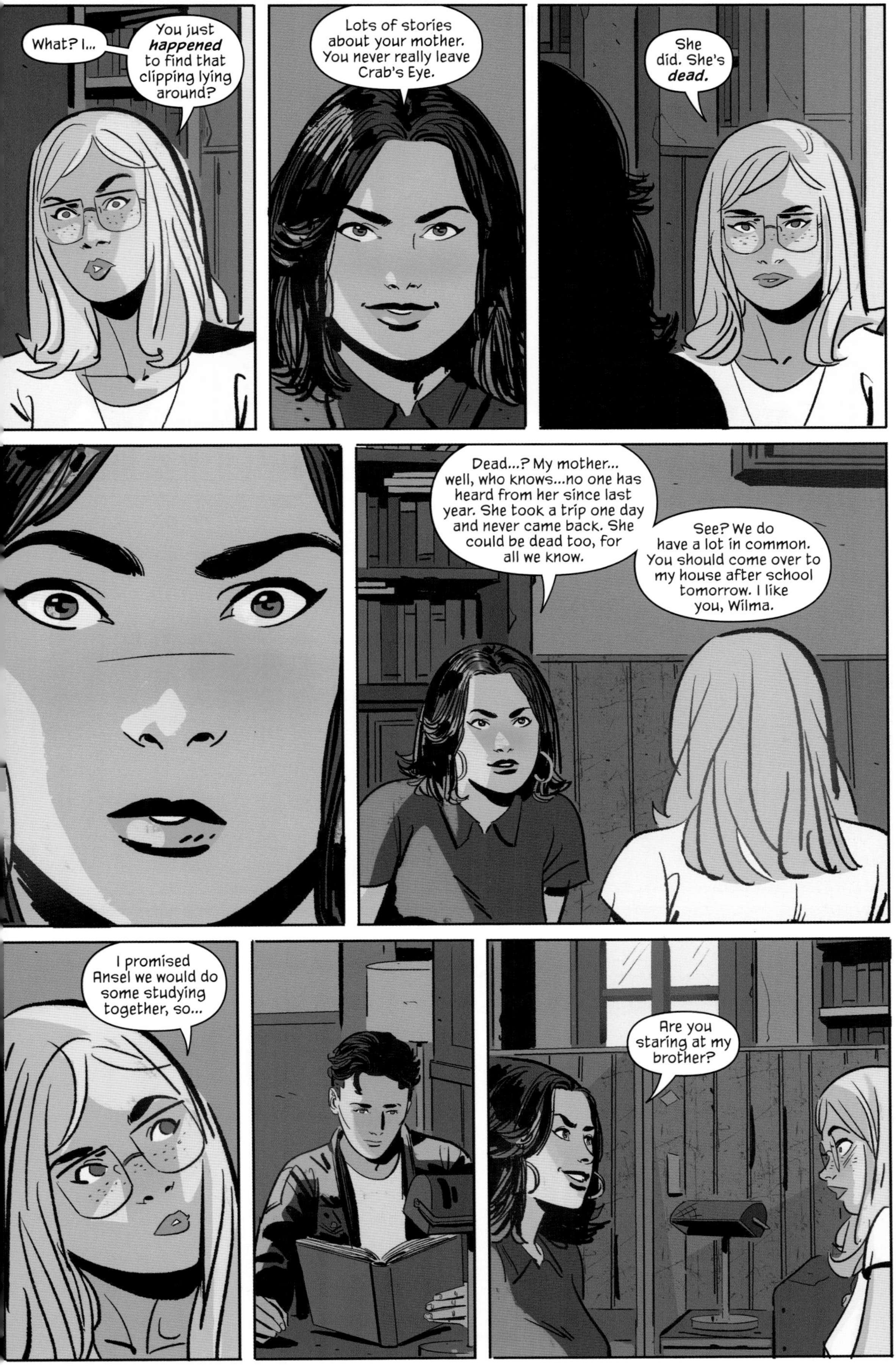
What? I...
You just *happened* to find that clipping lying around?
Lots of stories about your mother. You never really leave Crab's Eye.
She did. She's *dead.*
Dead...? My mother... well, who knows...no one has heard from her since last year. She took a trip one day and never came back. She could be dead too, for all we know.
See? We do have a lot in common. You should come over to my house after school tomorrow. I like you, Wilma.
I promised Ansel we would do some studying together, so...
Are you staring at my brother?

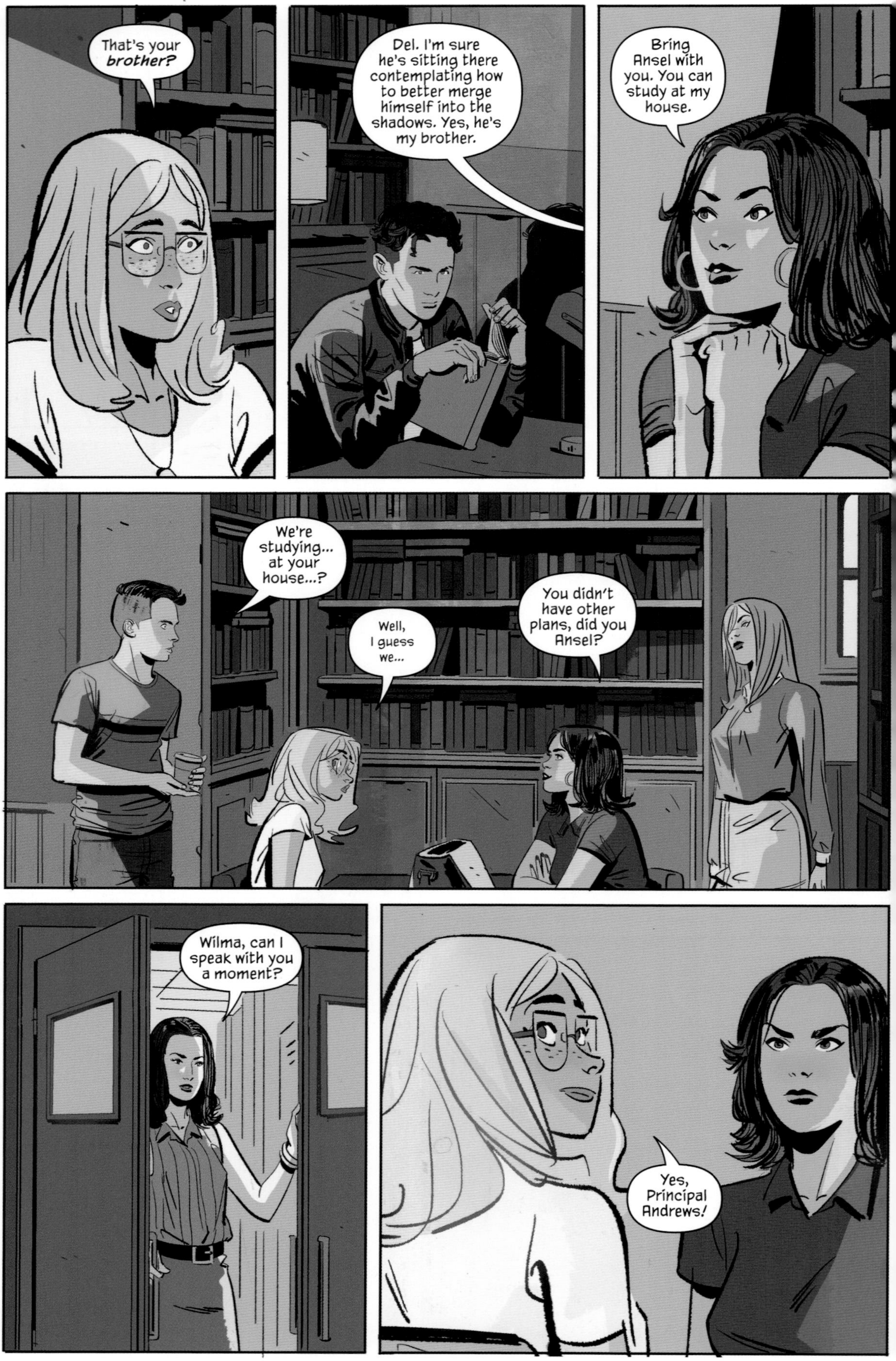

That's your *brother?*
Del. I'm sure he's sitting there contemplating how to better merge himself into the shadows. Yes, he's my brother.
Bring Ansel with you. You can study at my house.
We're studying... at your house...?
Well, I guess we...
You didn't have other plans, did you Ansel?
Wilma, can I speak with you a moment?
Yes, Principal Andrews!

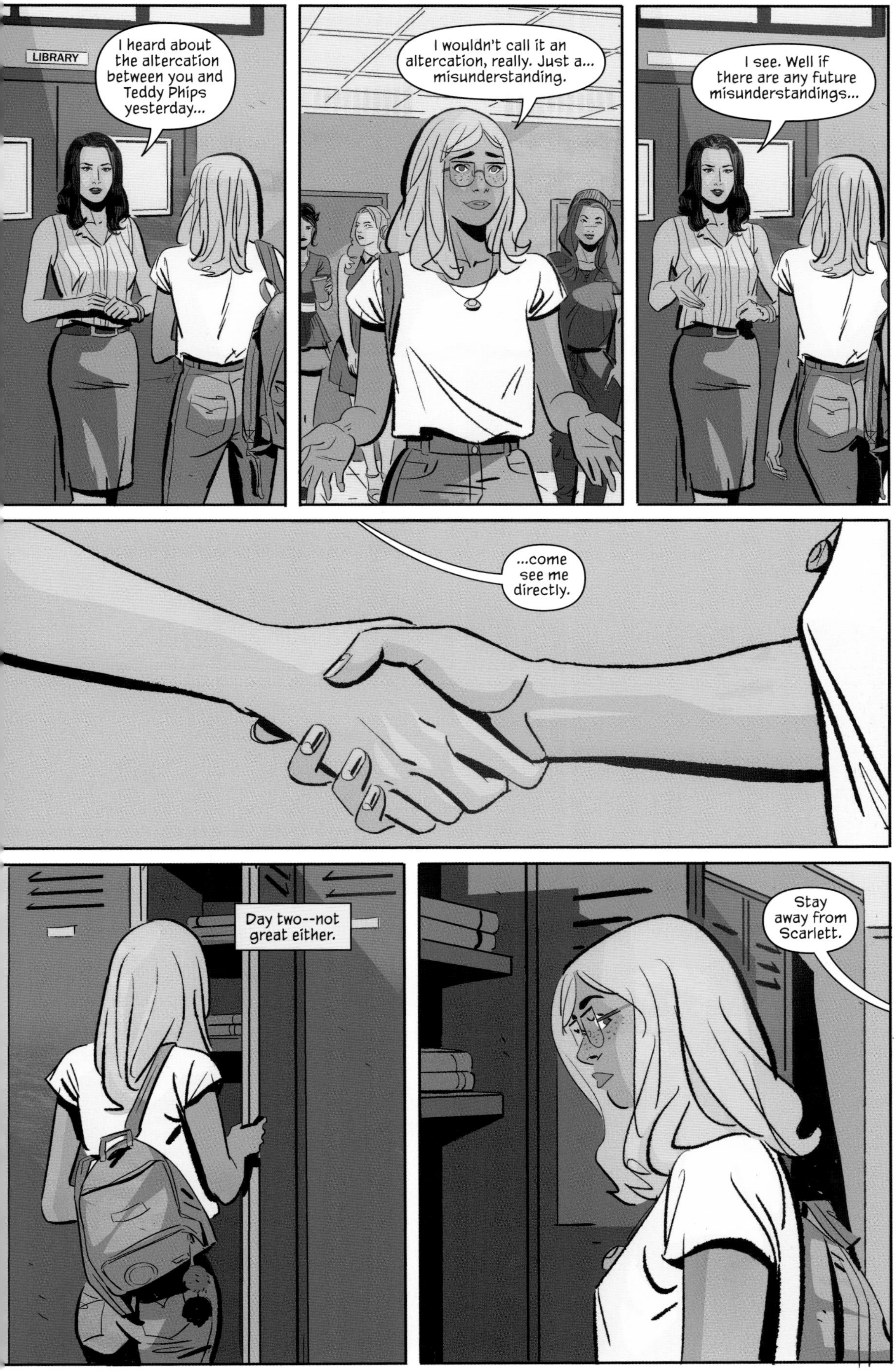
LIBRARY
I heard about the altercation between you and Teddy Phips yesterday...
I wouldn't call it an altercation, really. Just a... misunderstanding.
I see. Well if there are any future misunderstandings...
...come see me directly.
Day two--not great either.
Stay away from Scarlett.

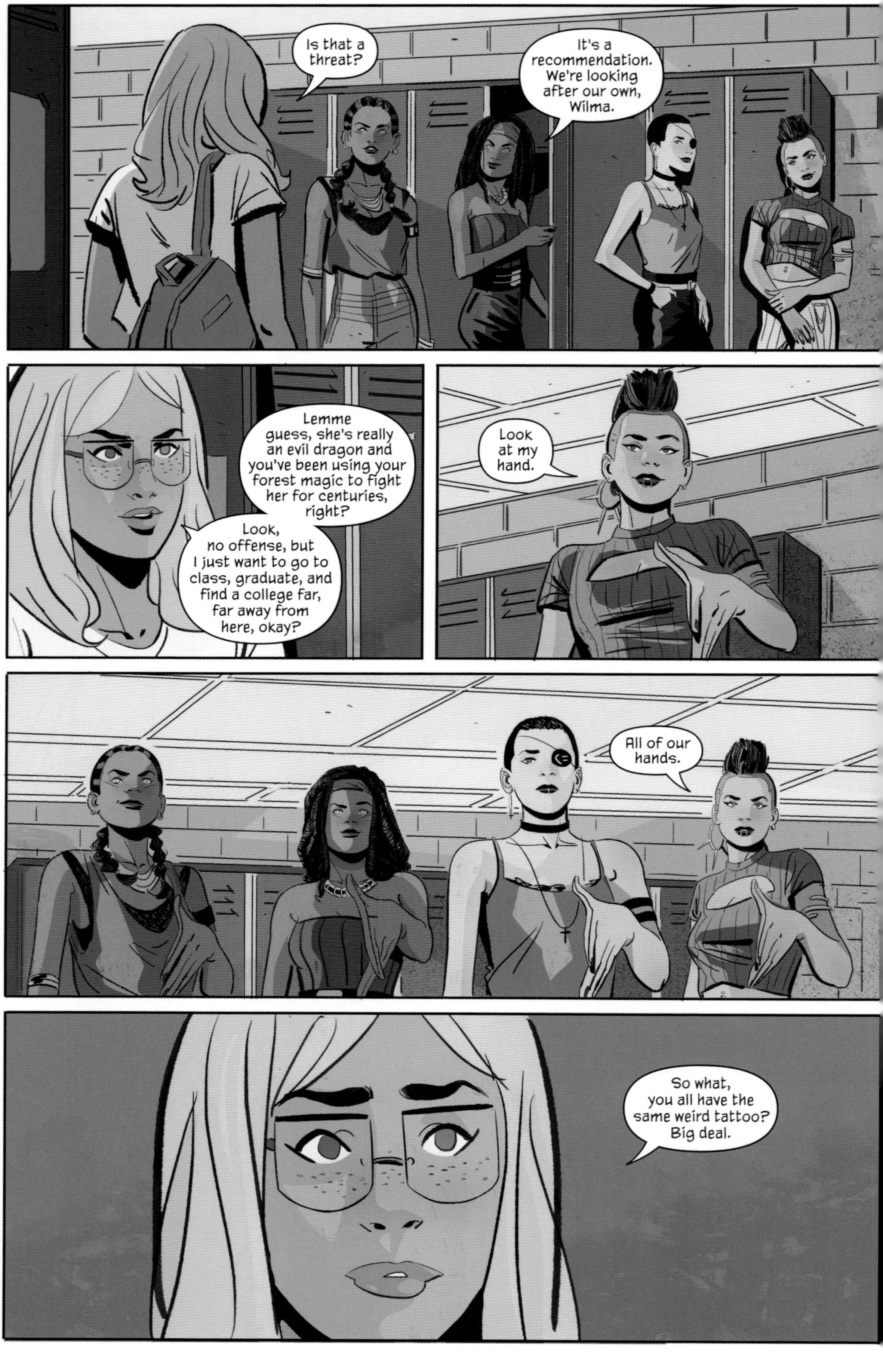
Is that a threat?
It's a recommendation. We're looking after our own, Wilma.
Lemme guess, she's really an evil dragon and you've been using your forest magic to fight her for centuries, right?
Look, no offense, but I just want to go to class, graduate, and find a college far, far away from here, okay?
Look at my hand.
All of our hands.
So what, you all have the same weird tattoo? Big deal.

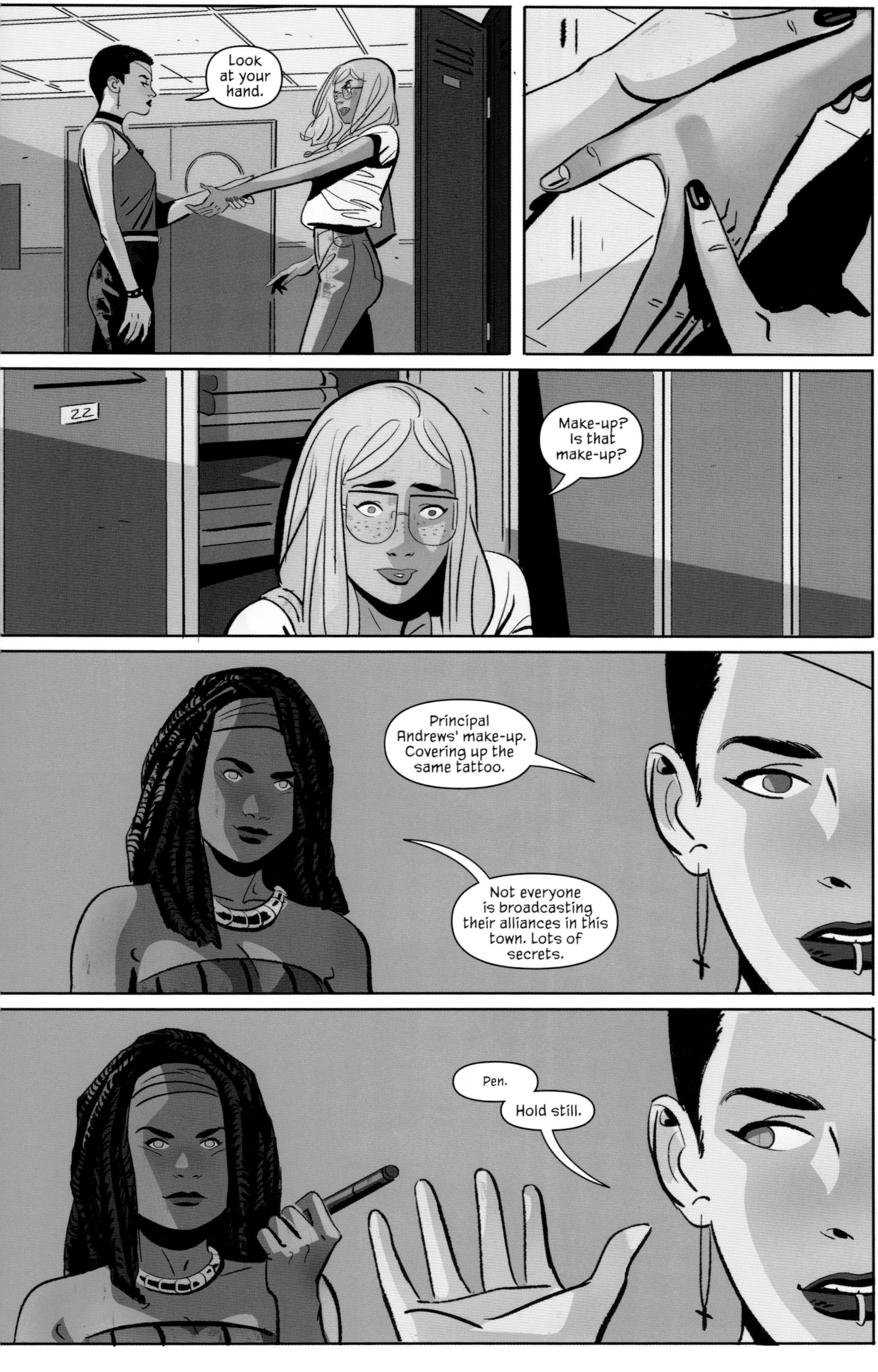
Look at your hand.
Make-up? Is that make-up?
Principal Andrews' make-up. Covering up the same tattoo.
Not everyone is broadcasting their alliances in this town. Lots of secrets.
Pen.
Hold still.
22

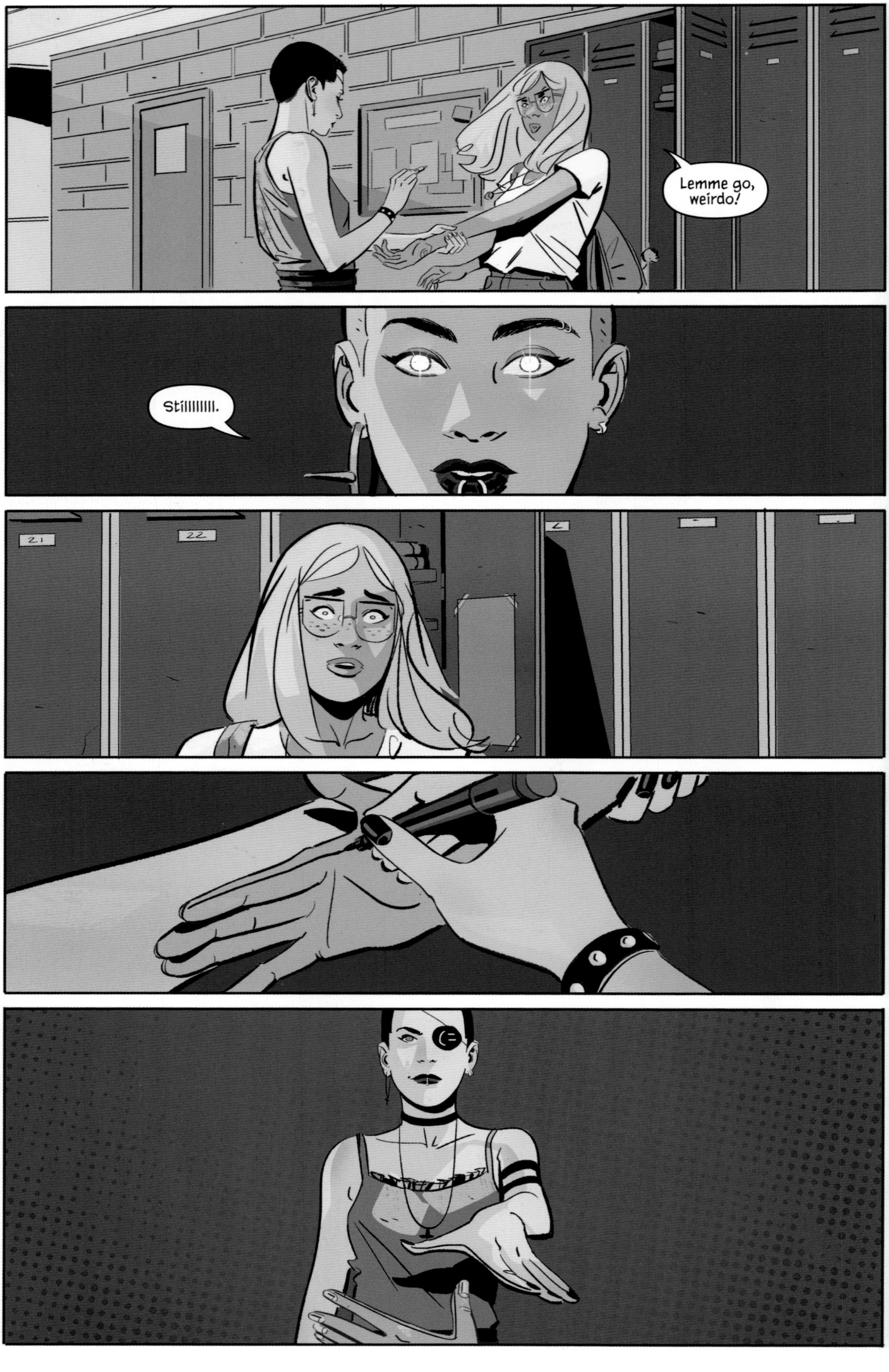
Lemme go, weirdo!
Stillllllll.

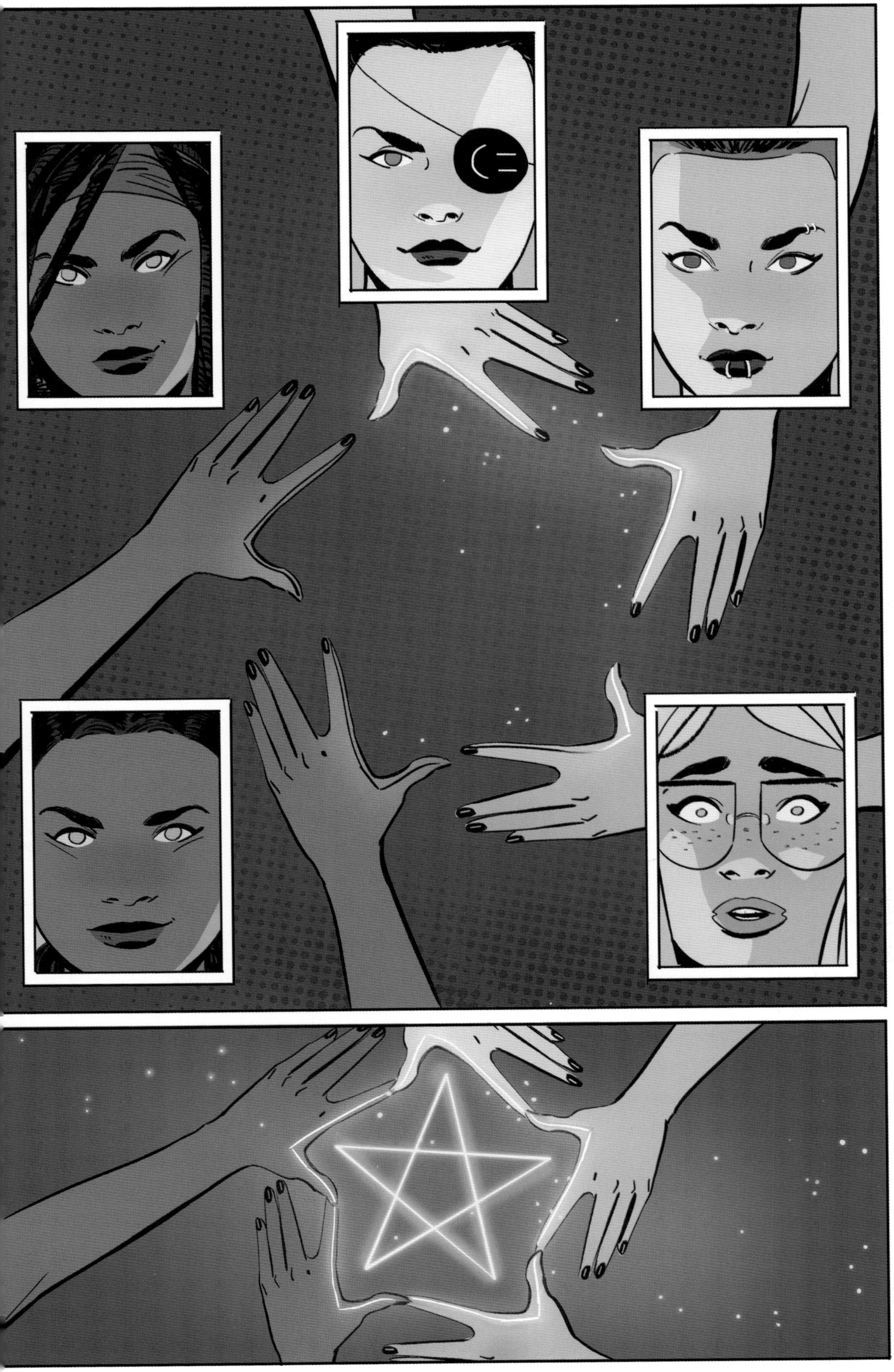

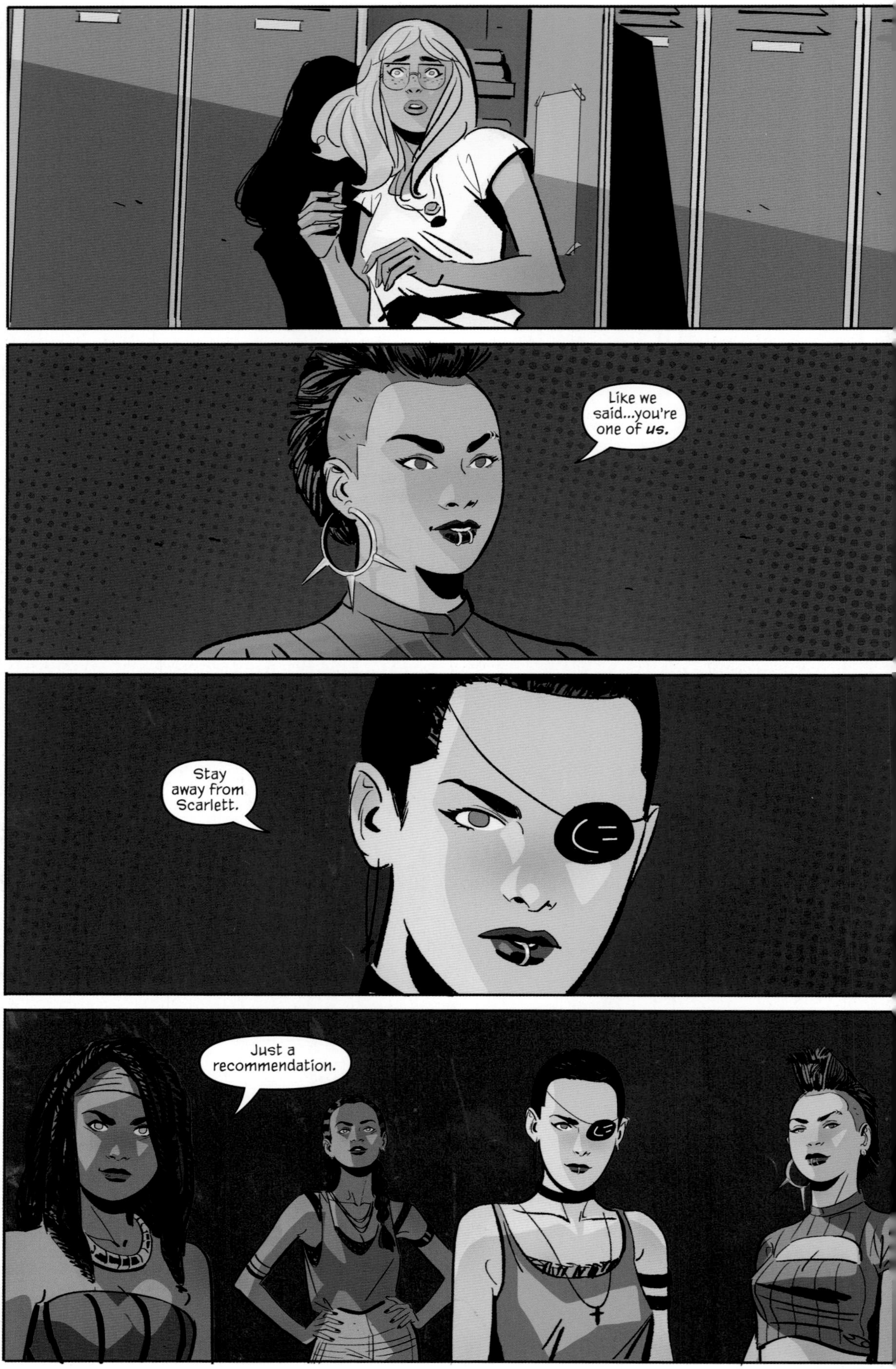

Like we said...you're one of *us.*
Stay away from Scarlett.
Just a recommendation.

V
H

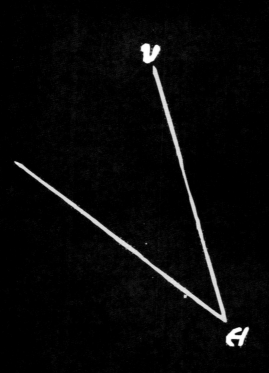

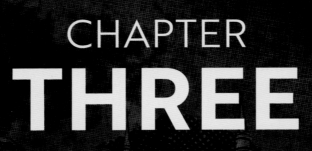

CHAPTER THREE

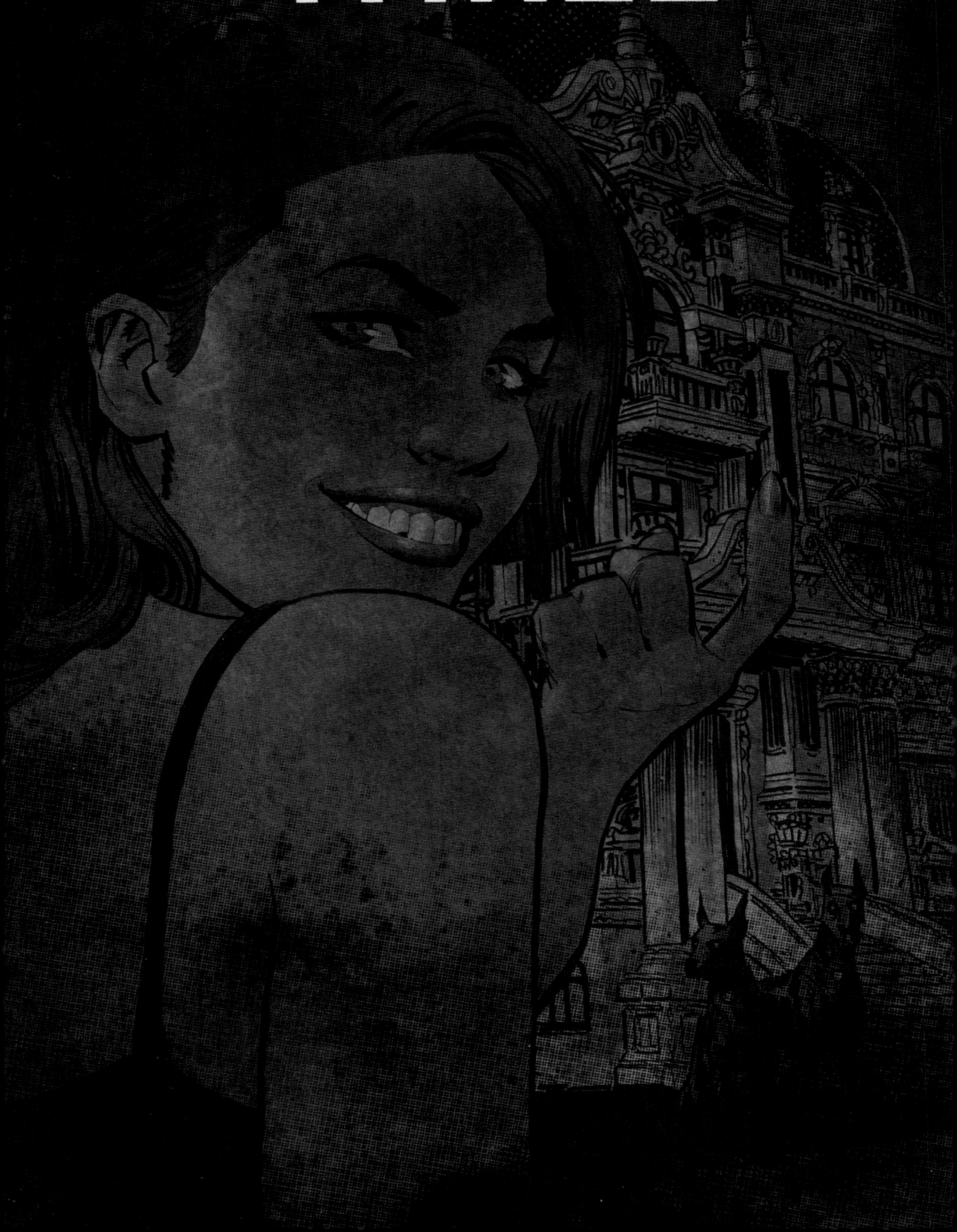

excerpts from

THE ABIGAIL HOUSE

a private hostelry

Where would I be without this handy compendium? Where would any of the Survivors be, for that matter? Keeping up with the Ravens has never been easy.

They're a secretive lot. Crab's Eye is not what you would call a big town. In fact, very few New Englanders have even heard of it. Not surprising, we've done our level best to keep things quiet here. It would be child's play too, but the Ravens love their plotting and scheming. They love multiplying as well...

This book is our little way of keeping tabs on them. All the who, what and where we can get our hands on. One day soon, we suspect, there will be a reckoning of sorts. Rumor has it, that day is fast approaching. It keeps me busy. Idle hands are the devil's playthings, as some say.

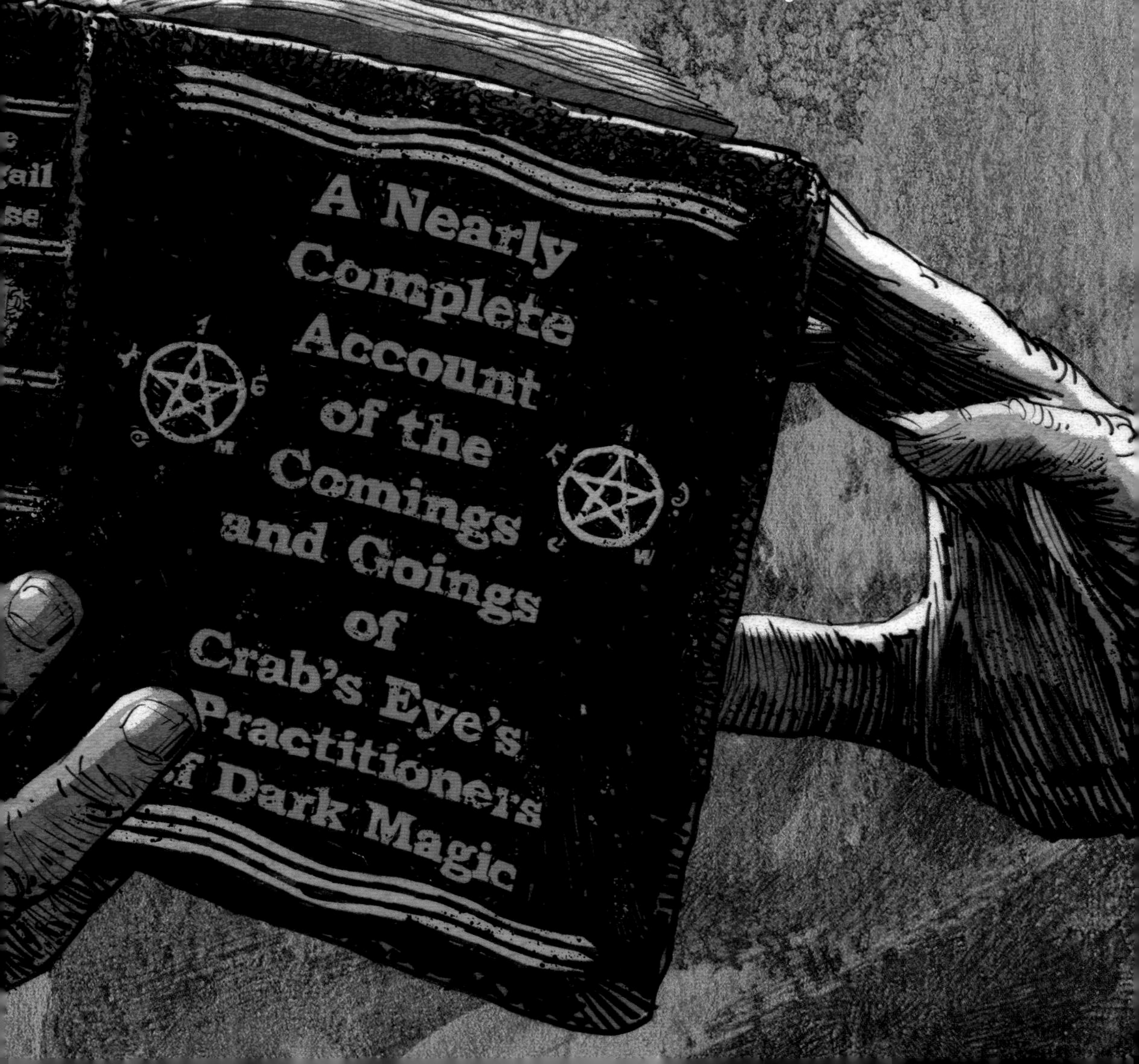
A Nearly
Complete
Account
of the
Comings
and Goings
of
Crab's Eye's
Practitioners
Dark Magic

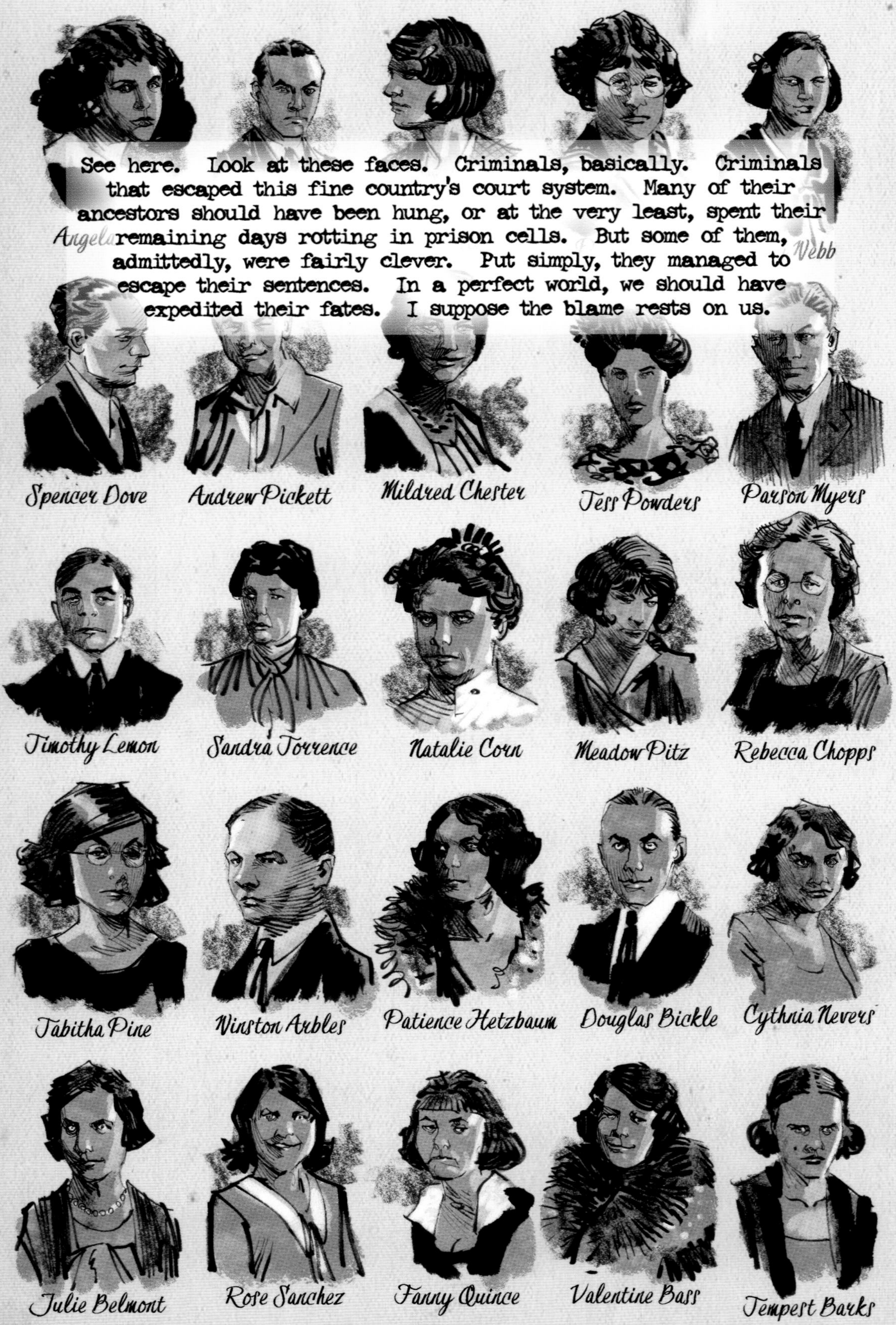

See here. Look at these faces. Criminals, basically. Criminals that escaped this fine country's court system. Many of their ancestors should have been hung, or at the very least, spent their remaining days rotting in prison cells. But some of them, admittedly, were fairly clever. Put simply, they managed to escape their sentences. In a perfect world, we should have expedited their fates. I suppose the blame rests on us.
Spencer Dove
Andrew Pickett
Mildred Chester
Tess Powders
Parson Myers
Timothy Lemon
Sandra Torrence
Natalie Corn
Meadow Pitz
Rebecca Chopps
Tabitha Pine
Winston Arbles
Patience Hetzbaum
Douglas Bickle
Cythnia Nevers
Julie Belmont
Rose Sanchez
Fanny Quince
Valentine Bass
Tempest Barks

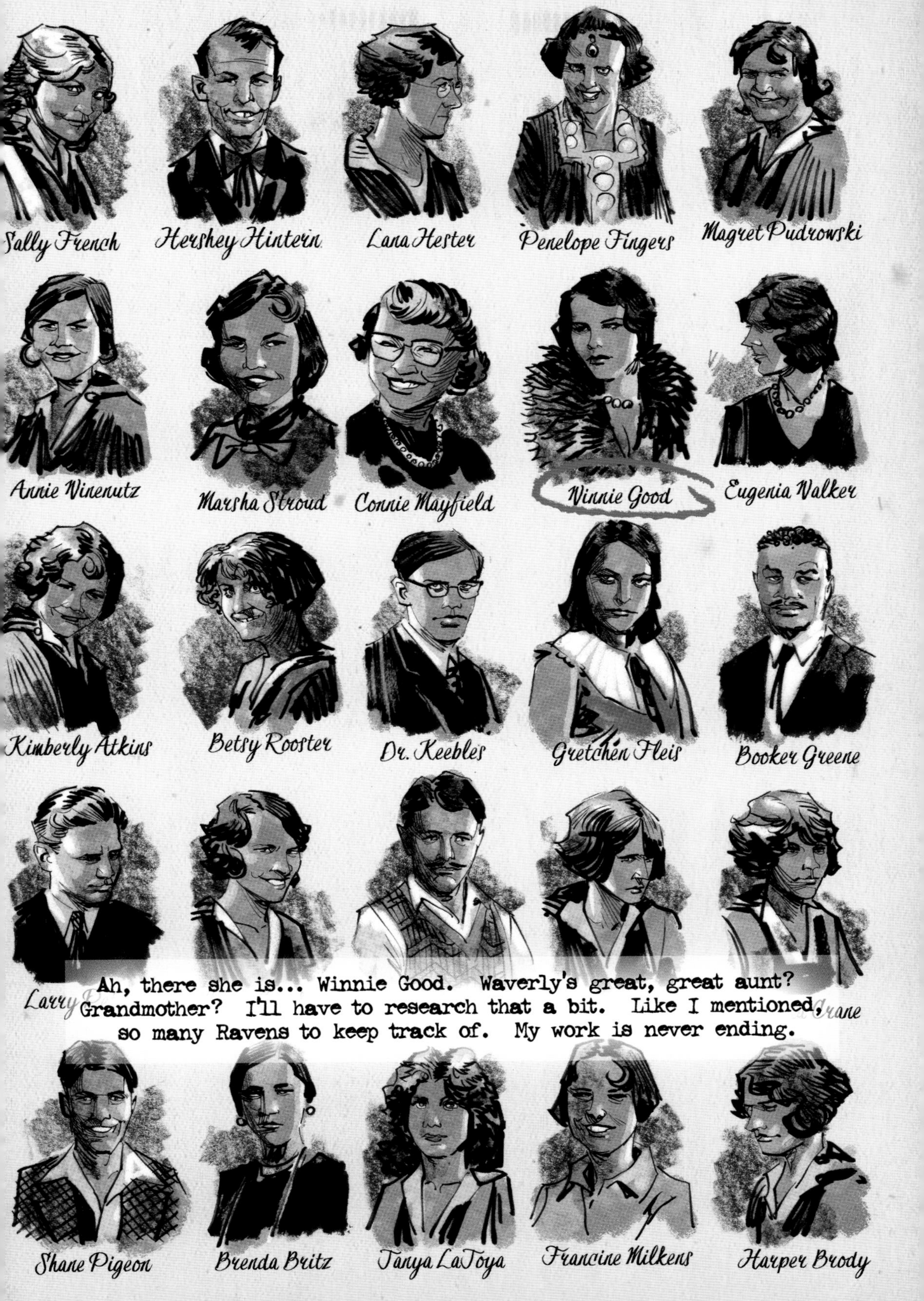
Sally French
Hershey Hintern
Lana Hester
Penelope Fingers
Magret Pudrowski
Annie Winenutz
Marsha Stroud
Connie Mayfield
Winnie Good
Eugenia Walker
Kimberly Atkins
Betsy Rooster
Dr. Keebles
Gretchen Fleis
Booker Greene
Larry
Crane
Ah, there she is... Winnie Good. Waverly's great, great aunt? Grandmother? I'll have to research that a bit. Like I mentioned, so many Ravens to keep track of. My work is never ending.
Shane Pigeon
Brenda Britz
Tanya LaToya
Francine Milkens
Harper Brody

No time to rest it would seem. The Dansforths' yearly gala is nearly upon us and they don't appreciate surprises.

And neither do their many and varied guests. They come from all over the world. It's quite the scene. The guest list is a who's who of industry, celebrity and the obscure. You may recognize a few here and there. And when they arrive, where do they rest their weary bones?

At the Abigail House, of course.

We highly recommend that guests R.S.V.P.

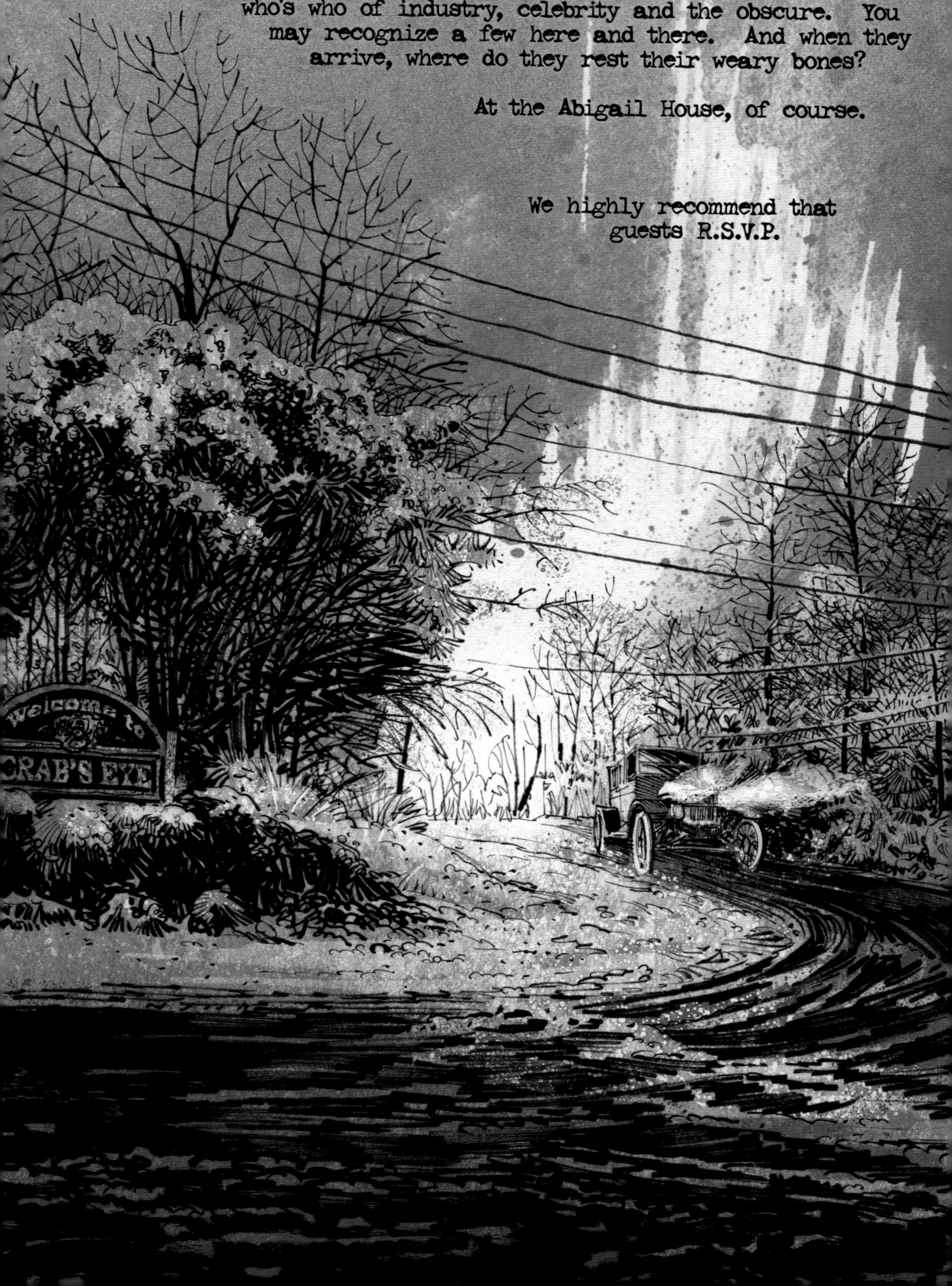
Welcome to
CRAB'S EYE

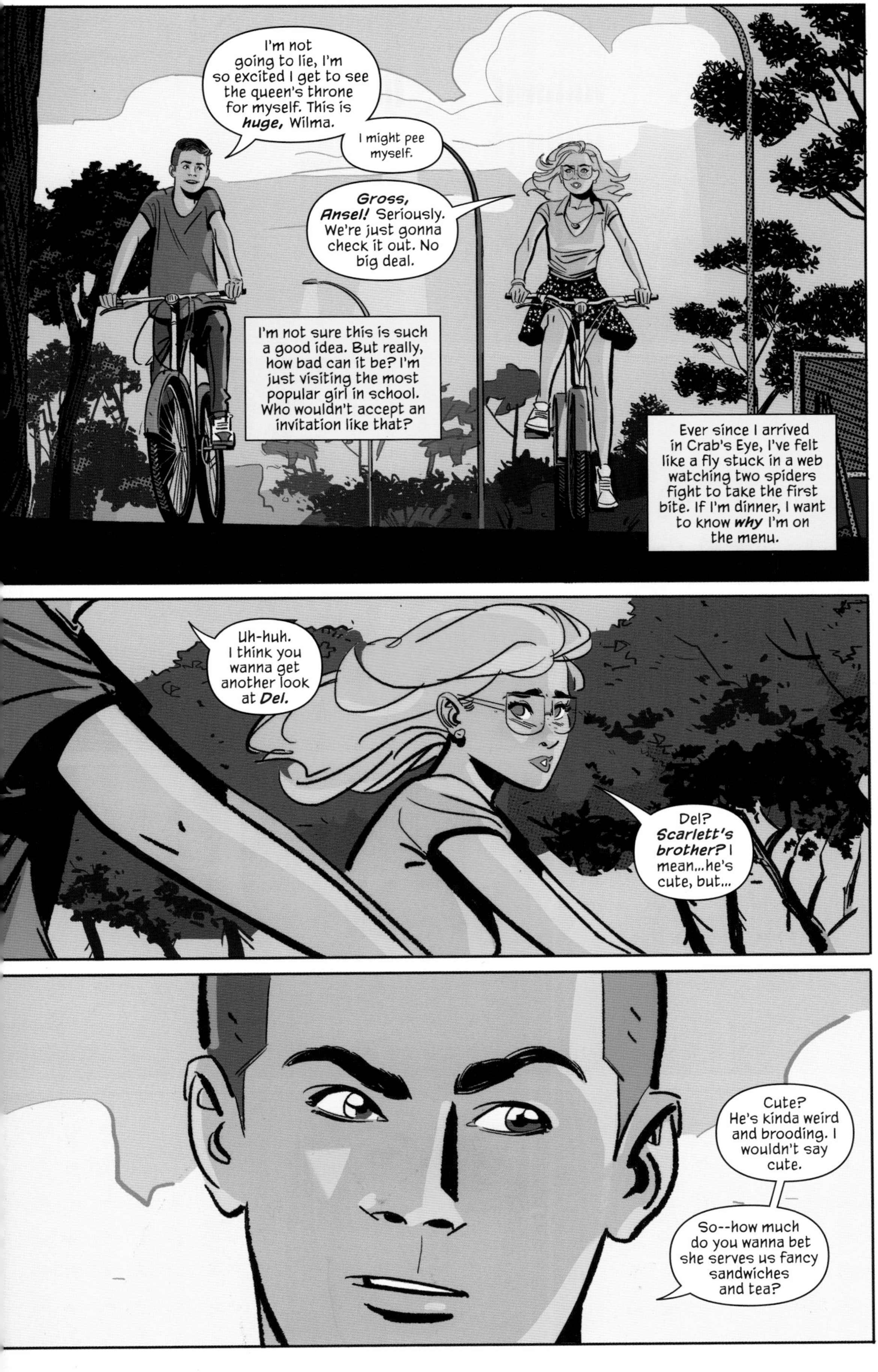
I'm not going to lie, I'm so excited I get to see the queen's throne for myself. This is **huge,** Wilma.
I might pee myself.
Gross, Ansel! Seriously. We're just gonna check it out. No big deal.
I'm not sure this is such a good idea. But really, how bad can it be? I'm just visiting the most popular girl in school. Who wouldn't accept an invitation like that?
Ever since I arrived in Crab's Eye, I've felt like a fly stuck in a web watching two spiders fight to take the first bite. If I'm dinner, I want to know ***why*** I'm on the menu.
Uh-huh. I think you wanna get another look at ***Del.***
Del? ***Scarlett's brother?*** I mean...he's cute, but...
Cute? He's kinda weird and brooding. I wouldn't say cute.
So--how much do you wanna bet she serves us fancy sandwiches and tea?

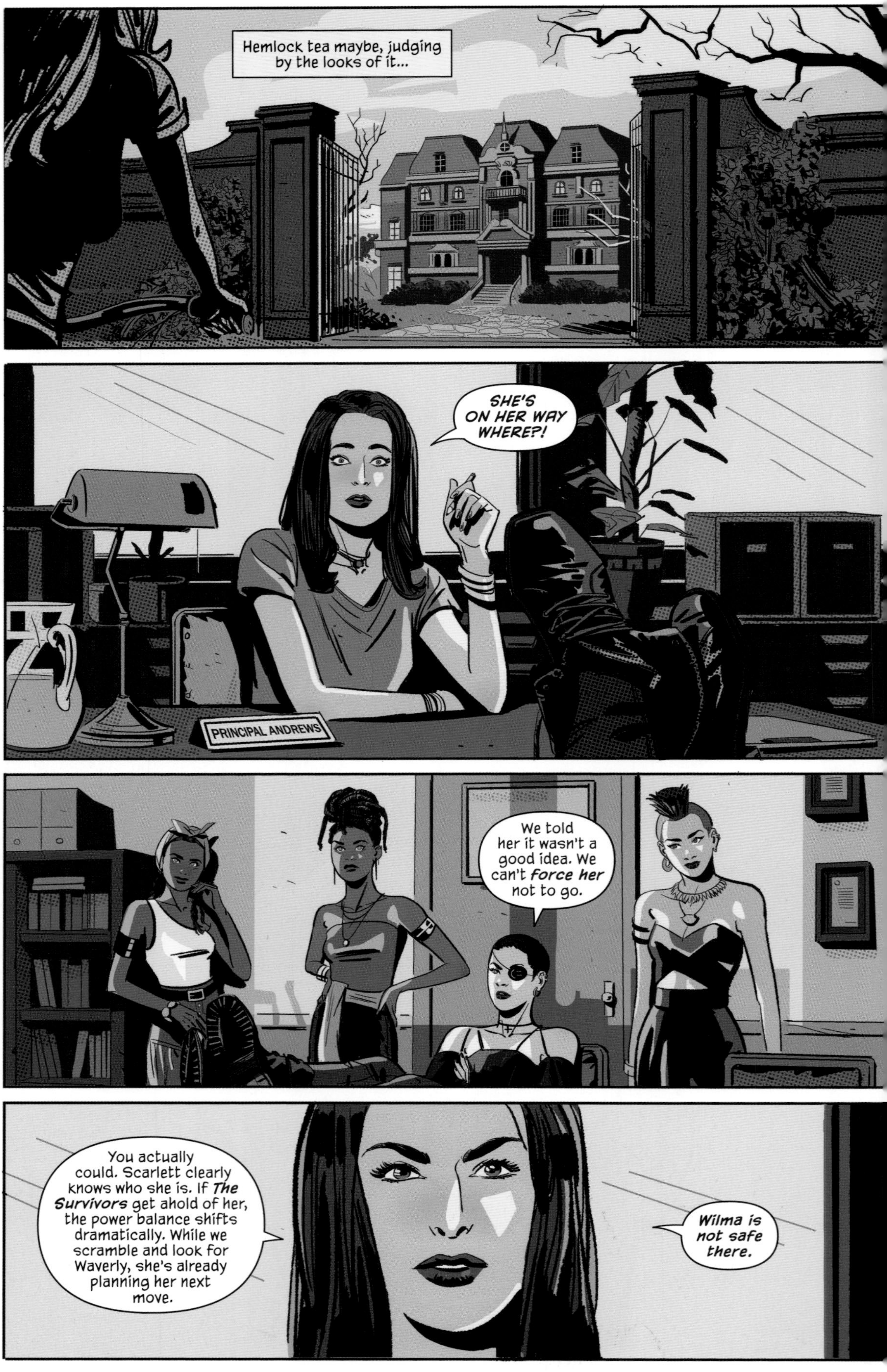
Hemlock tea maybe, judging by the looks of it...
SHE'S ON HER WAY WHERE?!
PRINCIPAL ANDREWS
We told her it wasn't a good idea. We can't *force her* not to go.
You actually could. Scarlett clearly knows who she is. If *The Survivors* get ahold of her, the power balance shifts dramatically. While we scramble and look for Waverly, she's already planning her next move.
Wilma is not safe there.

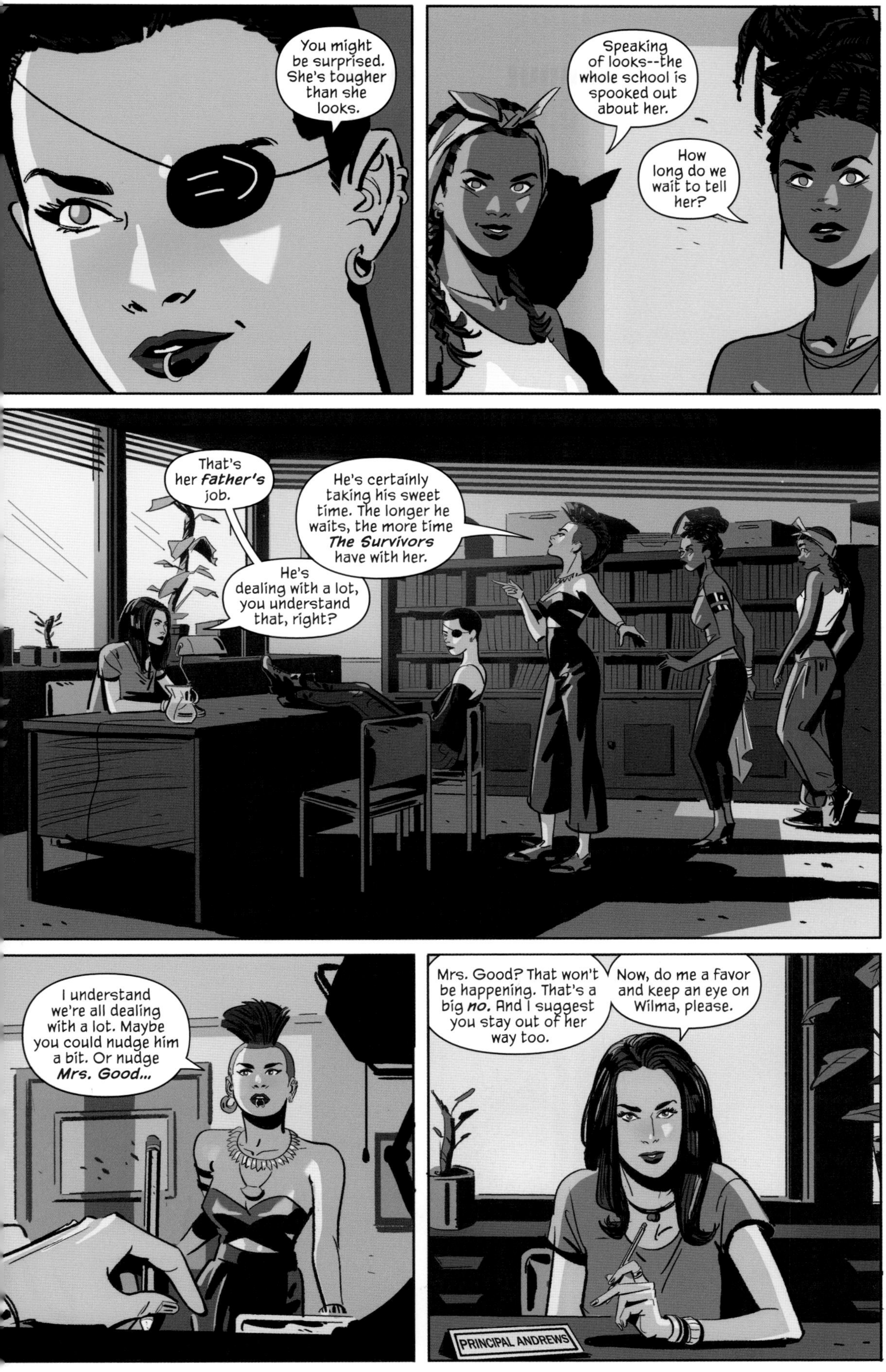
You might be surprised. She's tougher than she looks.
Speaking of looks--the whole school is spooked out about her.
How long do we wait to tell her?
That's her *father's* job.
He's certainly taking his sweet time. The longer he waits, the more time *The Survivors* have with her.
He's dealing with a lot, you understand that, right?
I understand we're all dealing with a lot. Maybe you could nudge him a bit. Or nudge *Mrs. Good...*
Mrs. Good? That won't be happening. That's a big *no.* And I suggest you stay out of her way too.
Now, do me a favor and keep an eye on Wilma, please.
PRINCIPAL ANDREWS

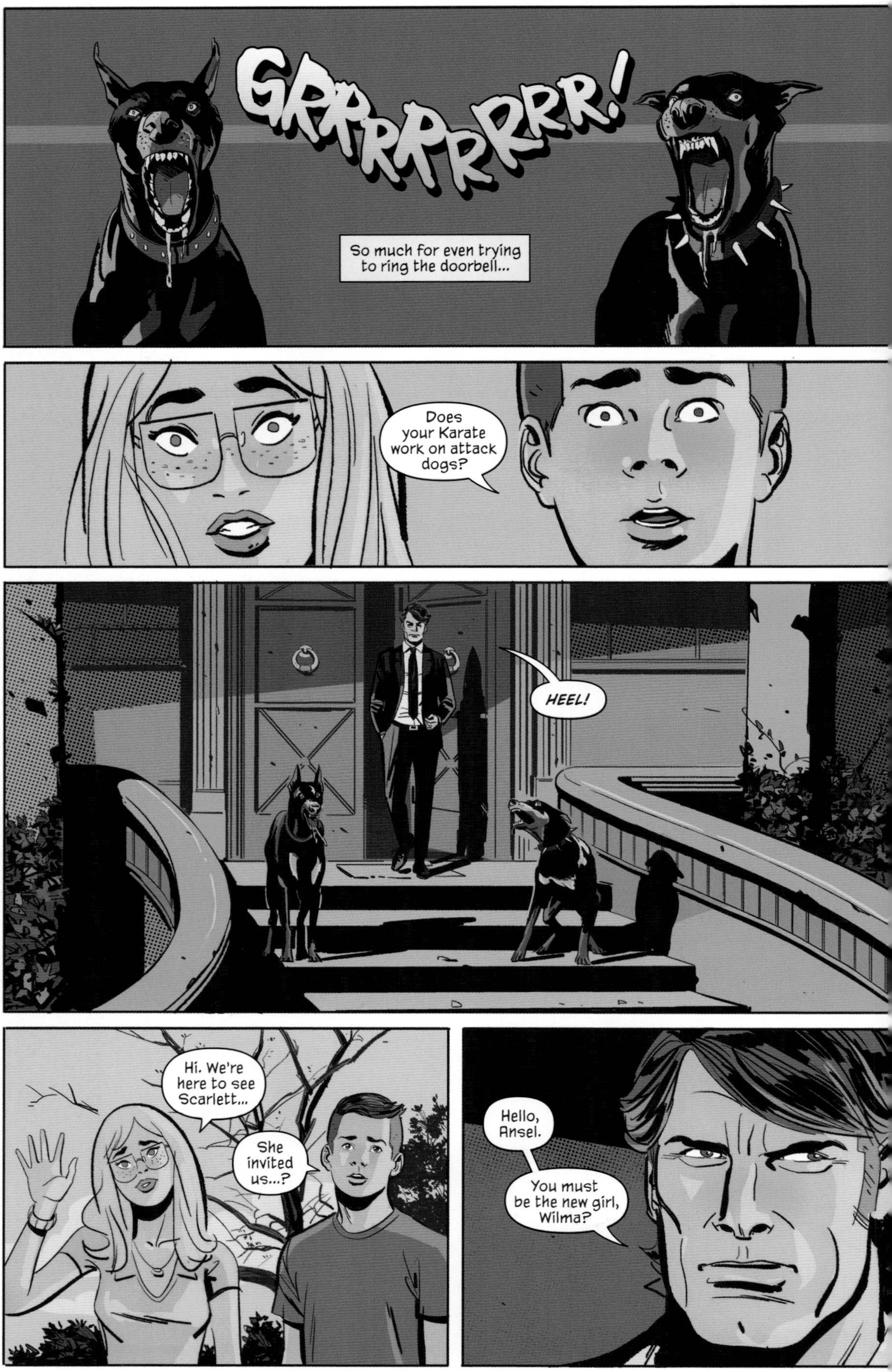
GRRRRRRR!
So much for even trying to ring the doorbell...
Does your Karate work on attack dogs?
HEEL!
Hi. We're here to see Scarlett...
She invited us...?
Hello, Ansel.
You must be the new girl, Wilma?

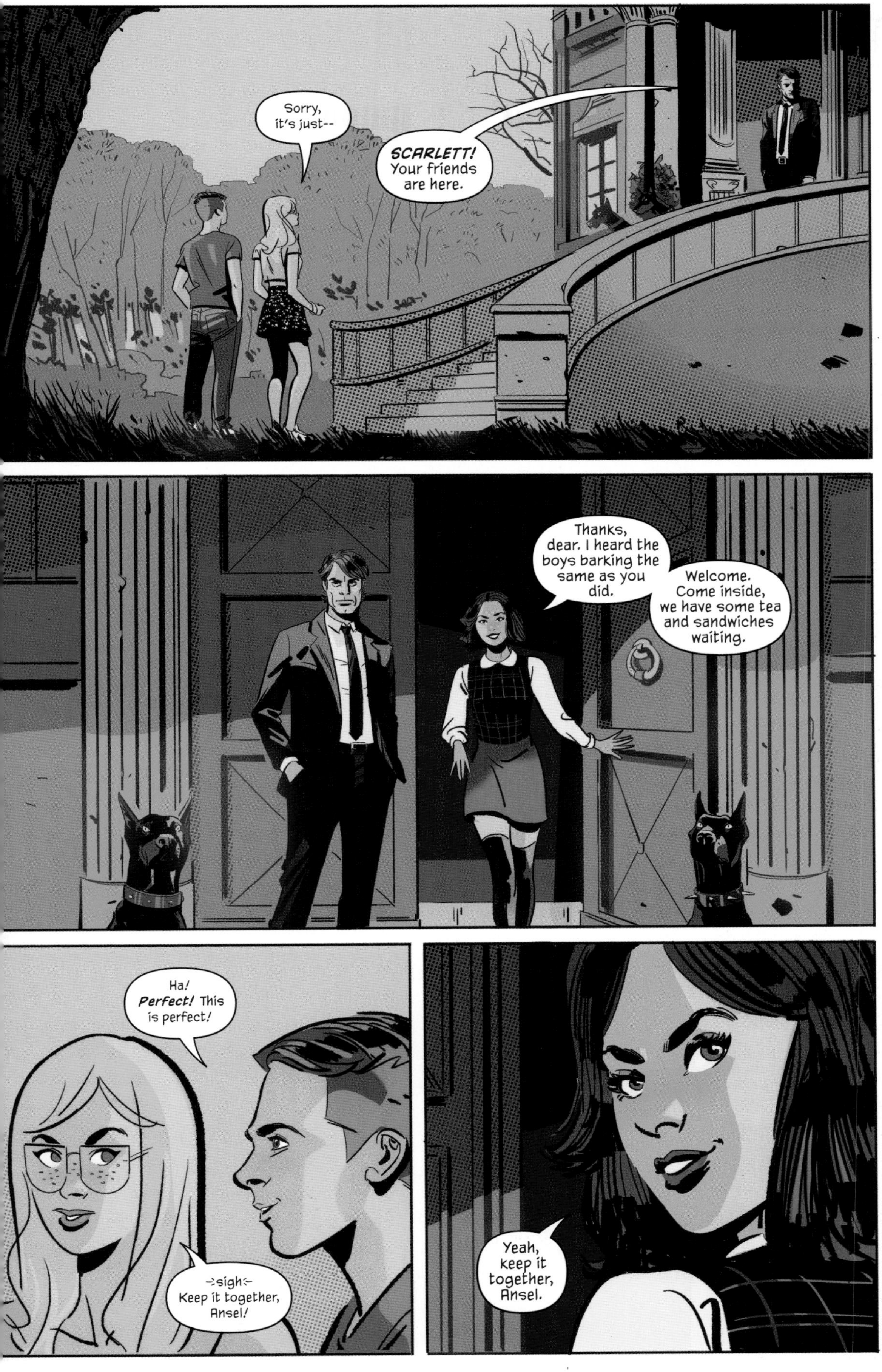
Sorry, it's just--
SCARLETT! Your friends are here.
Thanks, dear. I heard the boys barking the same as you did.
Welcome. Come inside, we have some tea and sandwiches waiting.
Ha! Perfect! This is perfect!
-sigh- Keep it together, Ansel!
Yeah, keep it together, Ansel.

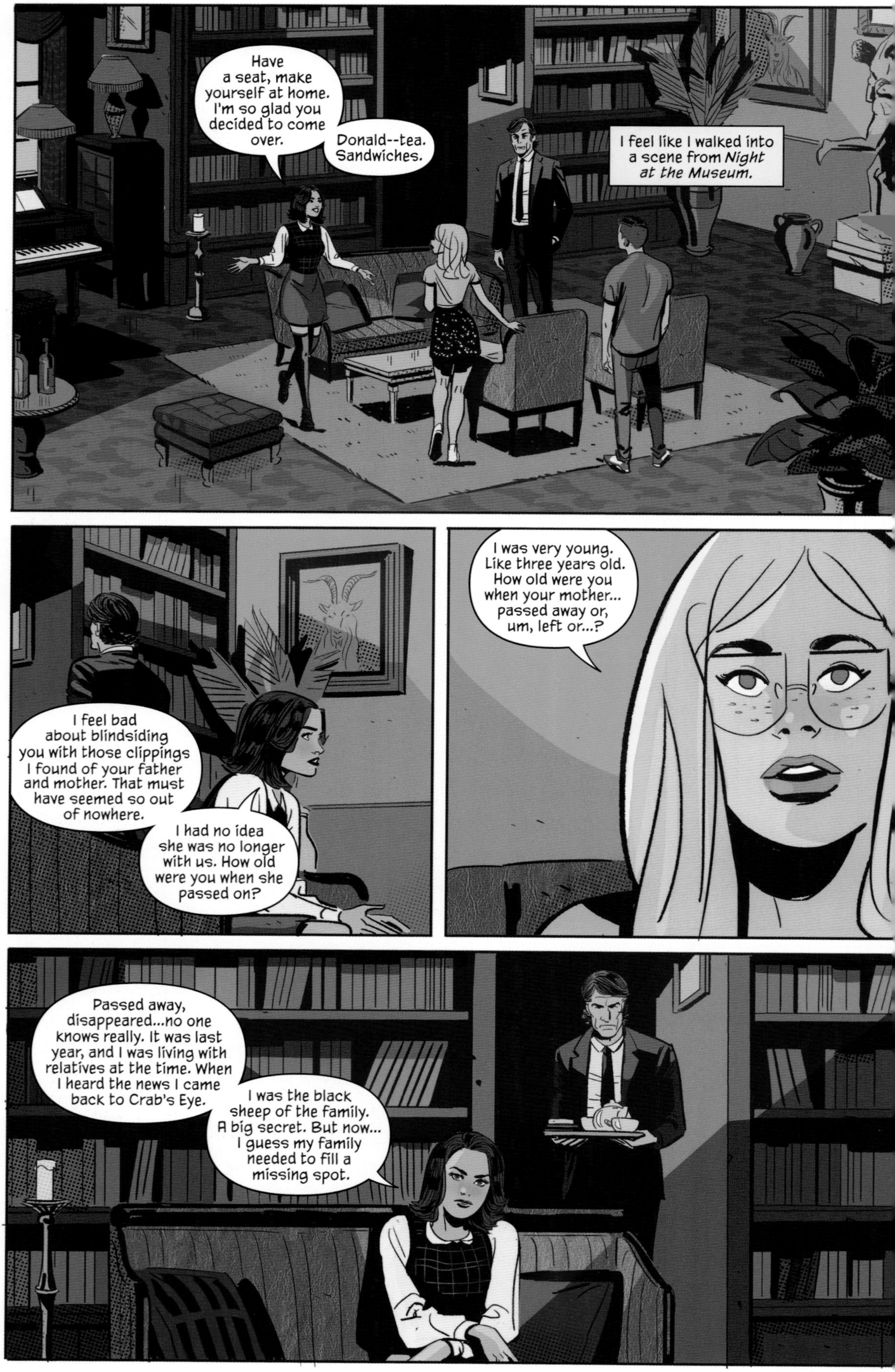
Have a seat, make yourself at home. I'm so glad you decided to come over.
Donald--tea. Sandwiches.
I feel like I walked into a scene from *Night at the Museum.*
I feel bad about blindsiding you with those clippings I found of your father and mother. That must have seemed so out of nowhere.
I had no idea she was no longer with us. How old were you when she passed on?
I was very young. Like three years old. How old were you when your mother... passed away or, um, left or...?
Passed away, disappeared...no one knows really. It was last year, and I was living with relatives at the time. When I heard the news I came back to Crab's Eye.
I was the black sheep of the family. A big secret. But now... I guess my family needed to fill a missing spot.

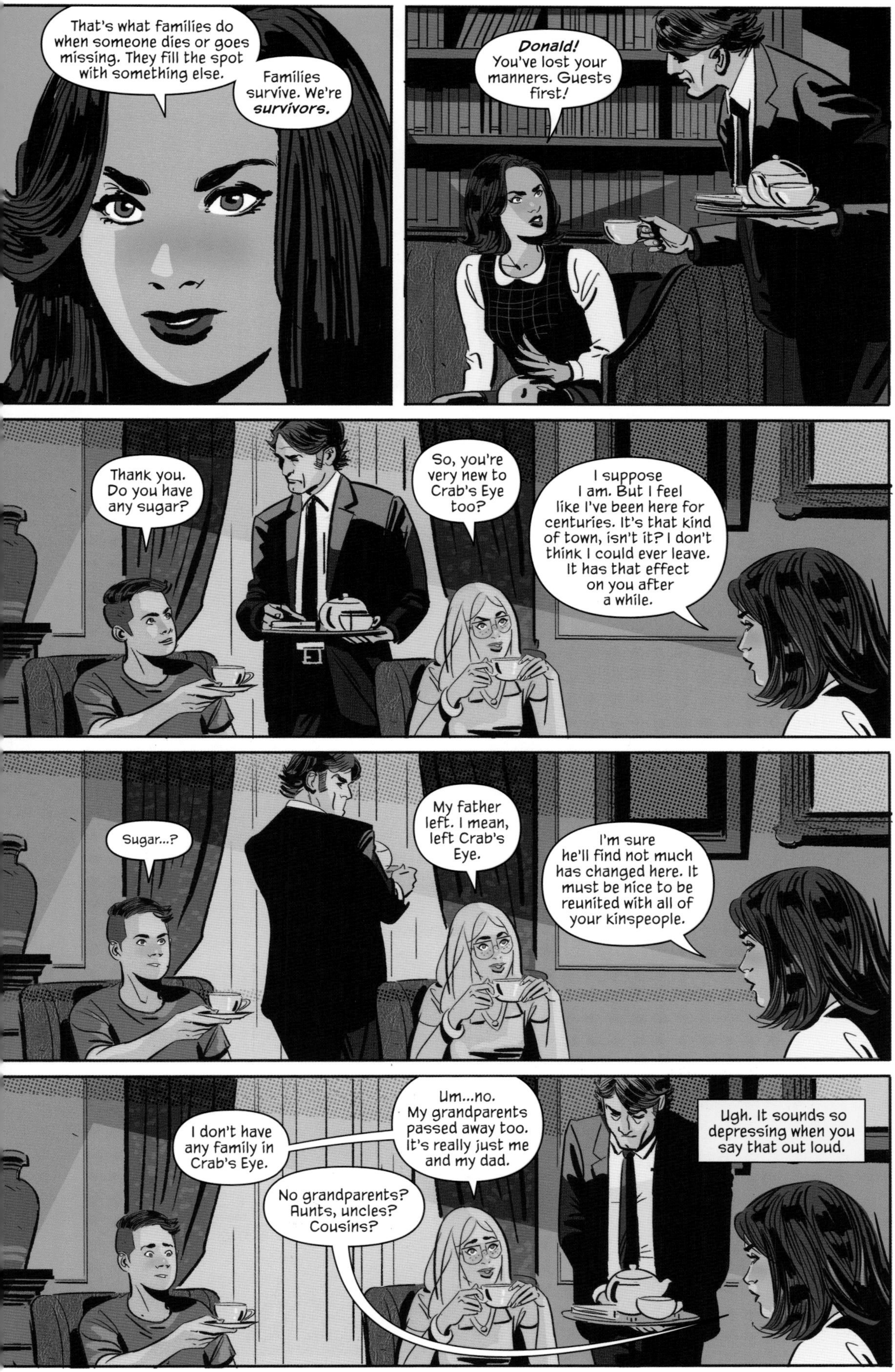
That's what families do when someone dies or goes missing. They fill the spot with something else.
Families survive. We're *survivors.*
Donald! You've lost your manners. Guests first!
Thank you. Do you have any sugar?
So, you're very new to Crab's Eye too?
I suppose I am. But I feel like I've been here for centuries. It's that kind of town, isn't it? I don't think I could ever leave. It has that effect on you after a while.
Sugar...?
My father left. I mean, left Crab's Eye.
I'm sure he'll find not much has changed here. It must be nice to be reunited with all of your kinspeople.
I don't have any family in Crab's Eye.
No grandparents? Aunts, uncles? Cousins?
Um...no. My grandparents passed away too. It's really just me and my dad.
Ugh. It sounds so depressing when you say that out loud.

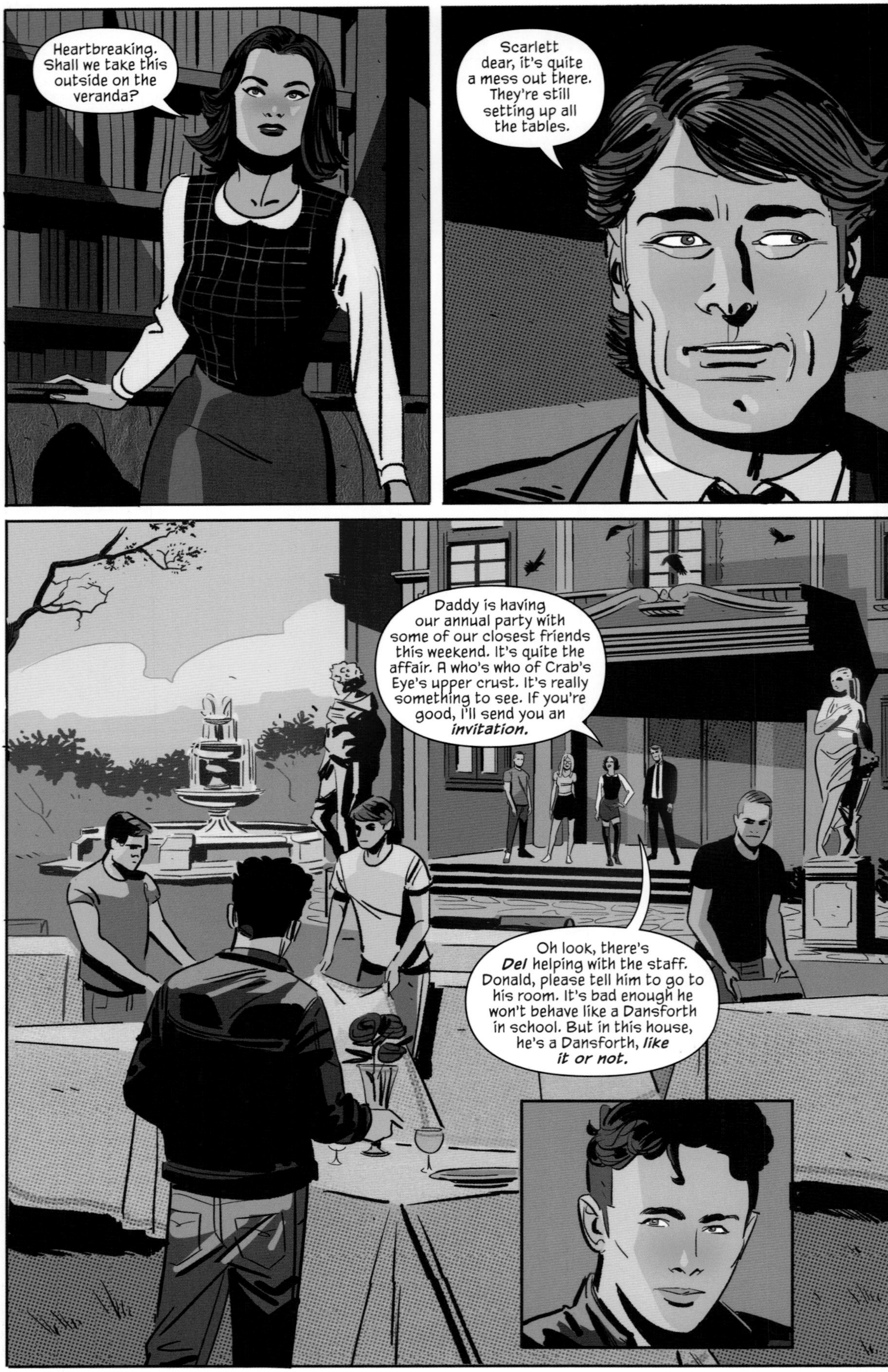
Heartbreaking. Shall we take this outside on the veranda?
Scarlett dear, it's quite a mess out there. They're still setting up all the tables.
Daddy is having our annual party with some of our closest friends this weekend. It's quite the affair. A who's who of Crab's Eye's upper crust. It's really something to see. If you're good, I'll send you an *invitation.*
Oh look, there's *Del* helping with the staff. Donald, please tell him to go to his room. It's bad enough he won't behave like a Dansforth in school. But in this house, he's a Dansforth, *like it or not.*

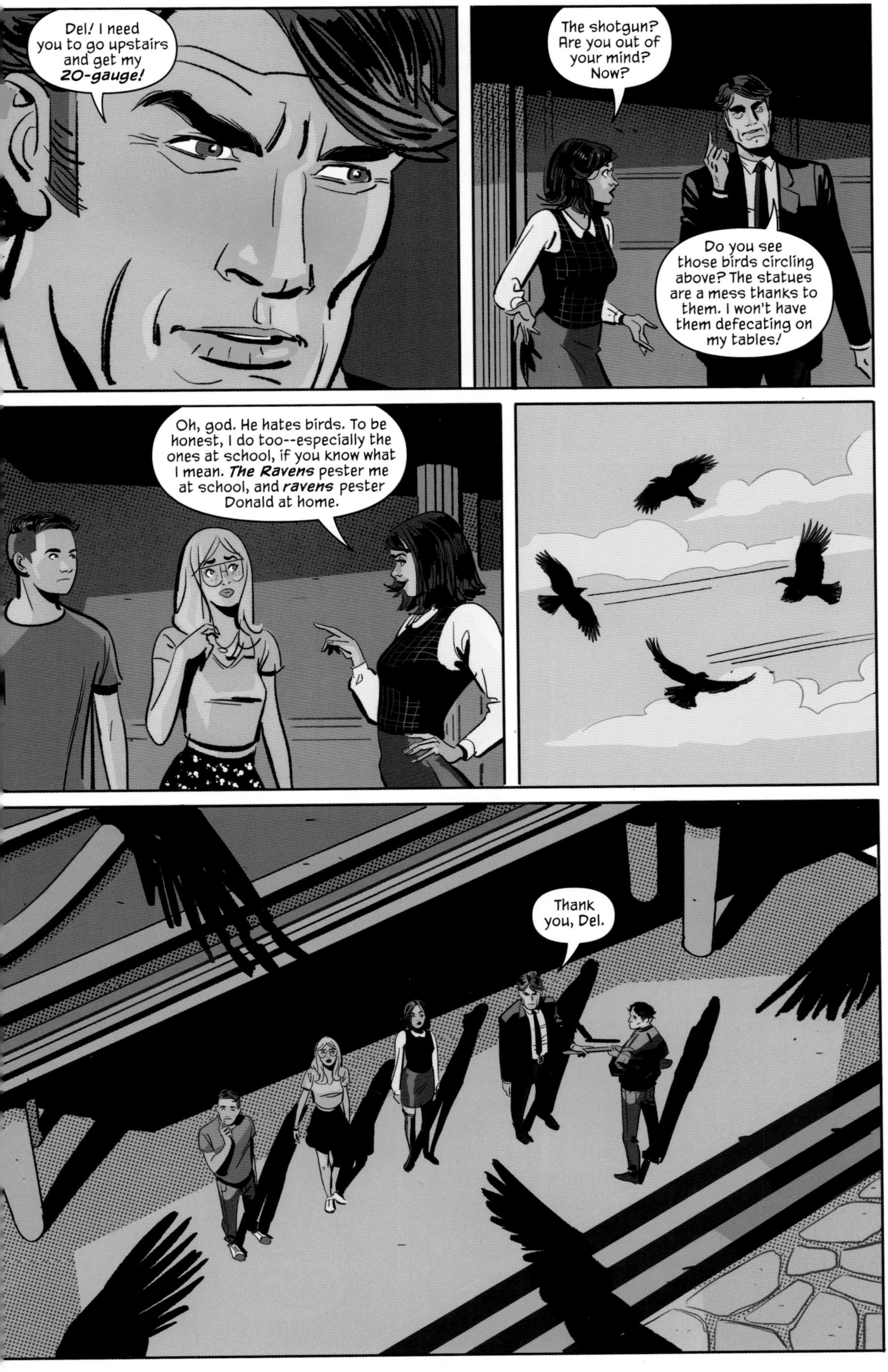
Del! I need you to go upstairs and get my 20-gauge!
The shotgun? Are you out of your mind? Now?
Do you see those birds circling above? The statues are a mess thanks to them. I won't have them defecating on my tables!
Oh, god. He hates birds. To be honest, I do too--especially the ones at school, if you know what I mean. The Ravens pester me at school, and ravens pester Donald at home.
Thank you, Del.

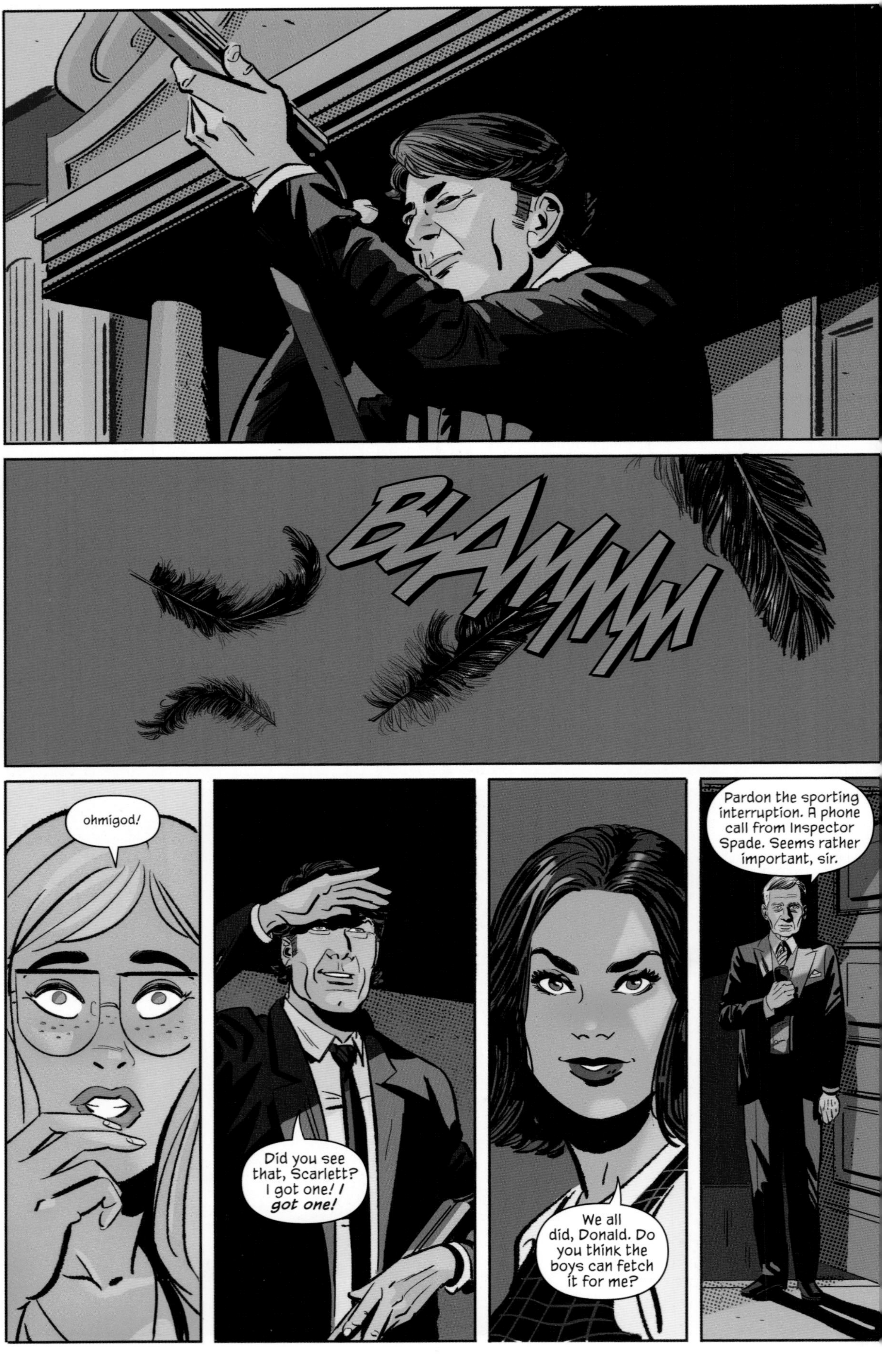
BLAMMM
ohmigod!
Did you see that, Scarlett? I got one! I got one!
We all did, Donald. Do you think the boys can fetch it for me?
Pardon the sporting interruption. A phone call from Inspector Spade. Seems rather important, sir.

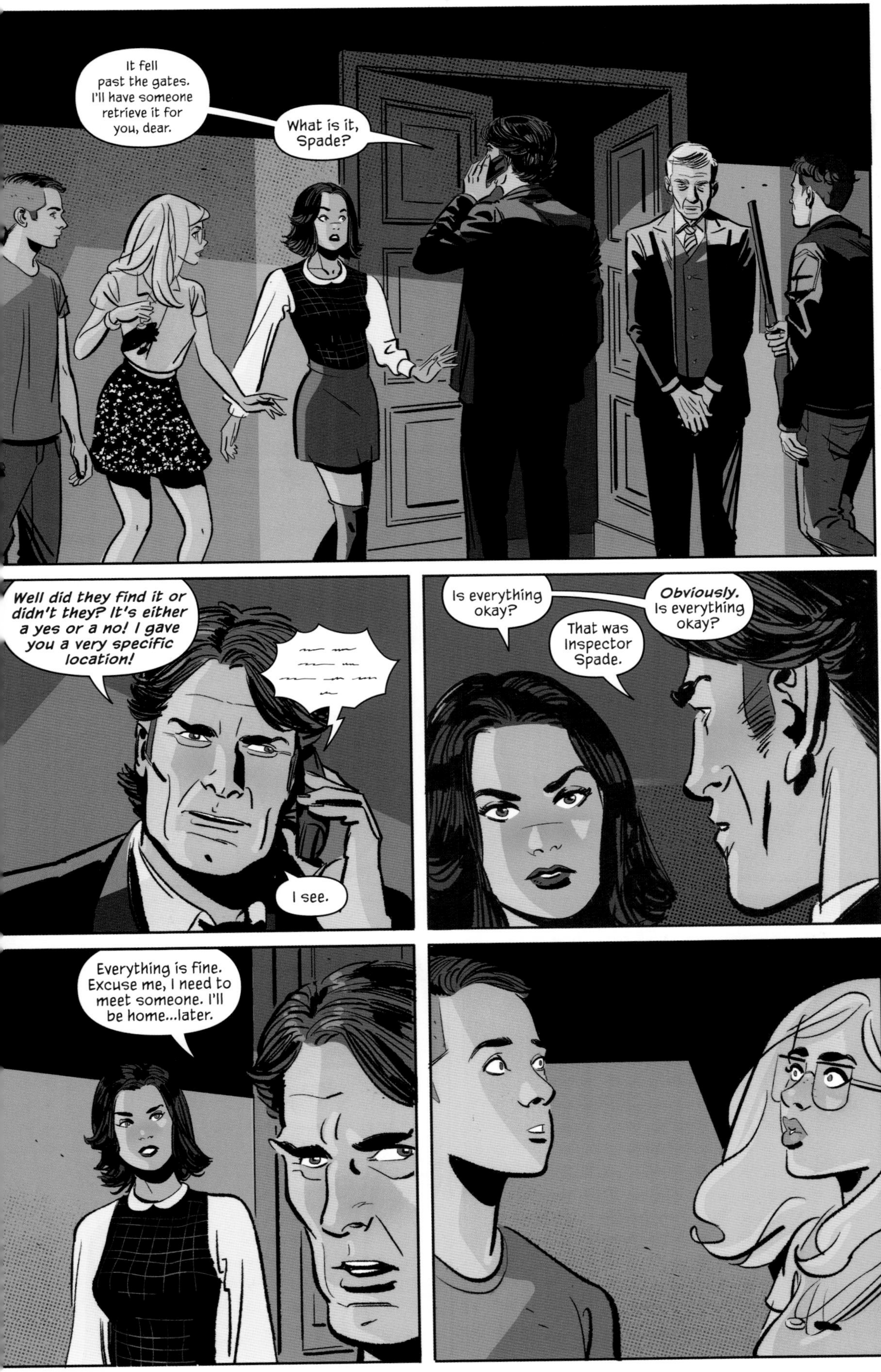

It fell past the gates. I'll have someone retrieve it for you, dear.
What is it, Spade?
Well did they find it or didn't they? It's either a yes or a no! I gave you a very specific location!
I see.
Is everything okay?
Obviously. Is everything okay?
That was Inspector Spade.
Everything is fine. Excuse me, I need to meet someone. I'll be home...later.

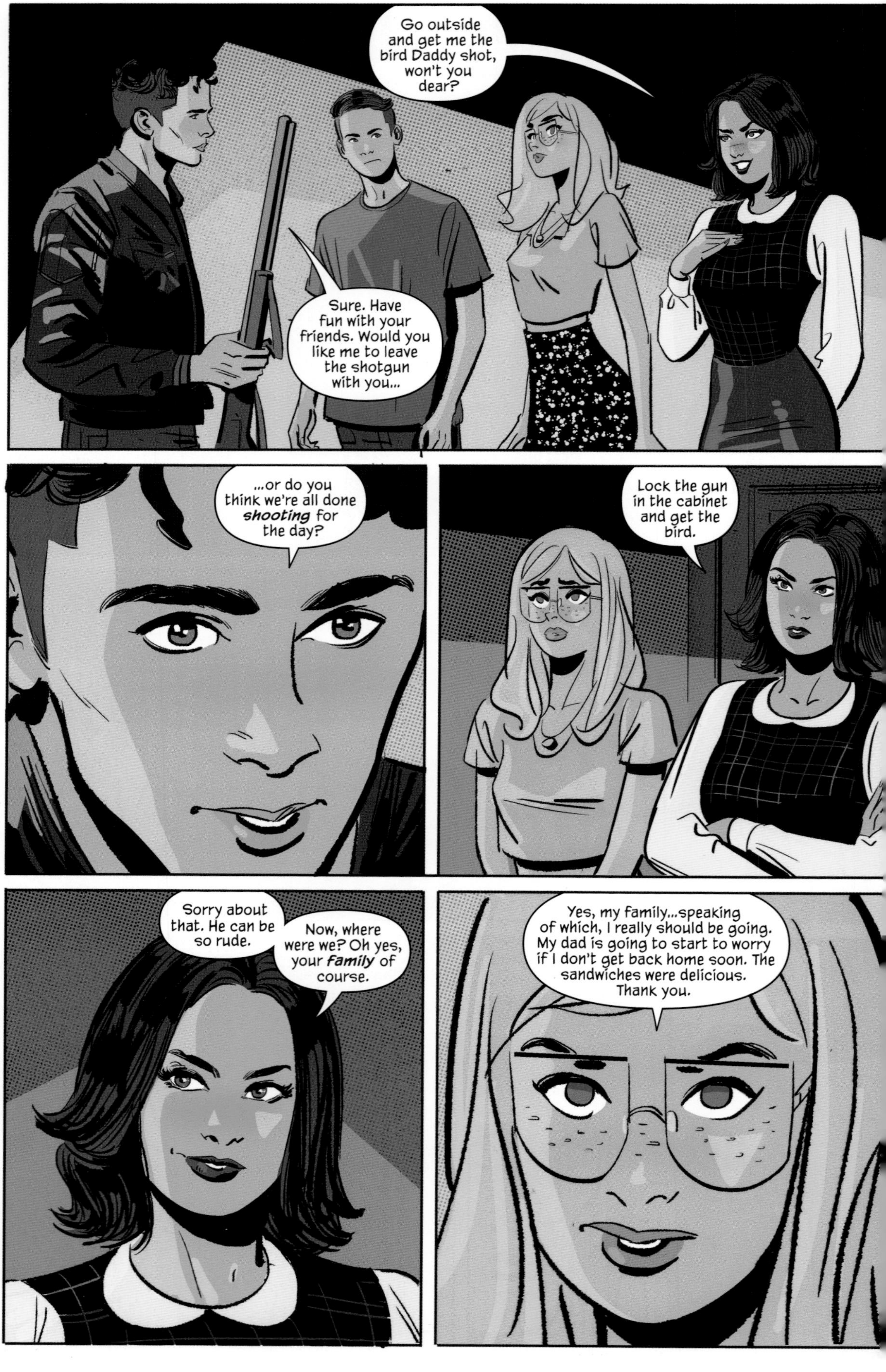
Go outside and get me the bird Daddy shot, won't you dear?
Sure. Have fun with your friends. Would you like me to leave the shotgun with you...
...or do you think we're all done *shooting* for the day?
Lock the gun in the cabinet and get the bird.
Sorry about that. He can be so rude.
Now, where were we? Oh yes, your *family* of course.
Yes, my family...speaking of which, I really should be going. My dad is going to start to worry if I don't get back home soon. The sandwiches were delicious. Thank you.

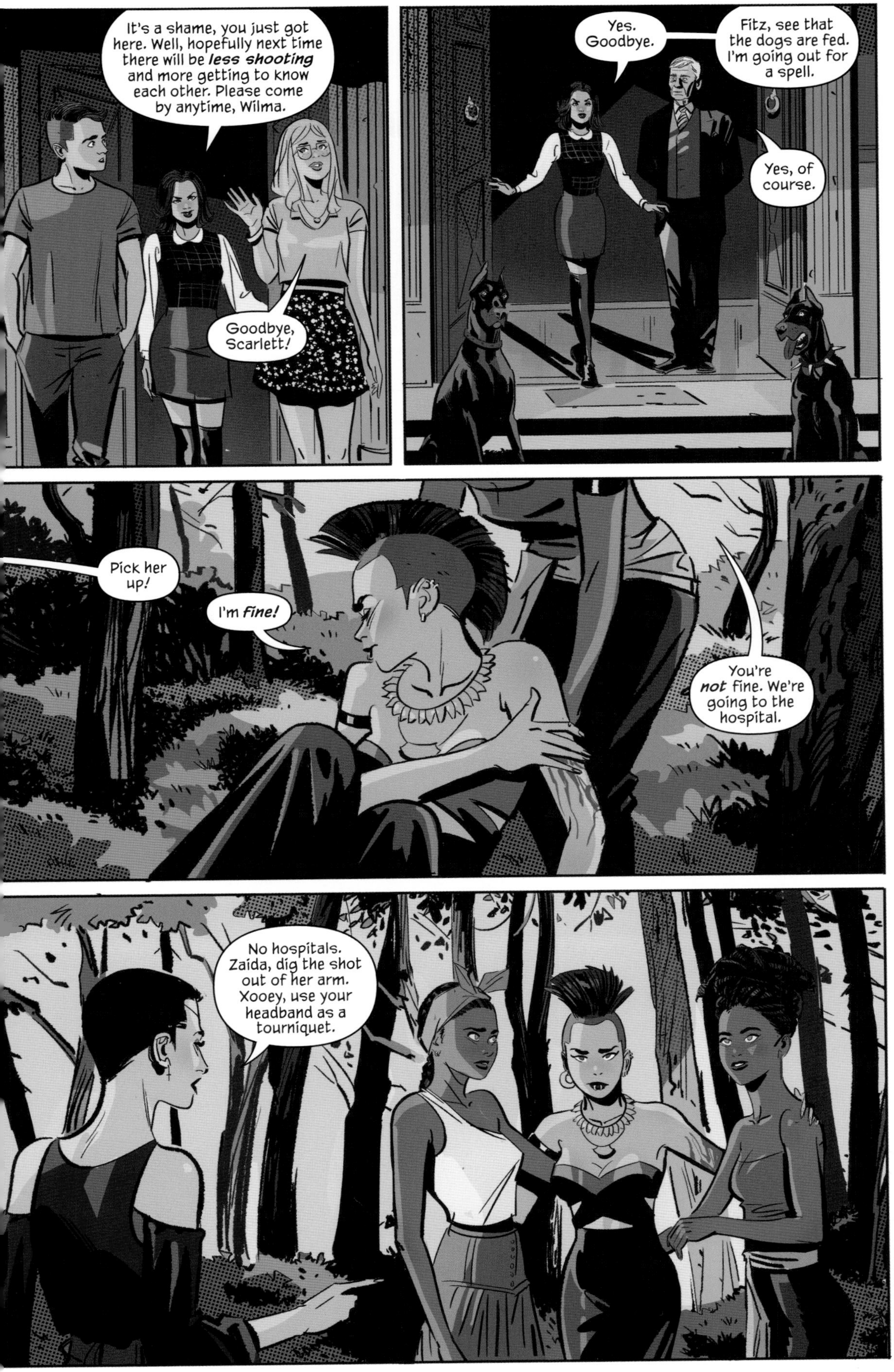
It's a shame, you just got here. Well, hopefully next time there will be *less shooting* and more getting to know each other. Please come by anytime, Wilma.
Goodbye, Scarlett!
Yes. Goodbye.
Fitz, see that the dogs are fed. I'm going out for a spell.
Yes, of course.
Pick her up!
I'm *fine!*
You're *not* fine. We're going to the hospital.
No hospitals. Zaida, dig the shot out of her arm. Xooey, use your headband as a tourniquet.

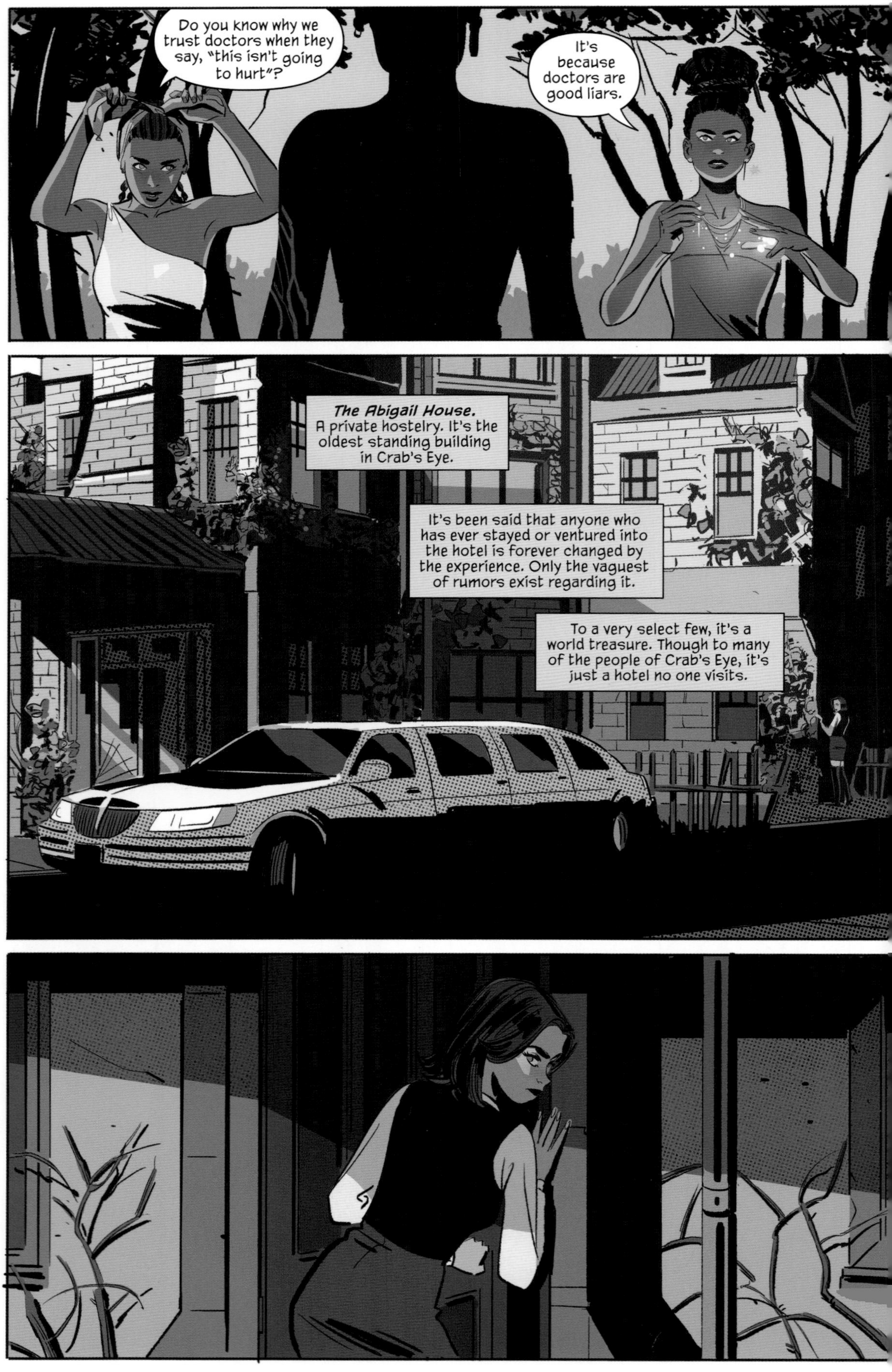
Do you know why we trust doctors when they say, "this isn't going to hurt"?
It's because doctors are good liars.
The Abigail House. A private hostelry. It's the oldest standing building in Crab's Eye.
It's been said that anyone who has ever stayed or ventured into the hotel is forever changed by the experience. Only the vaguest of rumors exist regarding it.
To a very select few, it's a world treasure. Though to many of the people of Crab's Eye, it's just a hotel no one visits.

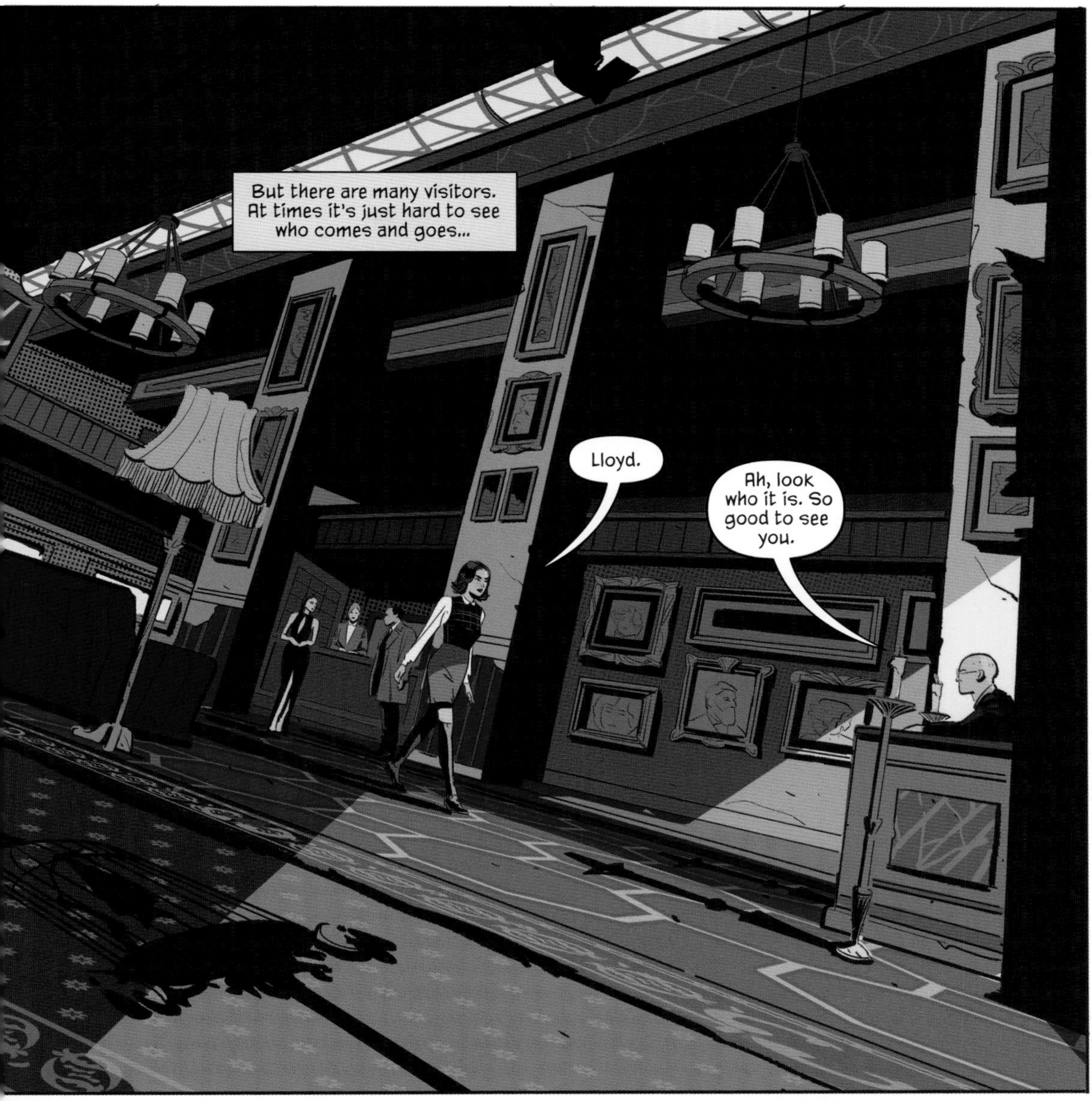
But there are many visitors. At times it's just hard to see who comes and goes...
Lloyd.
Ah, look who it is. So good to see you.

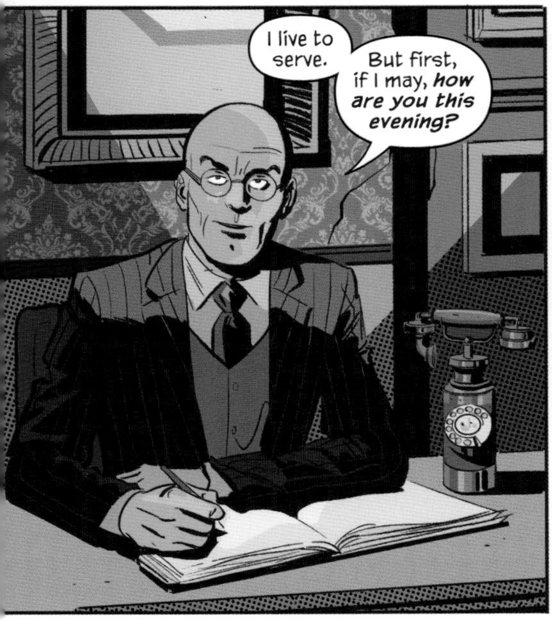
I live to serve.
But first, if I may, ***how are you this evening?***

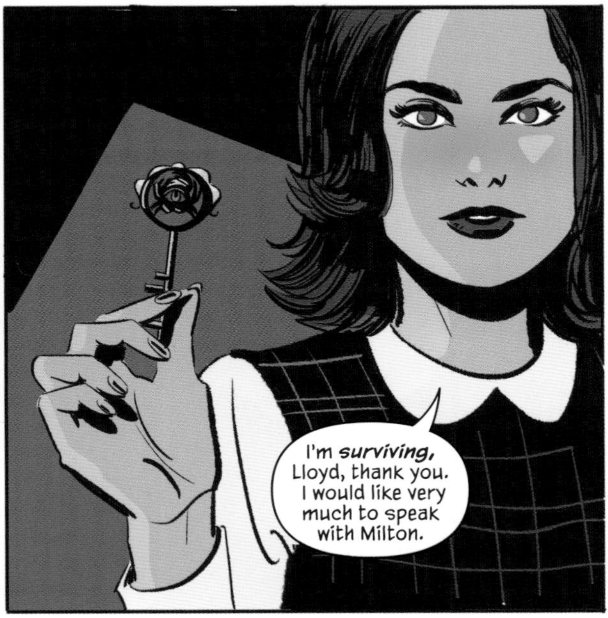
I'm ***surviving,*** Lloyd, thank you. I would like very much to speak with Milton.

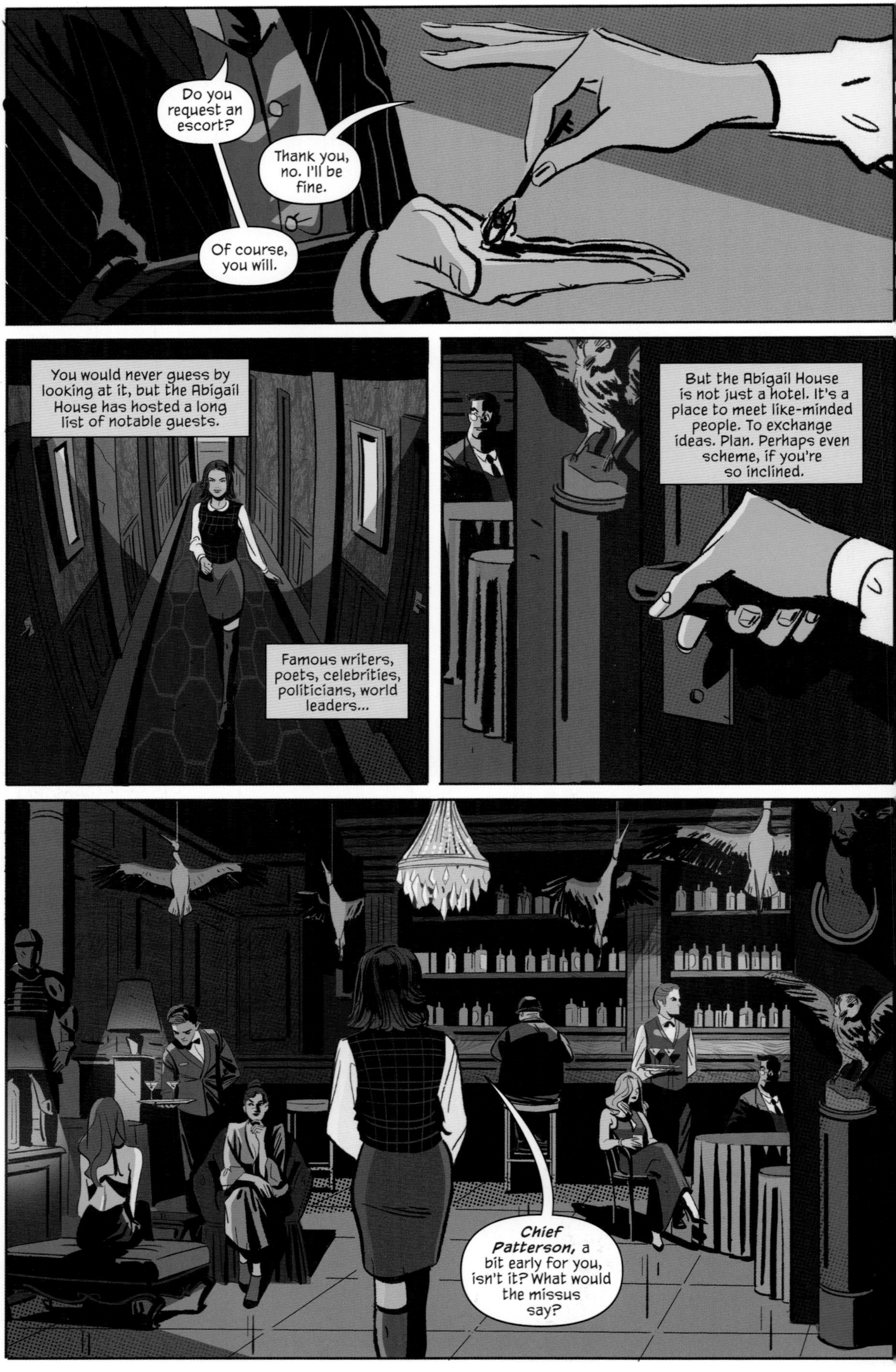
Do you request an escort?
Thank you, no. I'll be fine.
Of course, you will.
You would never guess by looking at it, but the Abigail House has hosted a long list of notable guests.
Famous writers, poets, celebrities, politicians, world leaders...
But the Abigail House is not just a hotel. It's a place to meet like-minded people. To exchange ideas. Plan. Perhaps even scheme, if you're so inclined.
Chief Patterson, a bit early for you, isn't it? What would the missus say?

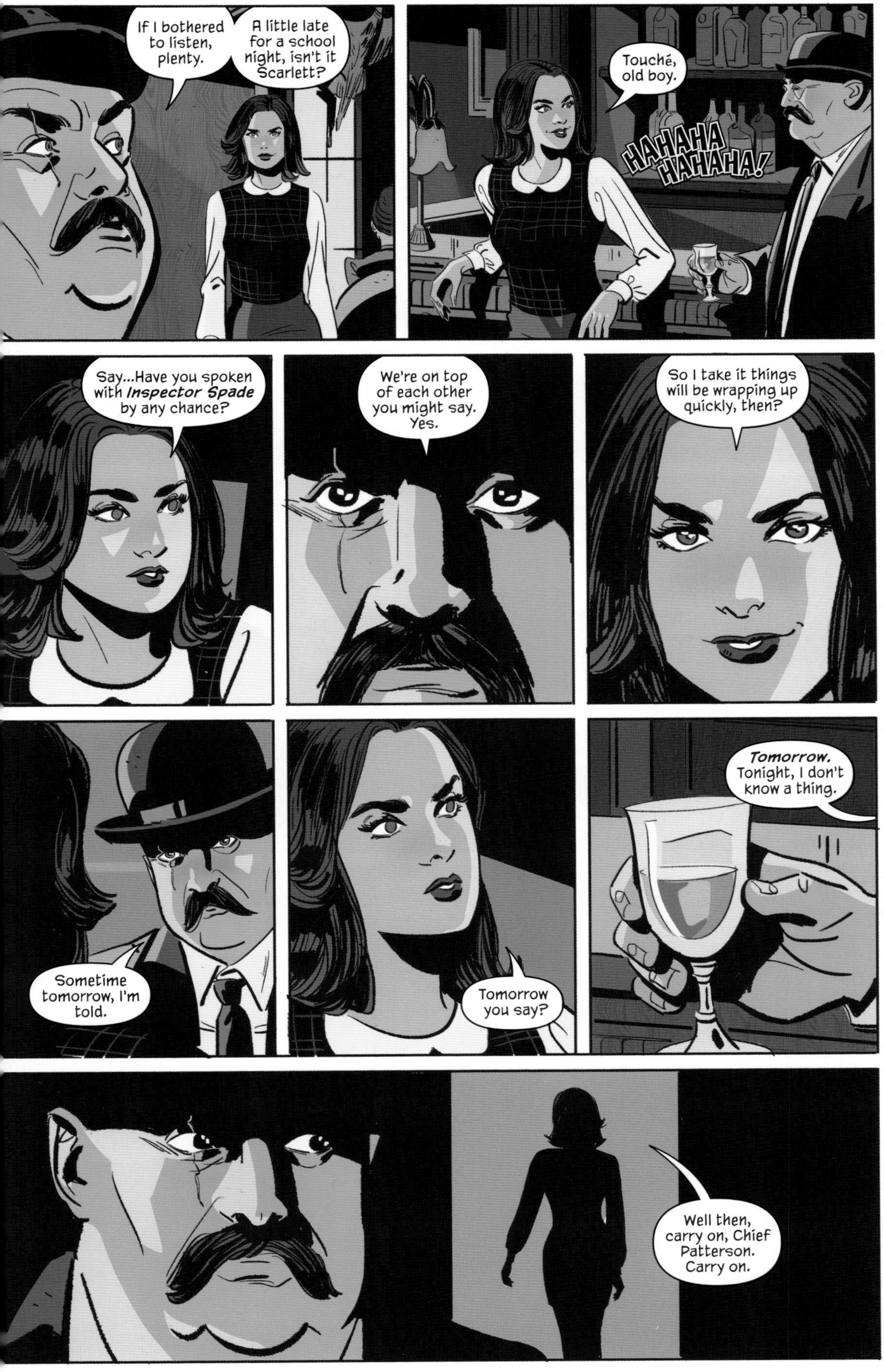

If I bothered to listen, plenty.
A little late for a school night, isn't it Scarlett?
Touché, old boy.
HAHAHA HAHAHA!
Say...Have you spoken with *Inspector Spade* by any chance?
We're on top of each other you might say. Yes.
So I take it things will be wrapping up quickly, then?
Sometime tomorrow, I'm told.
Tomorrow you say?
Tomorrow. Tonight, I don't know a thing.
Well then, carry on, Chief Patterson. Carry on.

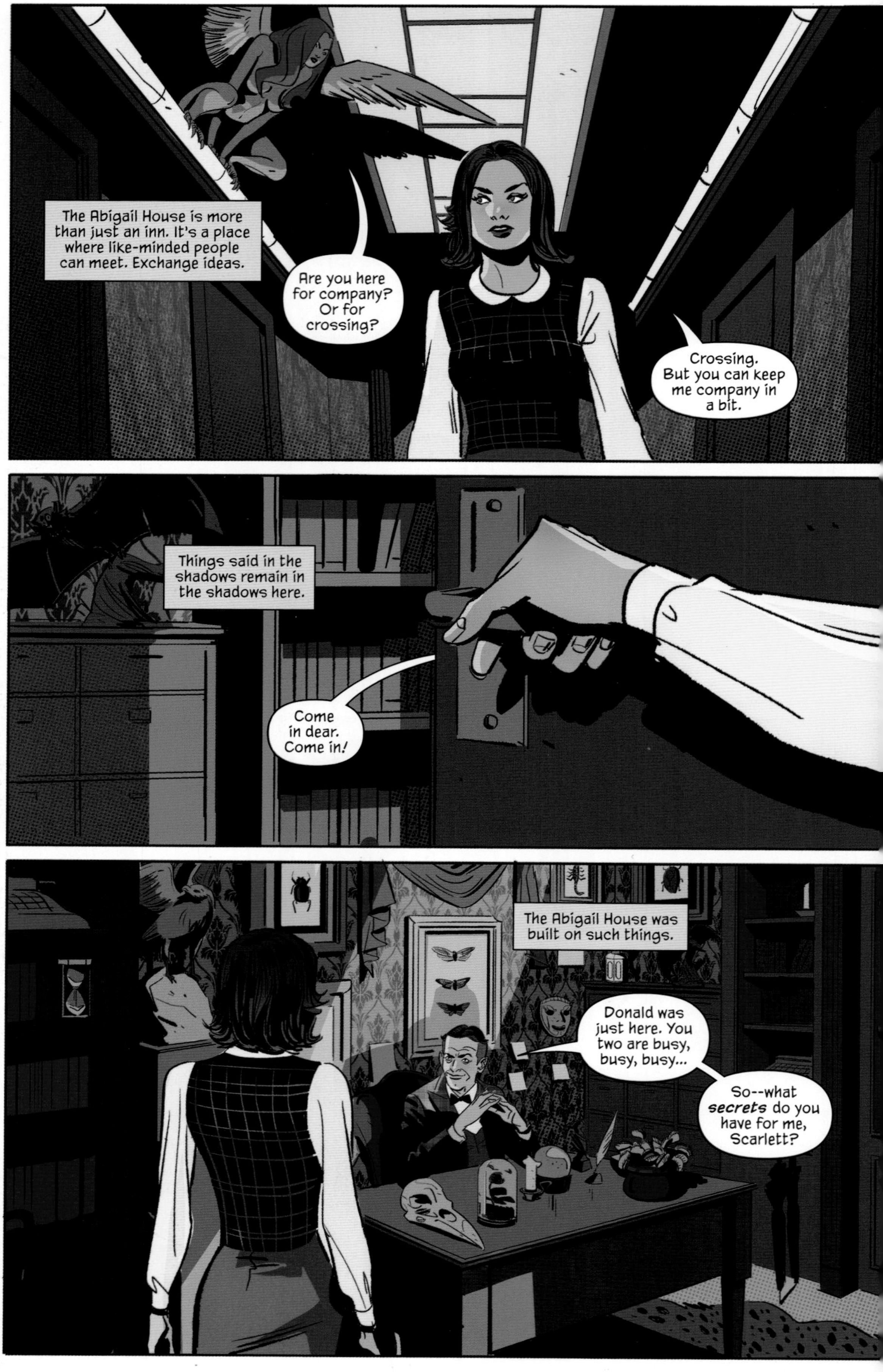

The Abigail House is more than just an inn. It's a place where like-minded people can meet. Exchange ideas.
Are you here for company? Or for crossing?
Crossing. But you can keep me company in a bit.
Things said in the shadows remain in the shadows here.
Come in dear. Come in!
The Abigail House was built on such things.
Donald was just here. You two are busy, busy, busy...
So--what *secrets* do you have for me, Scarlett?

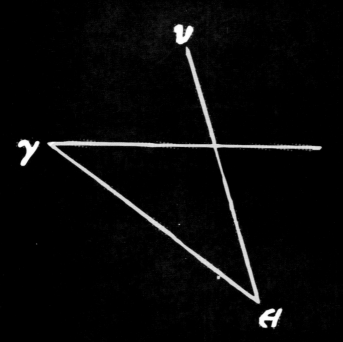

CHAPTER FOUR

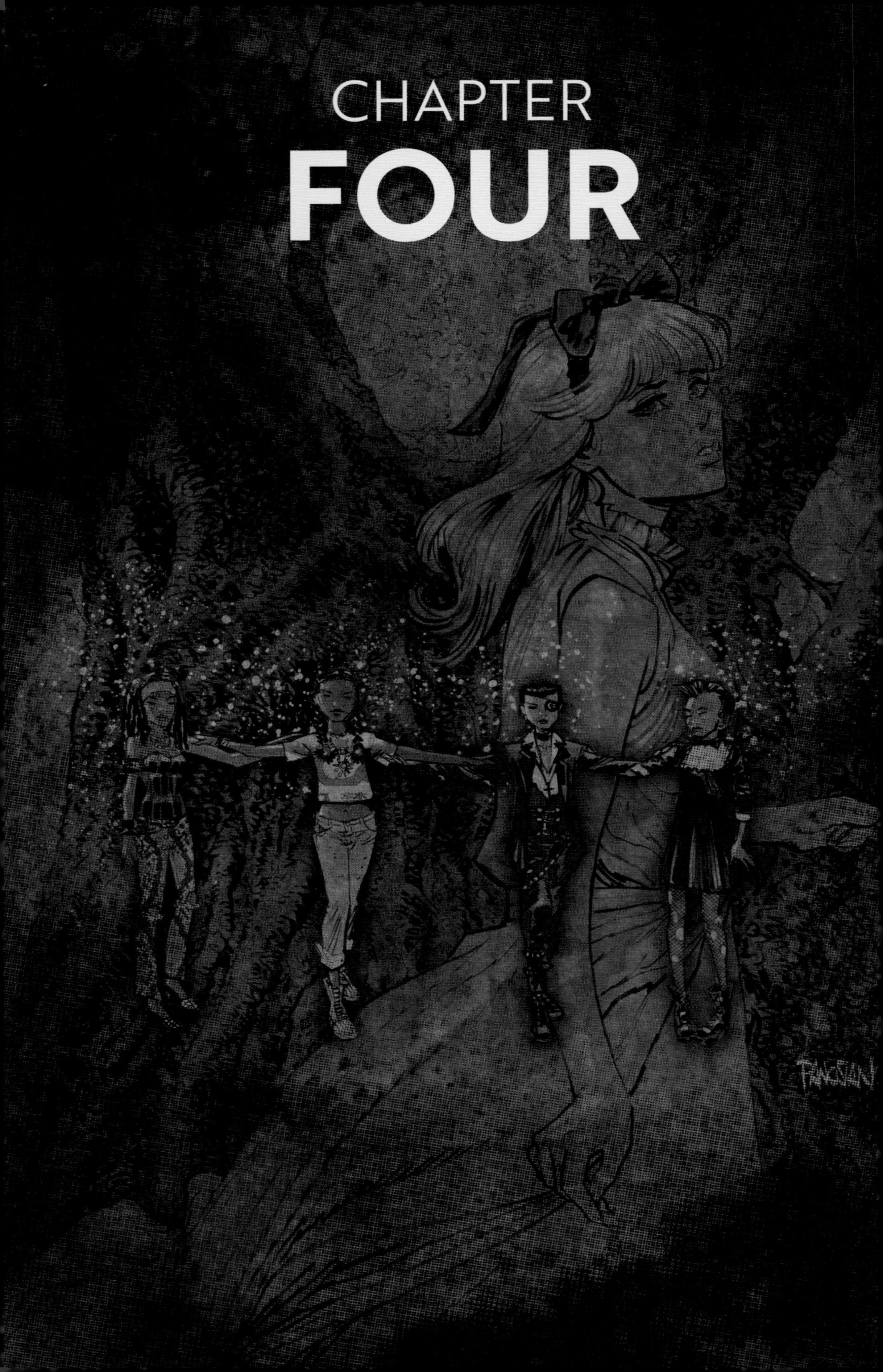

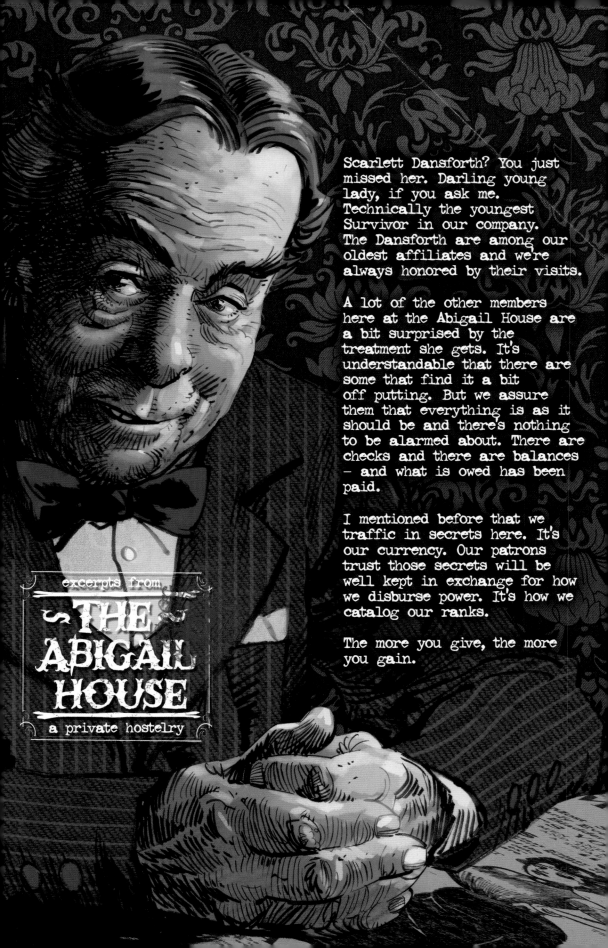

Scarlett Dansforth? You just missed her. Darling young lady, if you ask me. Technically the youngest Survivor in our company. The Dansforth are among our oldest affiliates and we're always honored by their visits.

A lot of the other members here at the Abigail House are a bit surprised by the treatment she gets. It's understandable that there are some that find it a bit off putting. But we assure them that everything is as it should be and there's nothing to be alarmed about. There are checks and there are balances — and what is owed has been paid.

I mentioned before that we traffic in secrets here. It's our currency. Our patrons trust those secrets will be well kept in exchange for how we disburse power. It's how we catalog our ranks.

The more you give, the more you gain.

excerpts from

THE ABIGAIL HOUSE

a private hostelry

Our system is completely paradoxical to the ethos of those uncouth Ravens. For them, it's all about family. Their ancestry dictates their rankings. A simple system really. Very easy to catalog and keep track of. It makes my job so much easier. Allow me to explain:

The pecking order, if you'll forgive the double entendre, goes as follows – the youngest Ravens, the ones that appear to be causing the biggest ruckus lately, they're the Black Ravens. Then there's the Blue Ravens. Followed by the Red Ravens. The older ones are the Grey Ravens and finally there's the White Ravens, the crones, if you will.

Five groups of five. It's no small coincidence there are also five sides to a pentagram. If you inspect their hands, they each have a little linear tattoo. When they connect their talons, they form their sacred five pointed star. A trifle gauche, in my opinion. But it certainly makes it easy to identify if you have a keen eye and you're looking for such things.

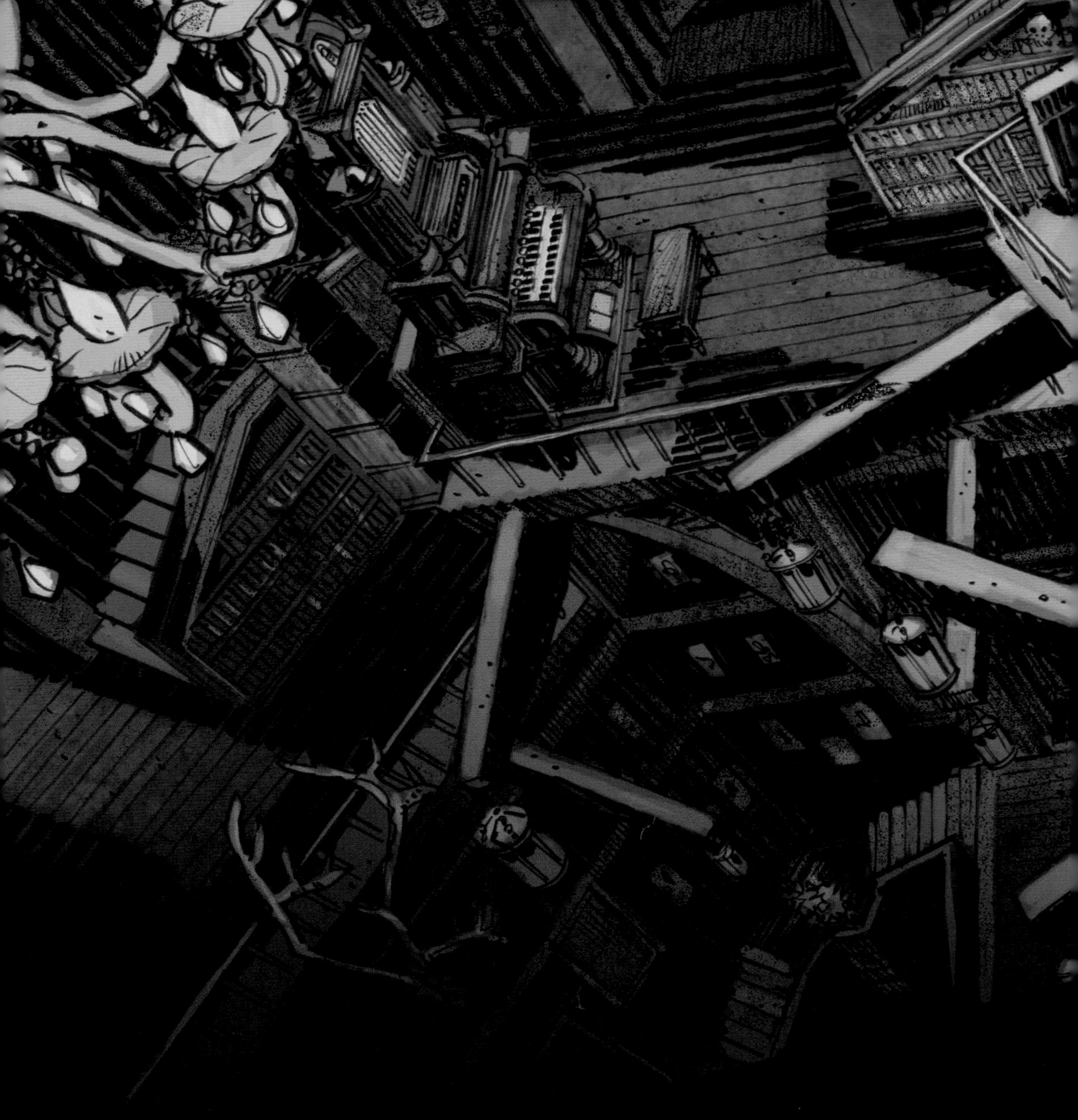

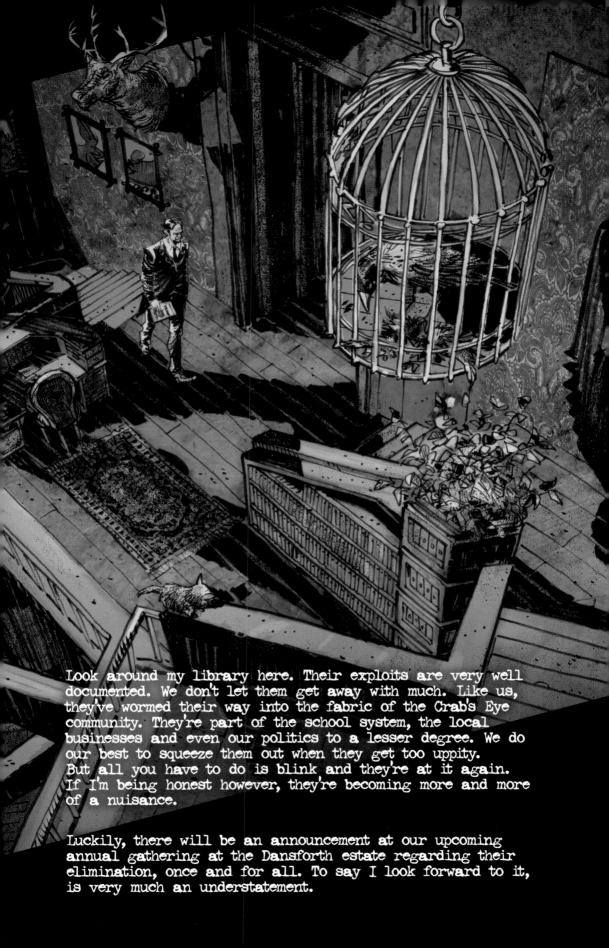

Look around my library here. Their exploits are very well
documented. We don't let them get away with much. Like us,
they've wormed their way into the fabric of the Crab's Eye
community. They're part of the school system, the local
businesses and even our politics to a lesser degree. We do
our best to squeeze them out when they get too uppity.
But all you have to do is blink and they're at it again.
If I'm being honest however, they're becoming more and more
of a nuisance.

Luckily, there will be an announcement at our upcoming
annual gathering at the Dansforth estate regarding their
elimination, once and for all. To say I look forward to it,
is very much an understatement.

But enough about the Ravens and back to Scarlett. As you can imagine, I enjoy doing research. Just like that unfortunate Raven, Waverly, Scarlett's mother is also missing. No one has heard from her in quite some time and quite frankly, I doubt they will at this rate.

Shortly after Ruth Dansforth took what many thought was just a brief holiday, Scarlett appeared and rejoined her family. She swept right in and basically picked up where her mother left off.

I must confess, I know just about everything that goes on in Crab's Eye – but even I wasn't aware that the Dansforth's had an additional child. I was mistakenly under the impression that Del was their only offspring. I suppose there are secrets in Crab's Eye that even I am not privy to.

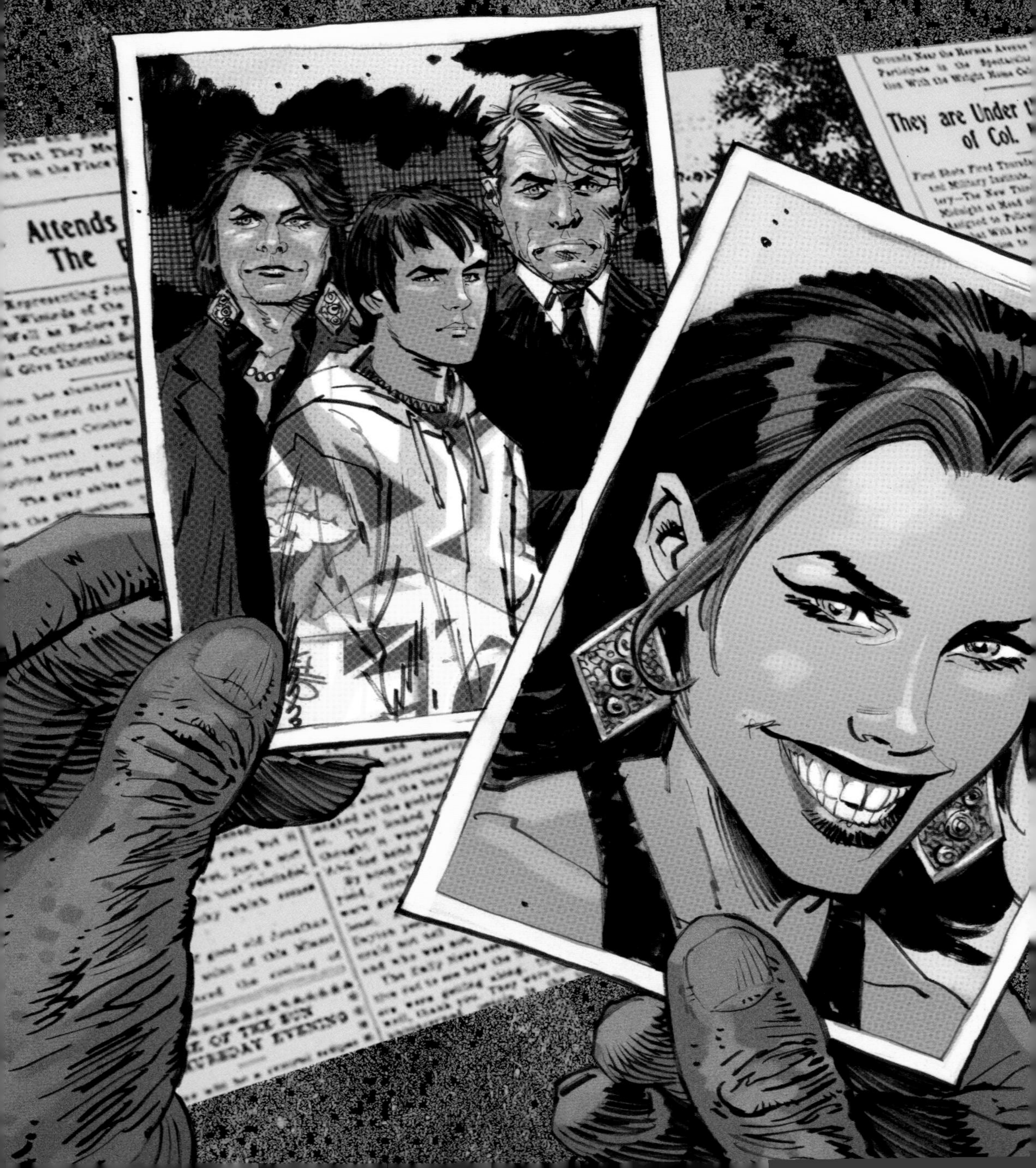
They are Under
of Col.
Attends
The

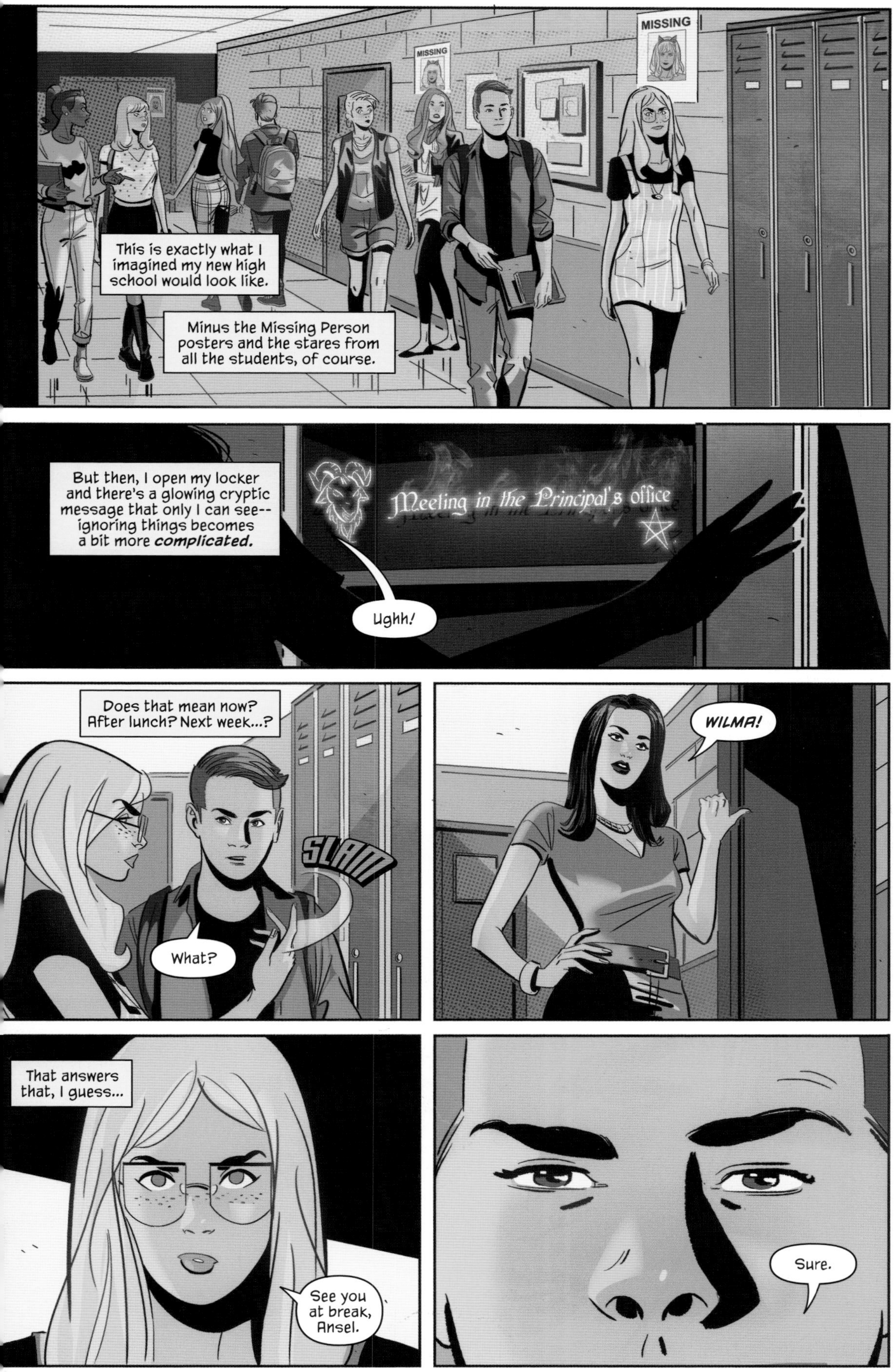
MISSING
MISSING
MISSING
This is exactly what I imagined my new high school would look like.
Minus the Missing Person posters and the stares from all the students, of course.
But then, I open my locker and there's a glowing cryptic message that only I can see--ignoring things becomes a bit more *complicated.*
Meeting in the Principal's office
Ughh!
Does that mean now? After lunch? Next week...?
SLAM
What?
WILMA!
That answers that, I guess...
See you at break, Ansel.
Sure.

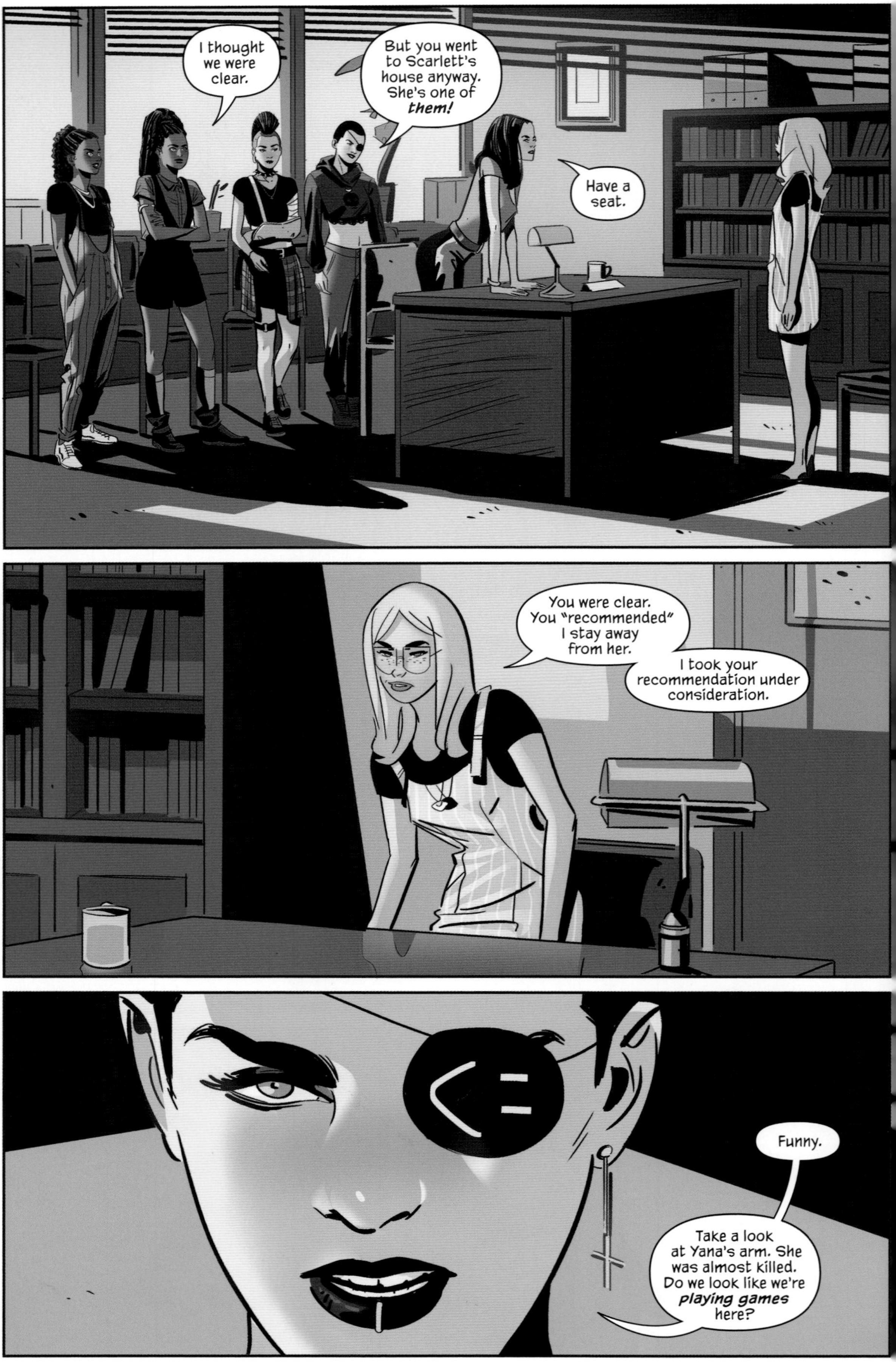
I thought we were clear.
But you went to Scarlett's house anyway. She's one of *them!*
Have a seat.
You were clear. You "recommended" I stay away from her.
I took your recommendation under consideration.
Funny.
Take a look at Yana's arm. She was almost killed. Do we look like we're *playing games* here?

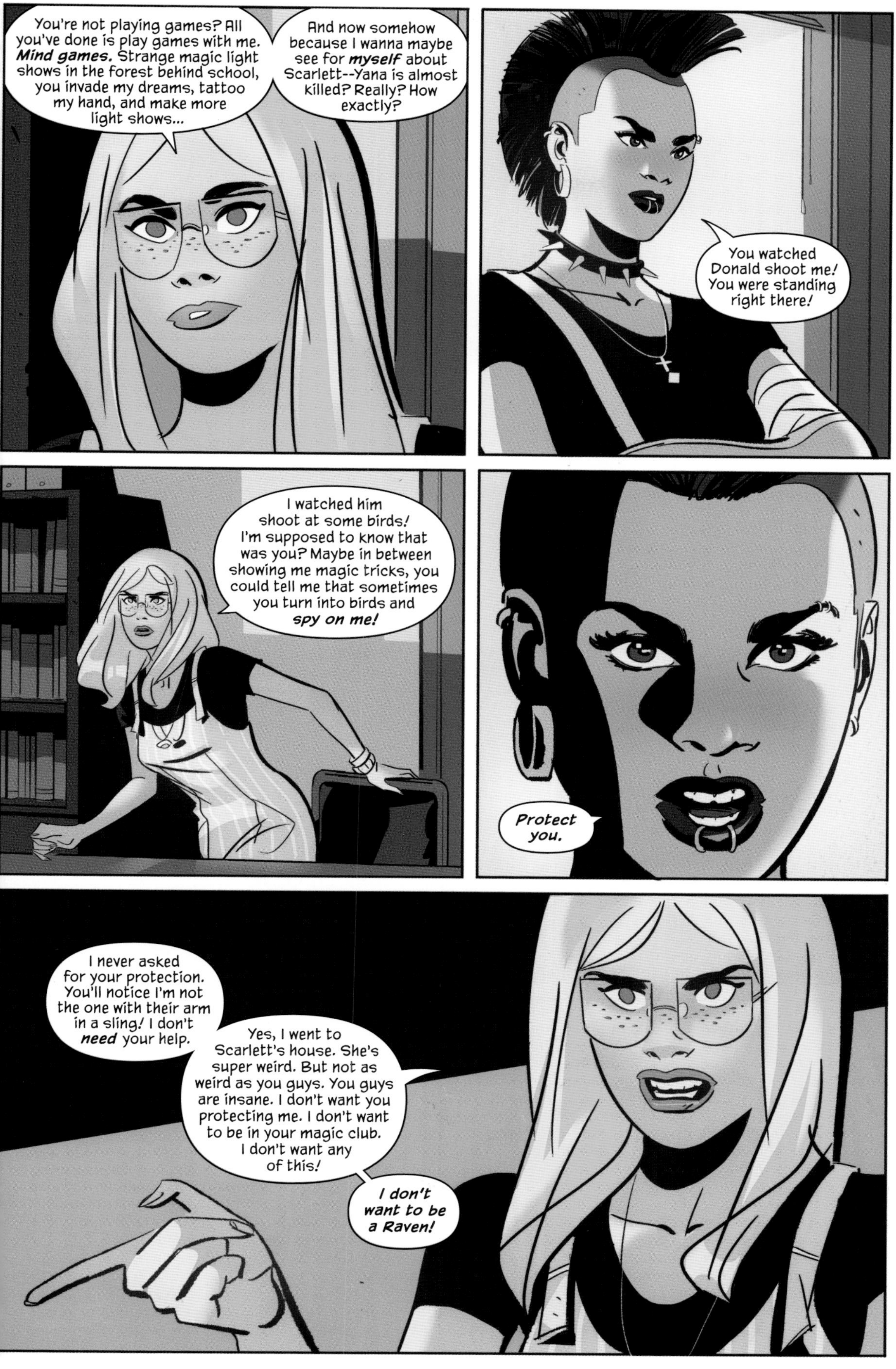

You're not playing games? All you've done is play games with me. ***Mind games.*** Strange magic light shows in the forest behind school, you invade my dreams, tattoo my hand, and make more light shows...
And now somehow because I wanna maybe see for ***myself*** about Scarlett--Yana is almost killed? Really? How exactly?
You watched Donald shoot me! You were standing right there!
I watched him shoot at some birds! I'm supposed to know that was you? Maybe in between showing me magic tricks, you could tell me that sometimes you turn into birds and ***spy on me!***
Protect you.
I never asked for your protection. You'll notice I'm not the one with their arm in a sling! I don't ***need*** your help.
Yes, I went to Scarlett's house. She's super weird. But not as weird as you guys. You guys are insane. I don't want you protecting me. I don't want to be in your magic club. I don't want any of this!
I don't want to be a Raven!

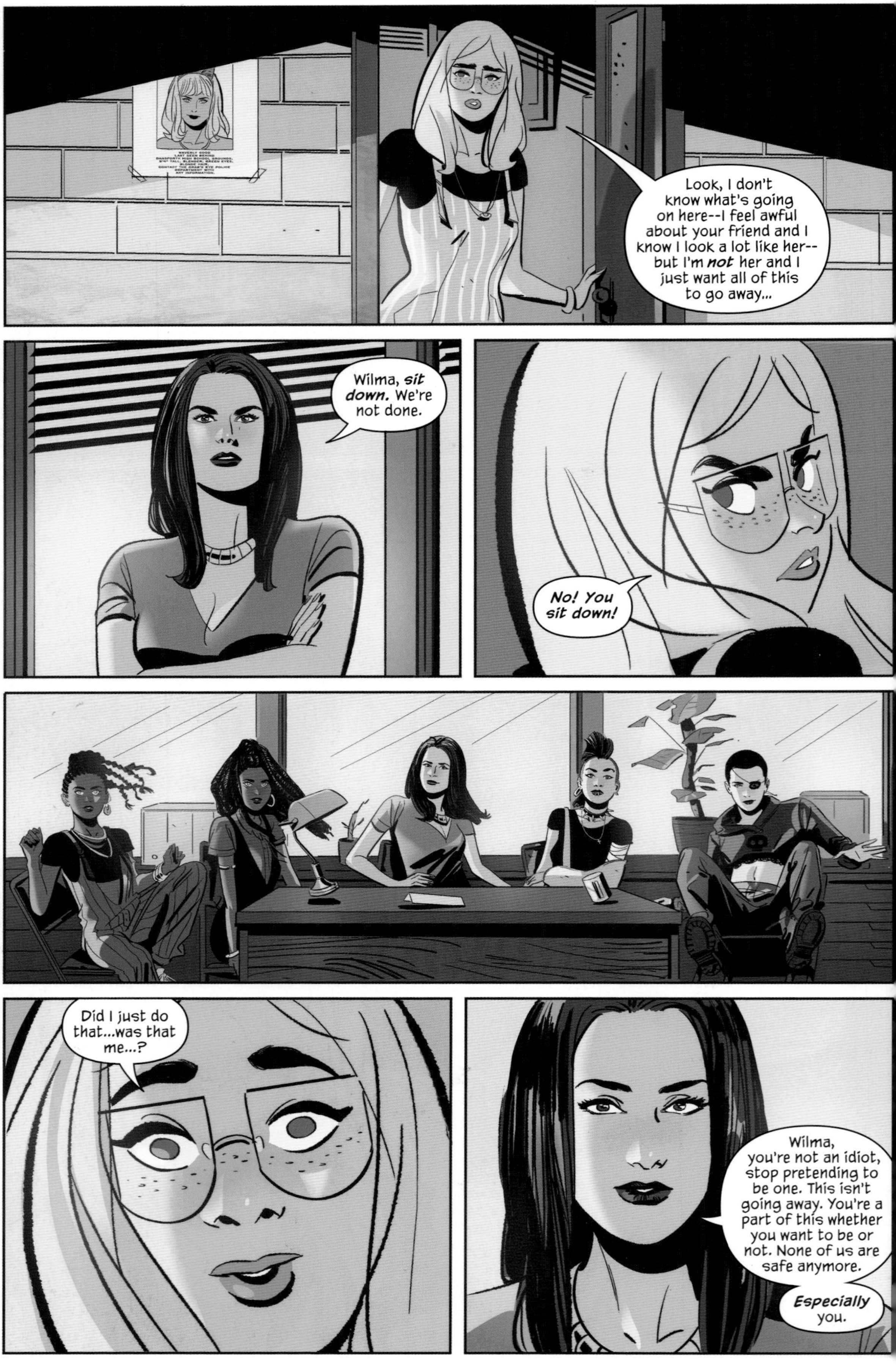
WAVERLY GOOD
LAST SEEN BEHIND
DANSFORTH HIGH SCHOOL GROUNDS.
5'4" TALL, SLENDER, GREEN EYES.
BLONDE HAIR.
CONTACT THE CRAB'S EYE POLICE
DEPARTMENT WITH
ANY INFORMATION.
Look, I don't know what's going on here--I feel awful about your friend and I know I look a lot like her--but I'm ***not*** her and I just want all of this to go away...
Wilma, ***sit down.*** We're not done.
No! You sit down!
Did I just do that...was that me...?
Wilma, you're not an idiot, stop pretending to be one. This isn't going away. You're a part of this whether you want to be or not. None of us are safe anymore.
Especially you.

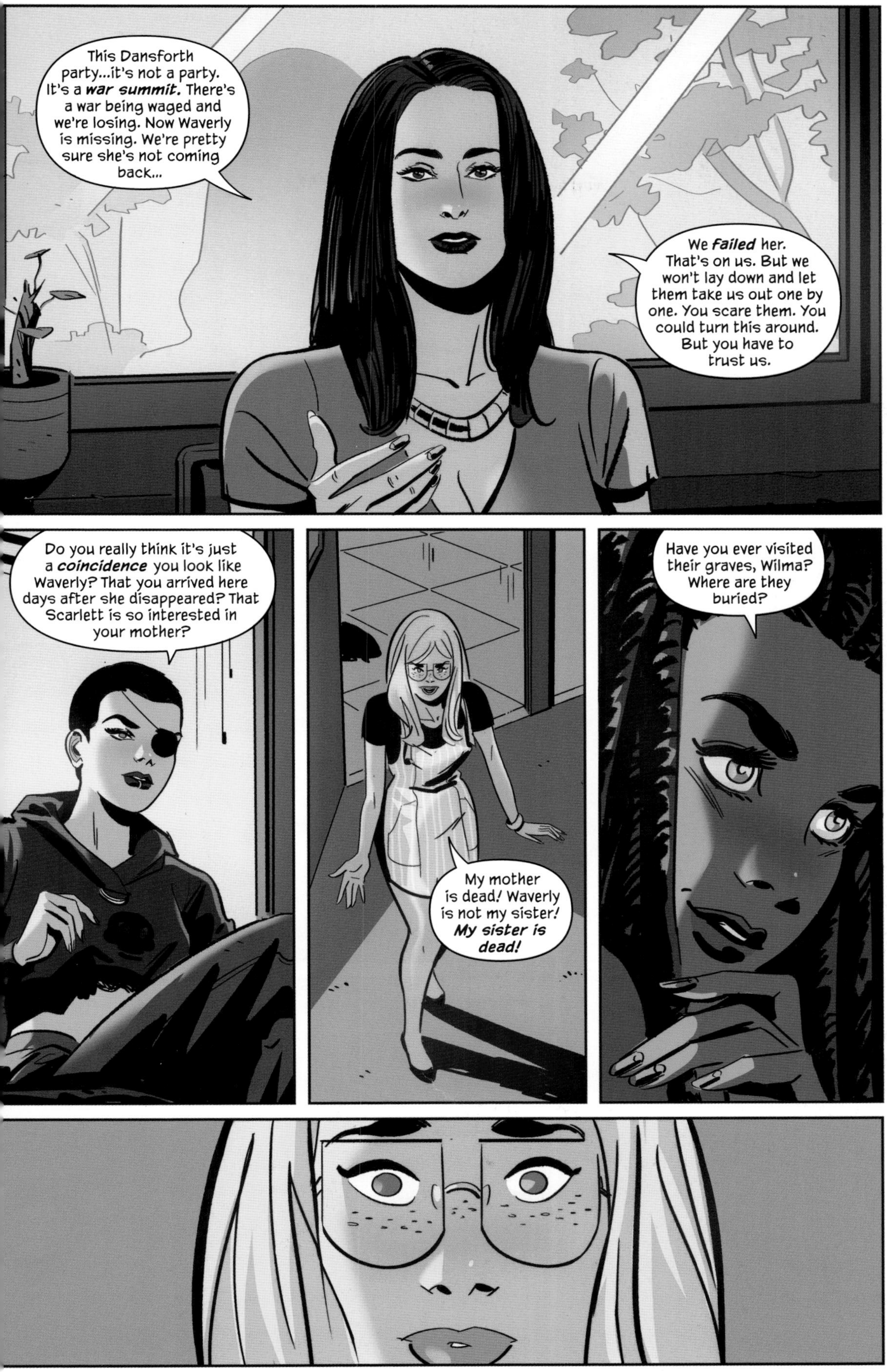
This Dansforth party...it's not a party. It's a ***war summit.*** There's a war being waged and we're losing. Now Waverly is missing. We're pretty sure she's not coming back...
We ***failed*** her. That's on us. But we won't lay down and let them take us out one by one. You scare them. You could turn this around. But you have to trust us.
Do you really think it's just a ***coincidence*** you look like Waverly? That you arrived here days after she disappeared? That Scarlett is so interested in your mother?
My mother is dead! Waverly is not my sister! ***My sister is dead!***
Have you ever visited their graves, Wilma? Where are they buried?

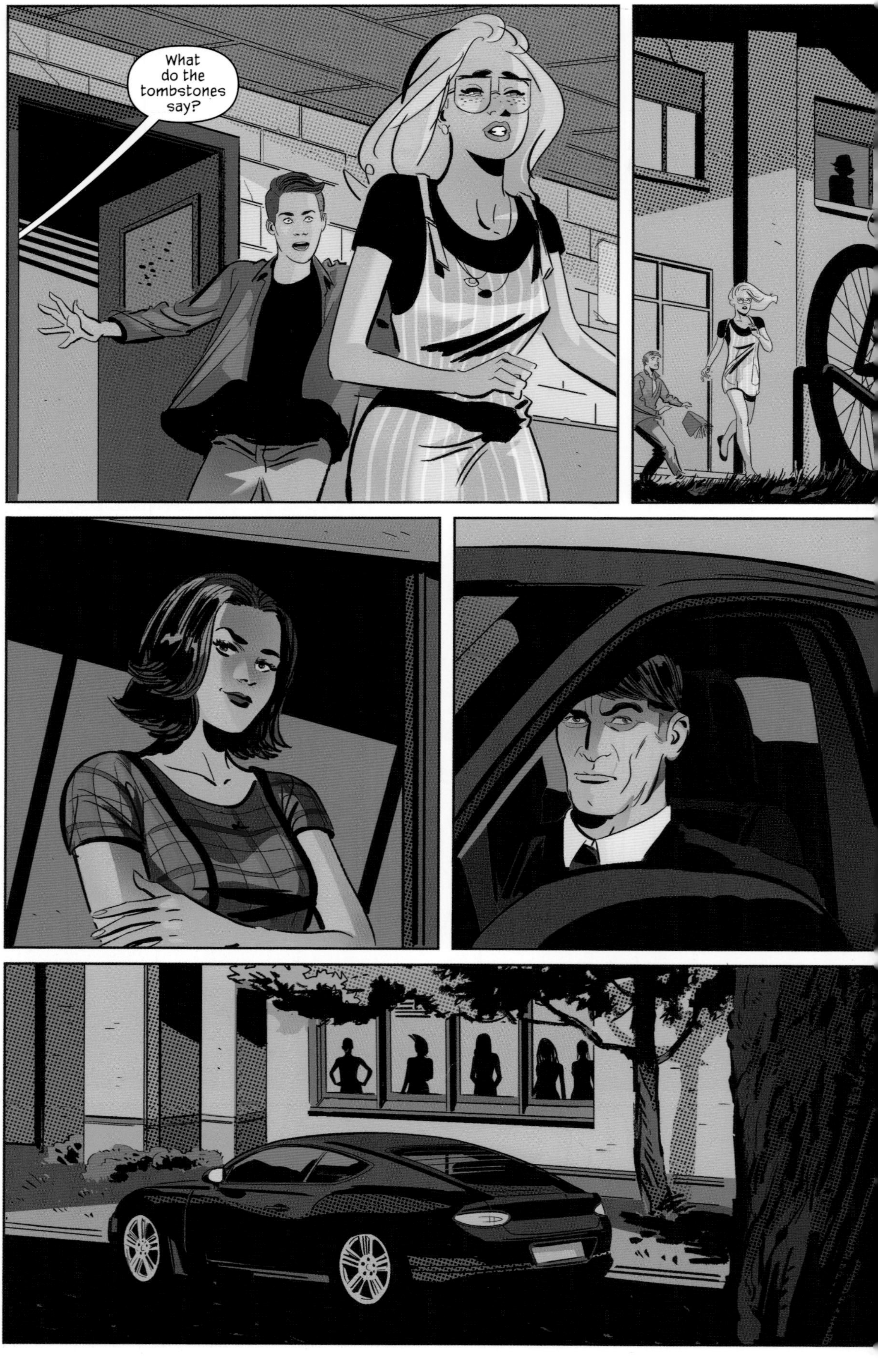
What do the tombstones say?

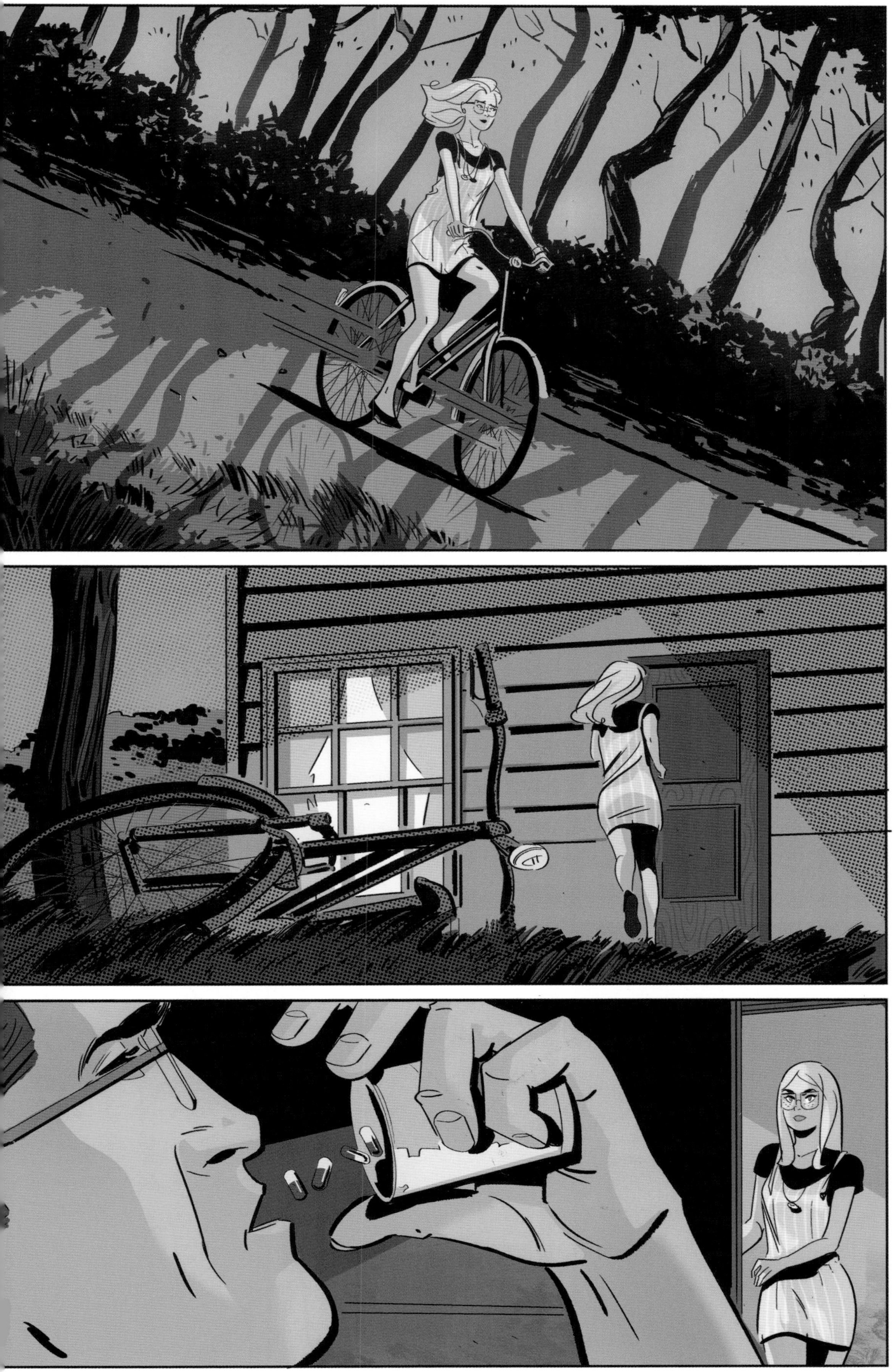

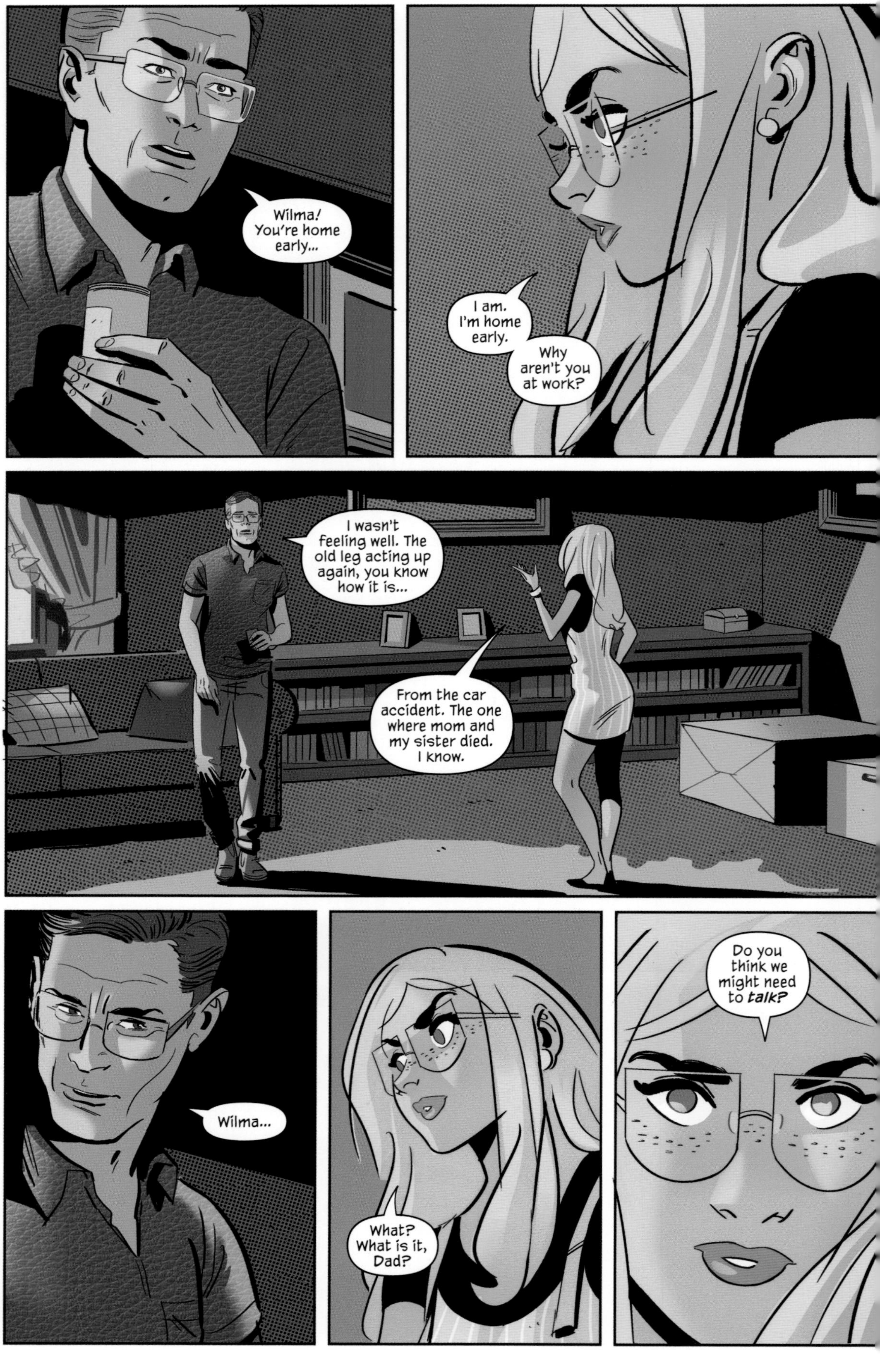

Wilma! You're home early...
I am. I'm home early.
Why aren't you at work?
I wasn't feeling well. The old leg acting up again, you know how it is...
From the car accident. The one where mom and my sister died. I know.
Wilma...
What? What is it, Dad?
Do you think we might need to *talk?*

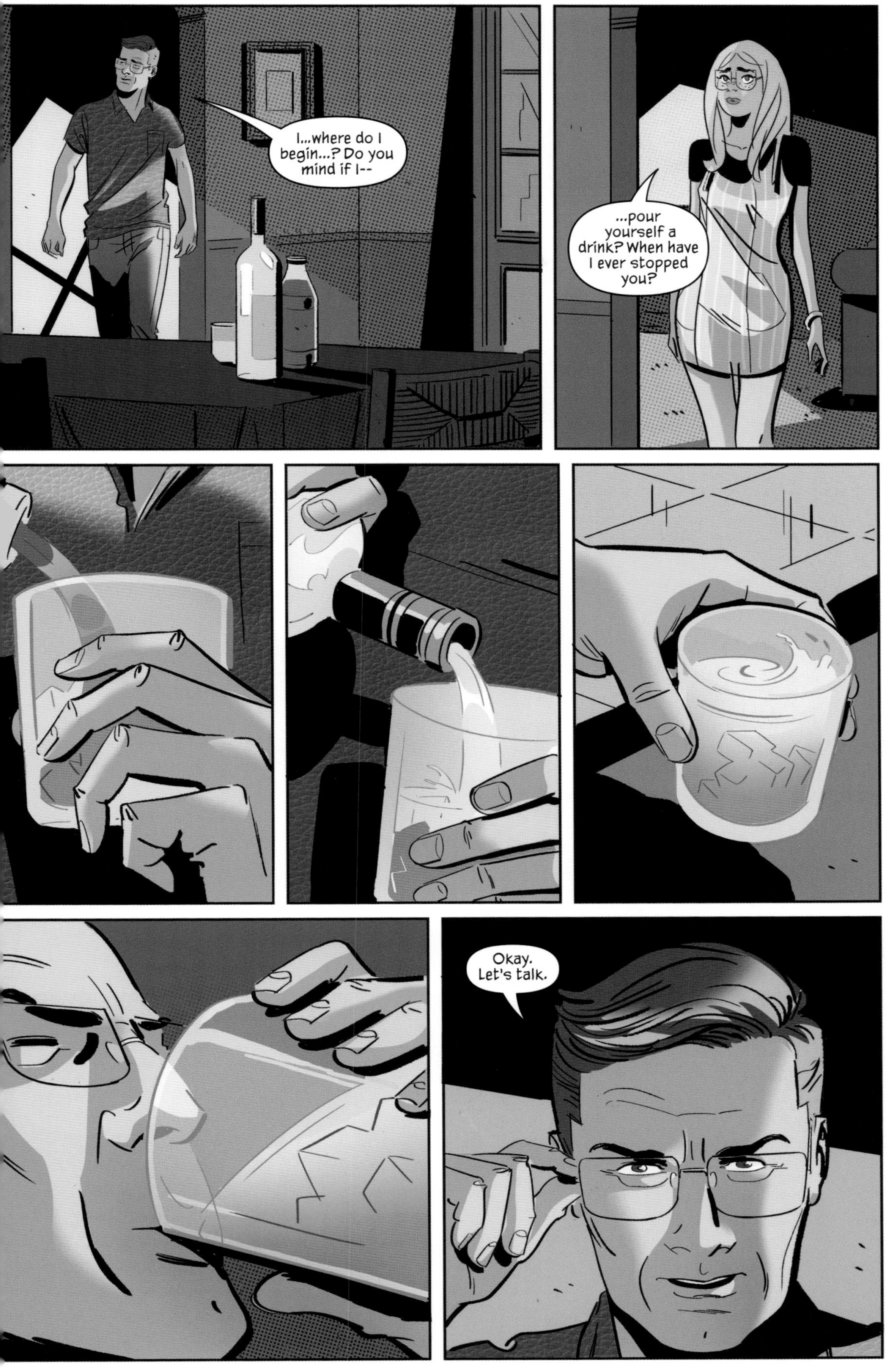
I...where do I begin...? Do you mind if I--
...pour yourself a drink? When have I ever stopped you?
Okay. Let's talk.

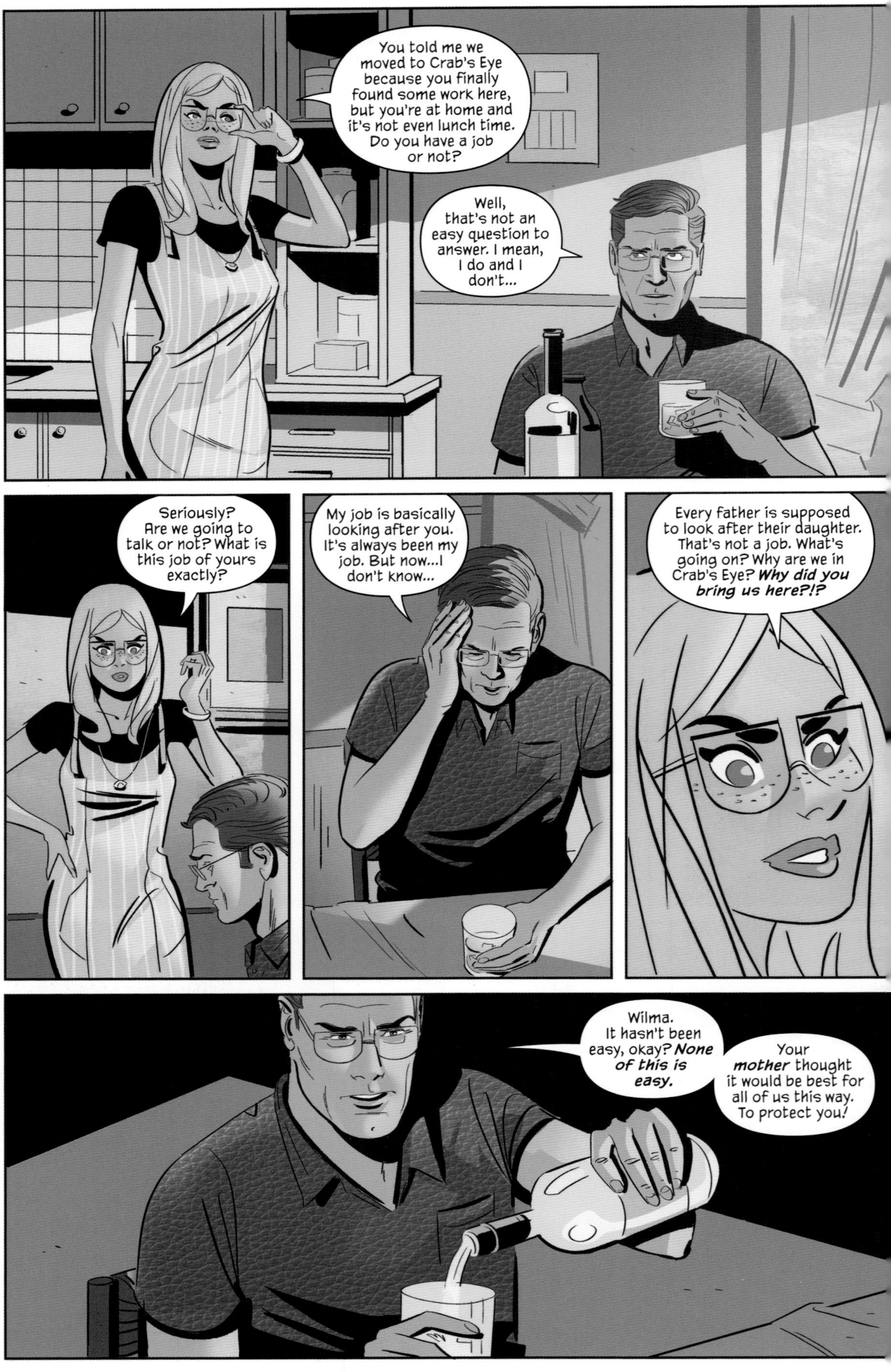

You told me we moved to Crab's Eye because you finally found some work here, but you're at home and it's not even lunch time. Do you have a job or not?
Well, that's not an easy question to answer. I mean, I do and I don't...
Seriously? Are we going to talk or not? What is this job of yours exactly?
My job is basically looking after you. It's always been my job. But now...I don't know...
Every father is supposed to look after their daughter. That's not a job. What's going on? Why are we in Crab's Eye? ***Why did you bring us here?!?***
Wilma. It hasn't been easy, okay? ***None of this is easy.***
Your ***mother*** thought it would be best for all of us this way. To protect you!

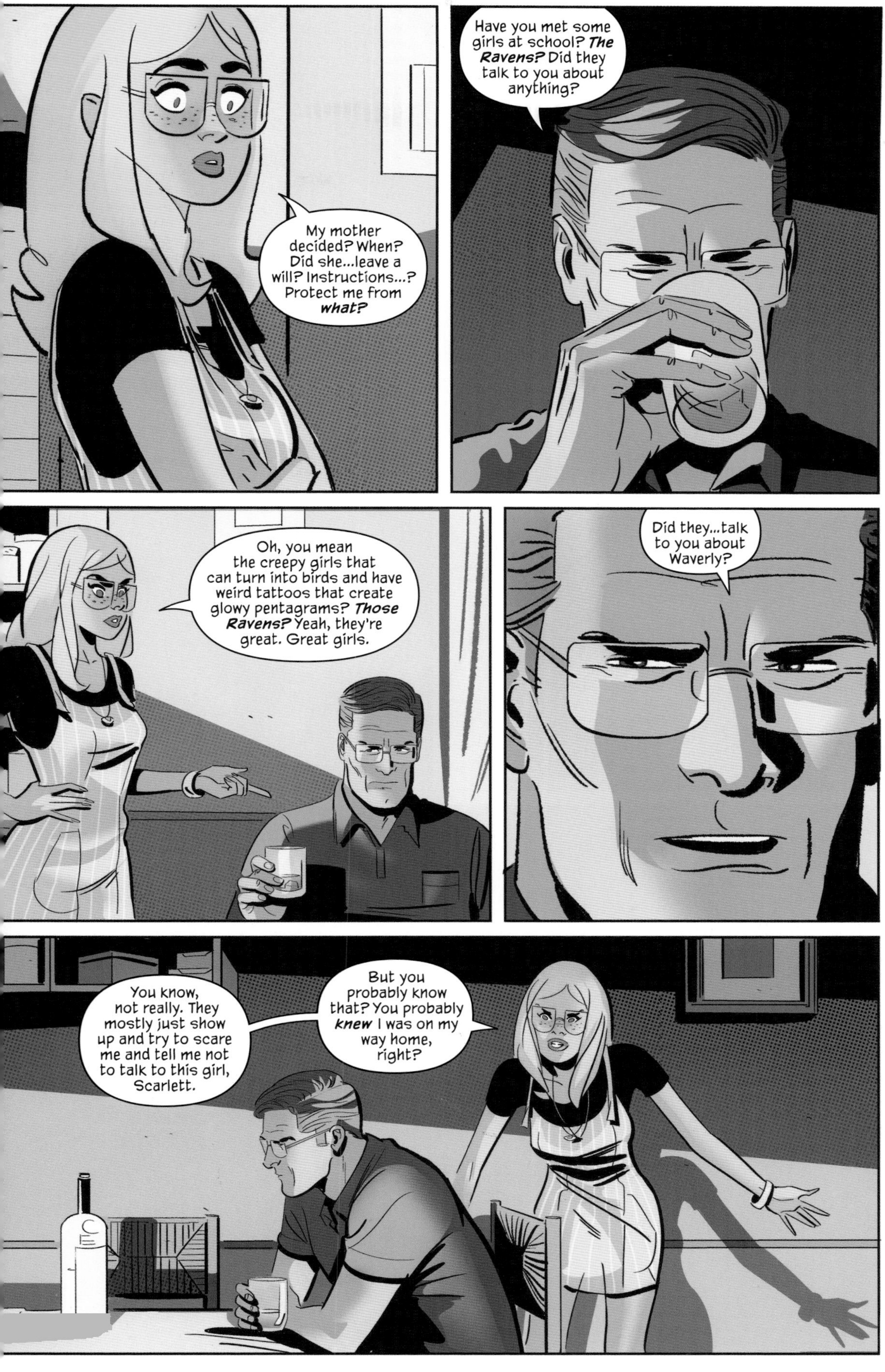
My mother decided? When? Did she...leave a will? Instructions...? Protect me from *what?*
Have you met some girls at school? *The Ravens?* Did they talk to you about anything?
Oh, you mean the creepy girls that can turn into birds and have weird tattoos that create glowy pentagrams? *Those Ravens?* Yeah, they're great. Great girls.
Did they...talk to you about Waverly?
You know, not really. They mostly just show up and try to scare me and tell me not to talk to this girl, Scarlett.
But you probably know that? You probably *knew* I was on my way home, right?

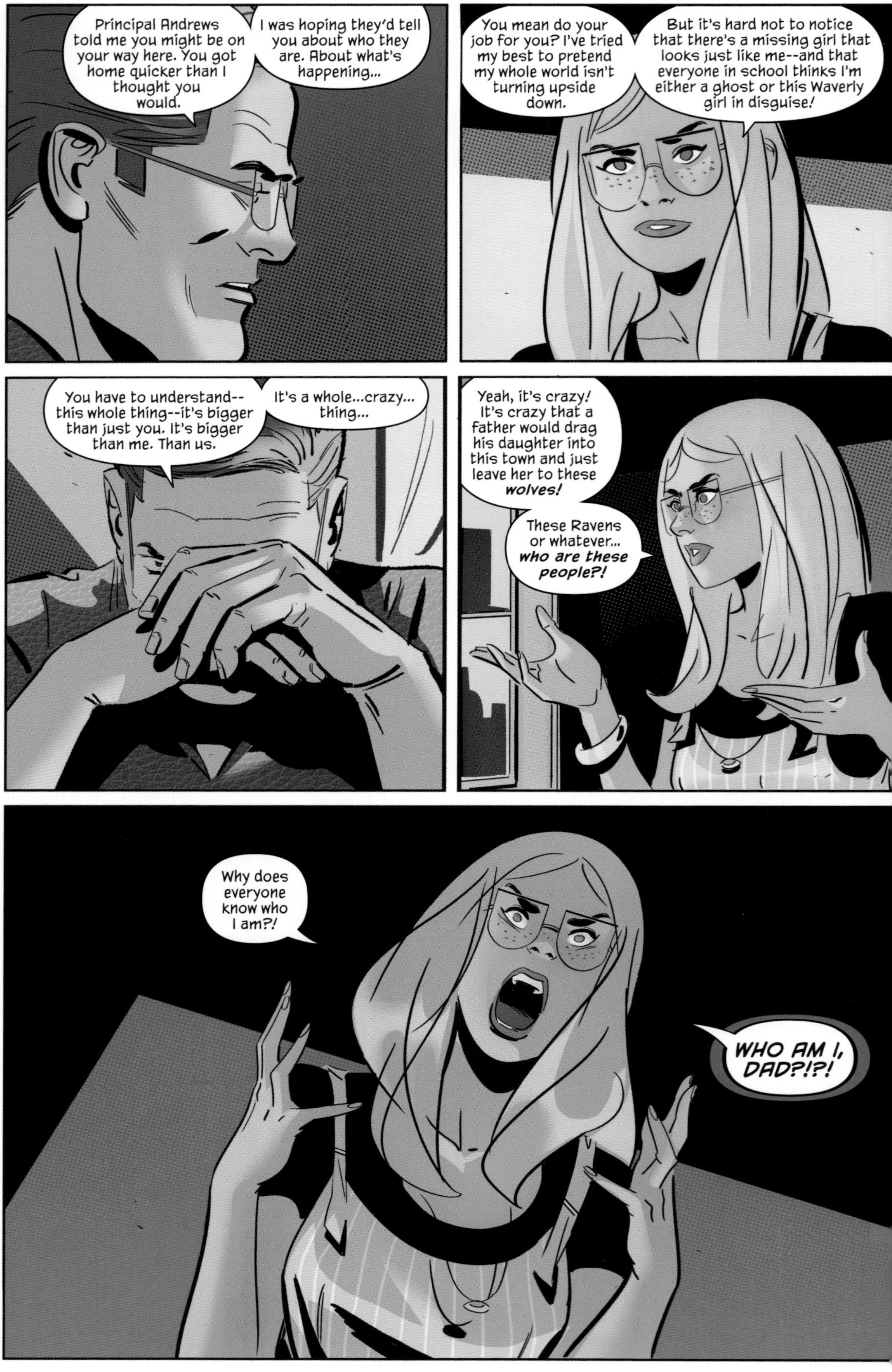
Principal Andrews told me you might be on your way here. You got home quicker than I thought you would.
I was hoping they'd tell you about who they are. About what's happening...
You mean do your job for you? I've tried my best to pretend my whole world isn't turning upside down.
But it's hard not to notice that there's a missing girl that looks just like me--and that everyone in school thinks I'm either a ghost or this Waverly girl in disguise!
You have to understand--this whole thing--it's bigger than just you. It's bigger than me. Than us.
It's a whole...crazy... thing...
Yeah, it's crazy! It's crazy that a father would drag his daughter into this town and just leave her to these *wolves!*
These Ravens or whatever... *who are these people?!*
Why does everyone know who I am?!
WHO AM I, DAD?!?!

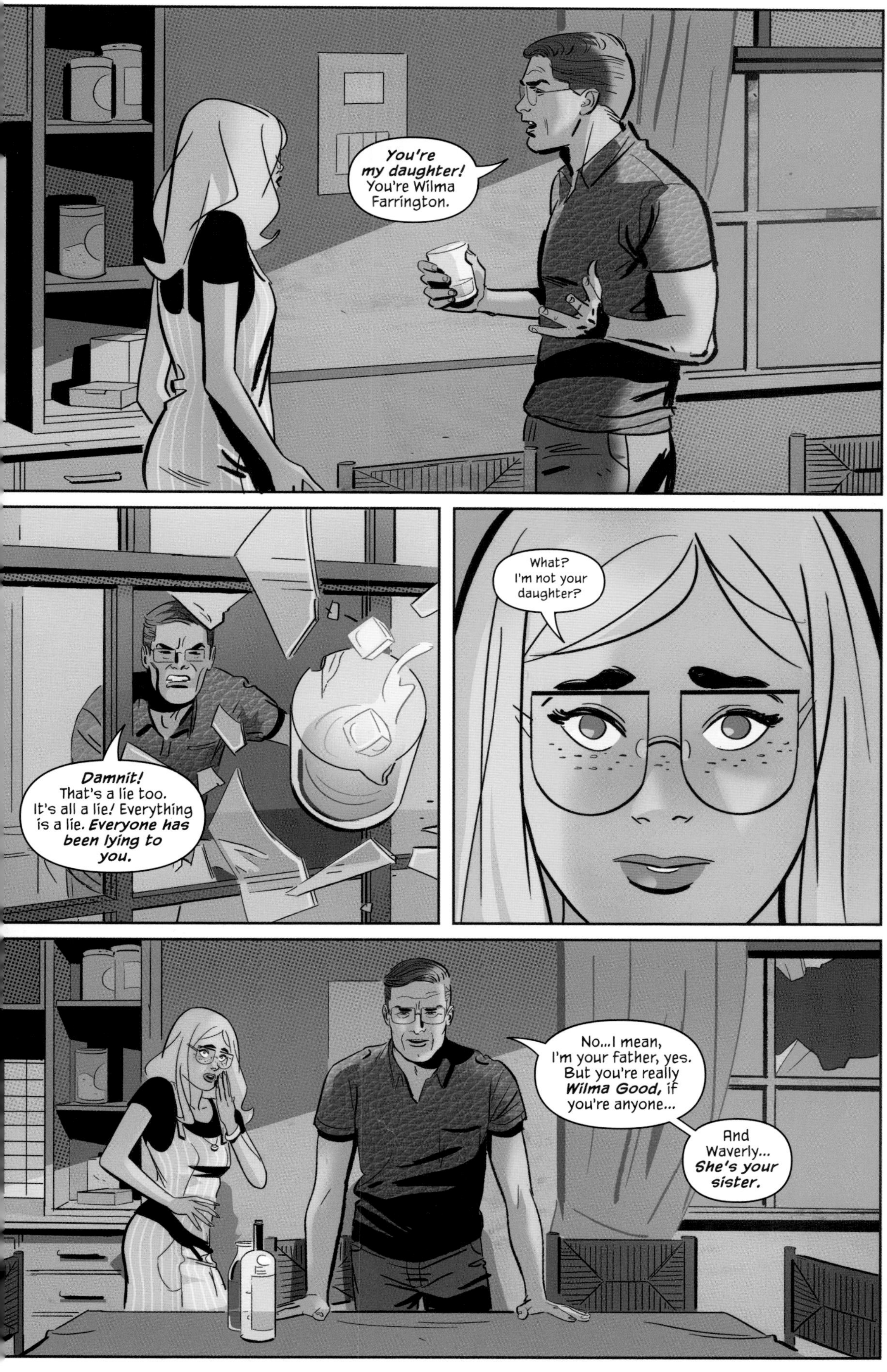
You're my daughter! You're Wilma Farrington.
What? I'm not your daughter?
Damnit! That's a lie too. It's all a lie! Everything is a lie. *Everyone has been lying to you.*
No...I mean, I'm your father, yes. But you're really *Wilma Good,* if you're anyone...
And Waverly... *She's your sister.*

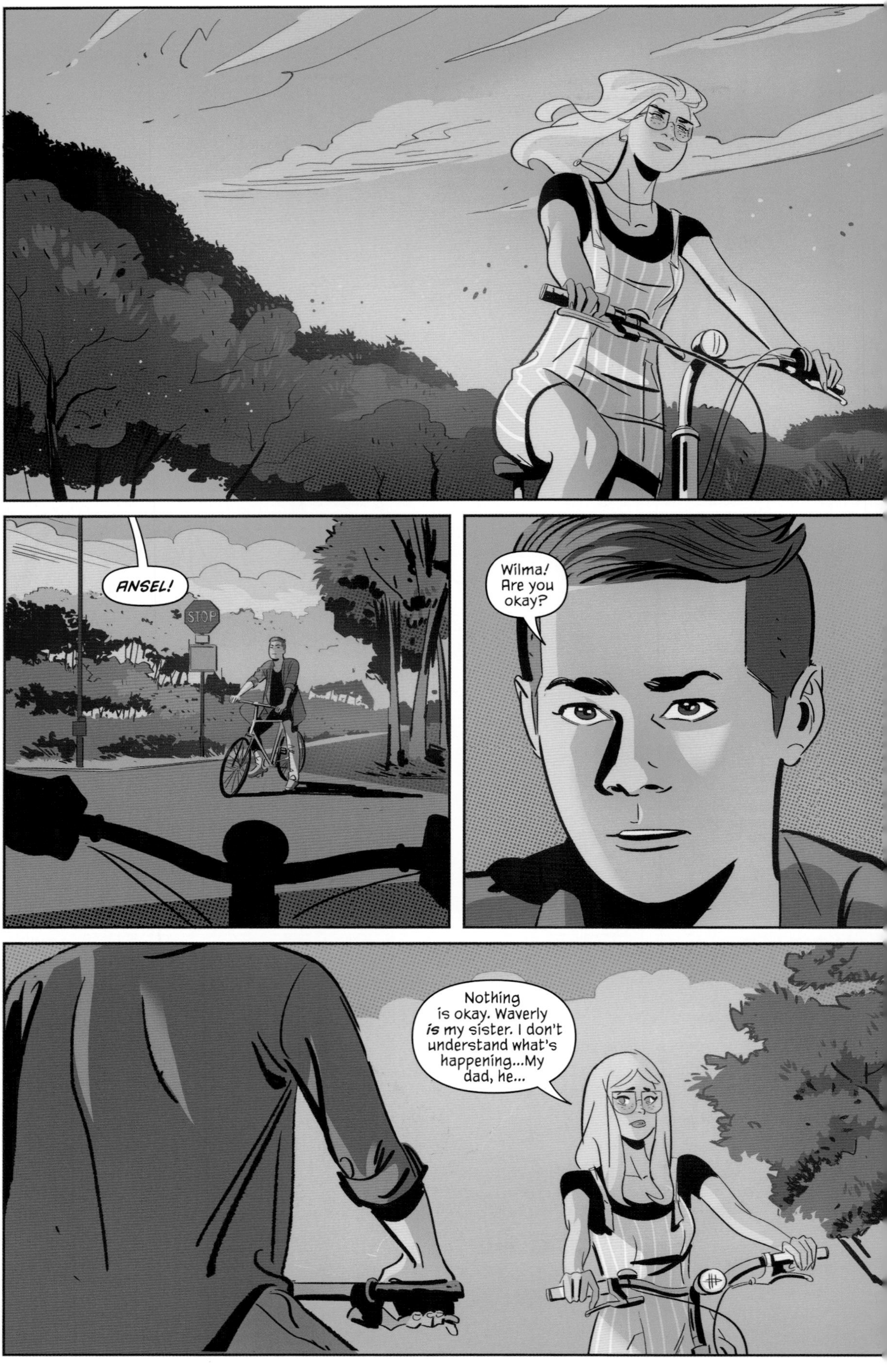
ANSEL!
Wilma! Are you okay?
Nothing is okay. Waverly *is* my sister. I don't understand what's happening...My dad, he...

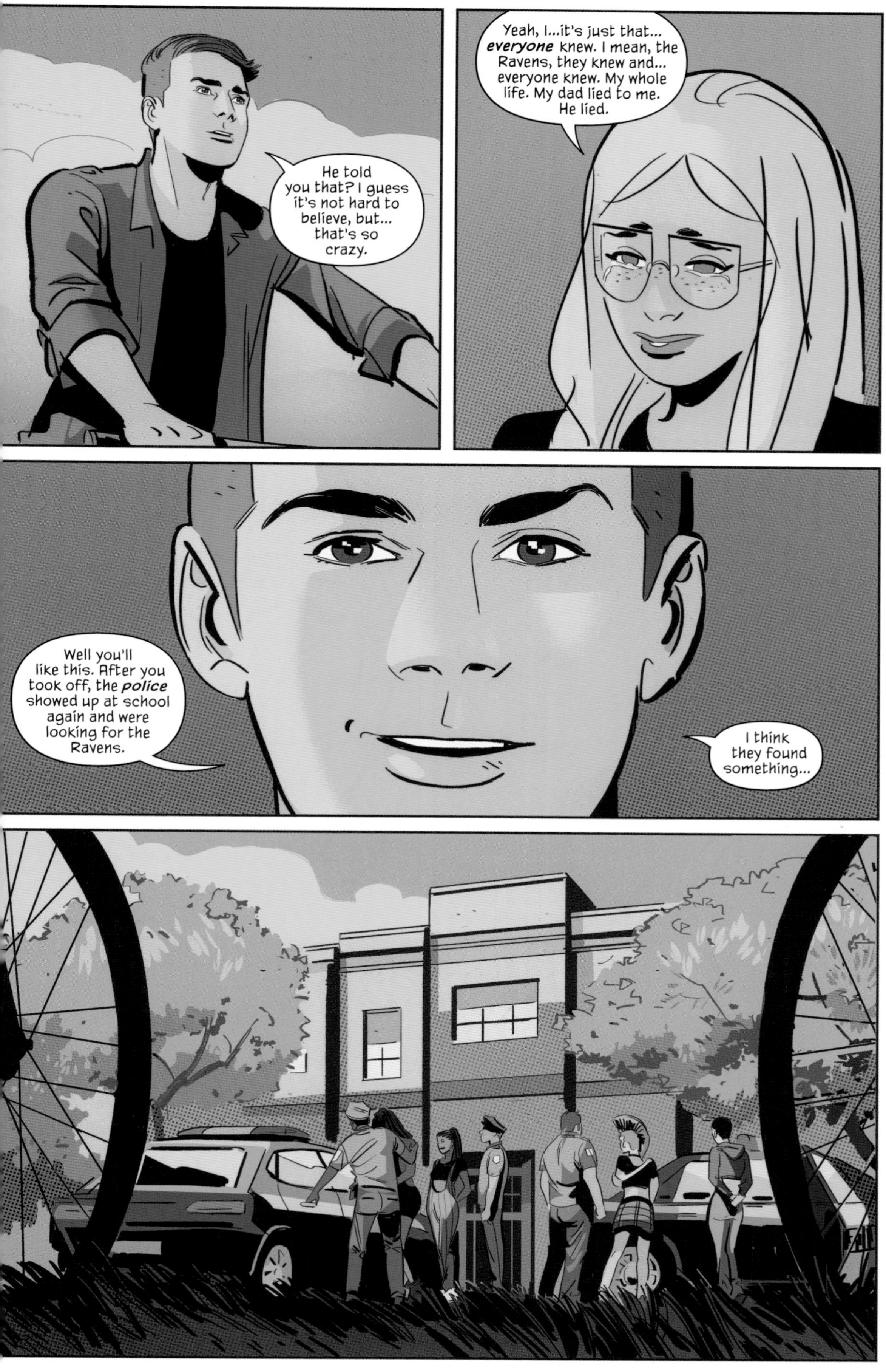
He told you that? I guess it's not hard to believe, but... that's so crazy.
Yeah, I...it's just that... *everyone* knew. I mean, the Ravens, they knew and... everyone knew. My whole life. My dad lied to me. He lied.
Well you'll like this. After you took off, the *police* showed up at school again and were looking for the Ravens.
I think they found something...

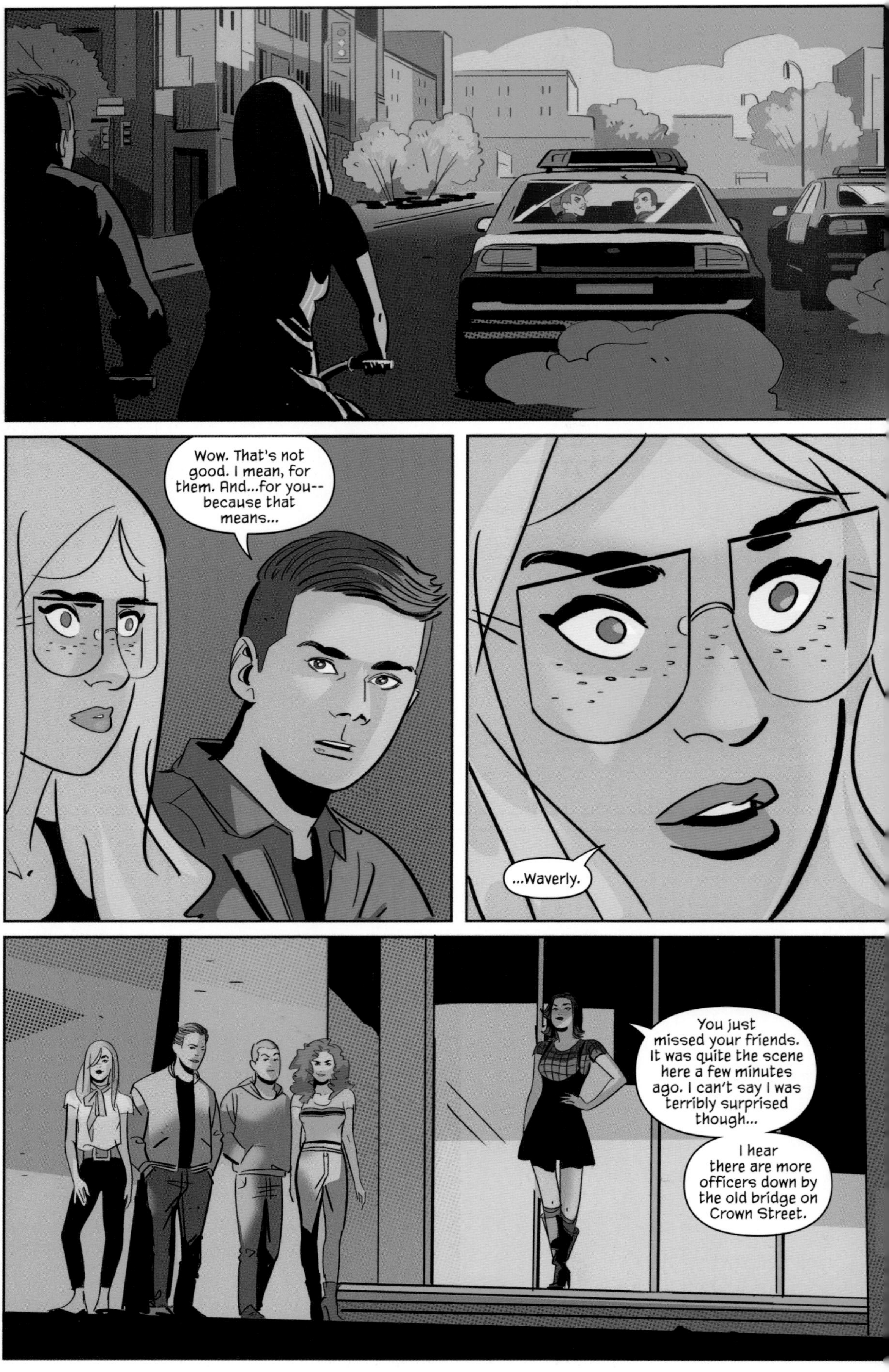
Wow. That's not good. I mean, for them. And...for you-- because that means...
...Waverly.
You just missed your friends. It was quite the scene here a few minutes ago. I can't say I was terribly surprised though...
I hear there are more officers down by the old bridge on Crown Street.

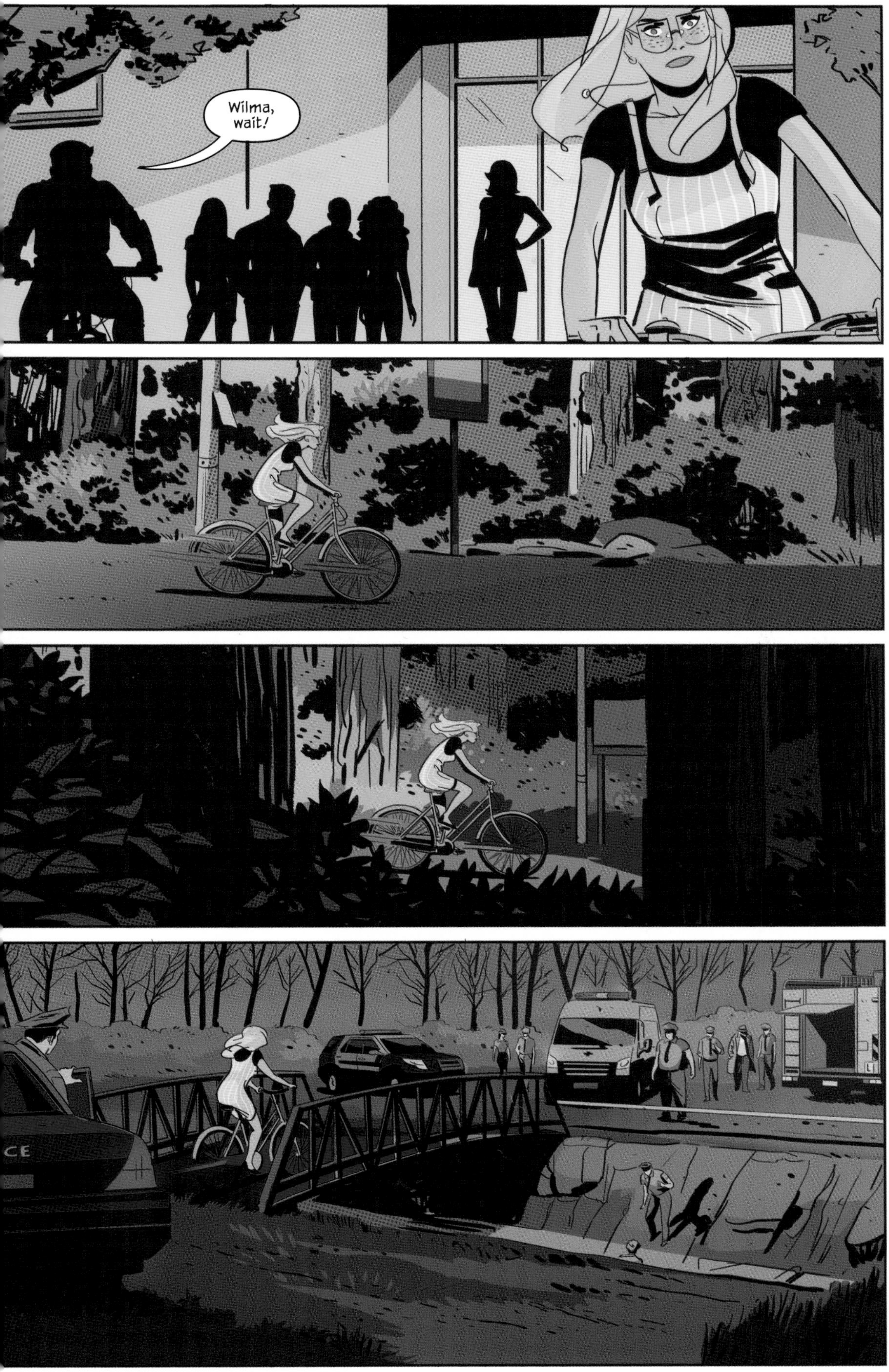
Wilma, wait!
CE

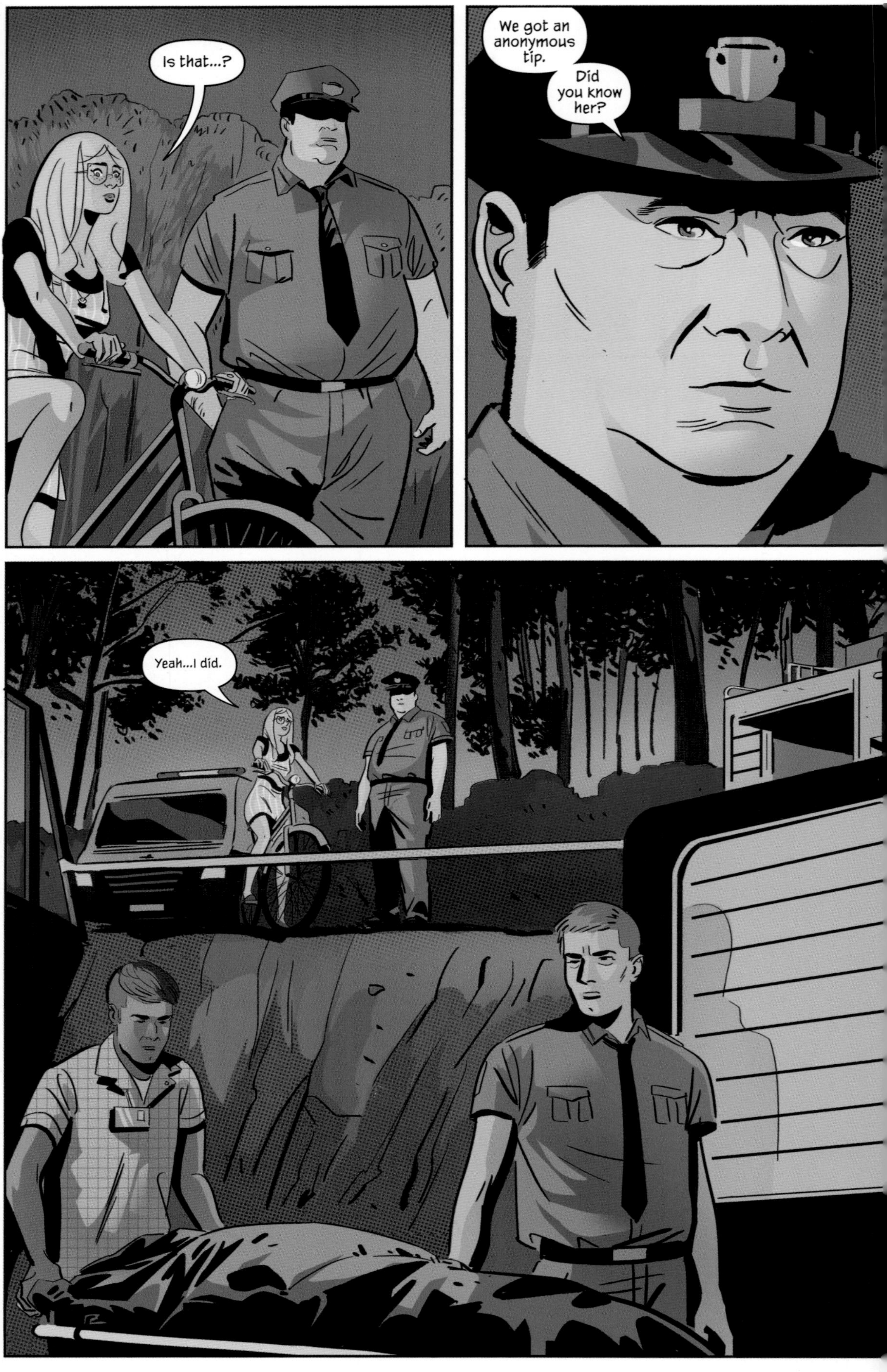
Is that...?
We got an anonymous tip.
Did you know her?
Yeah...I did.

υ
γ
α
ϵ

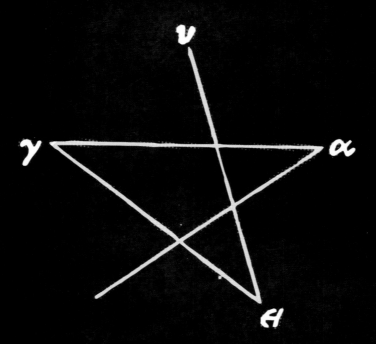

CHAPTER FIVE

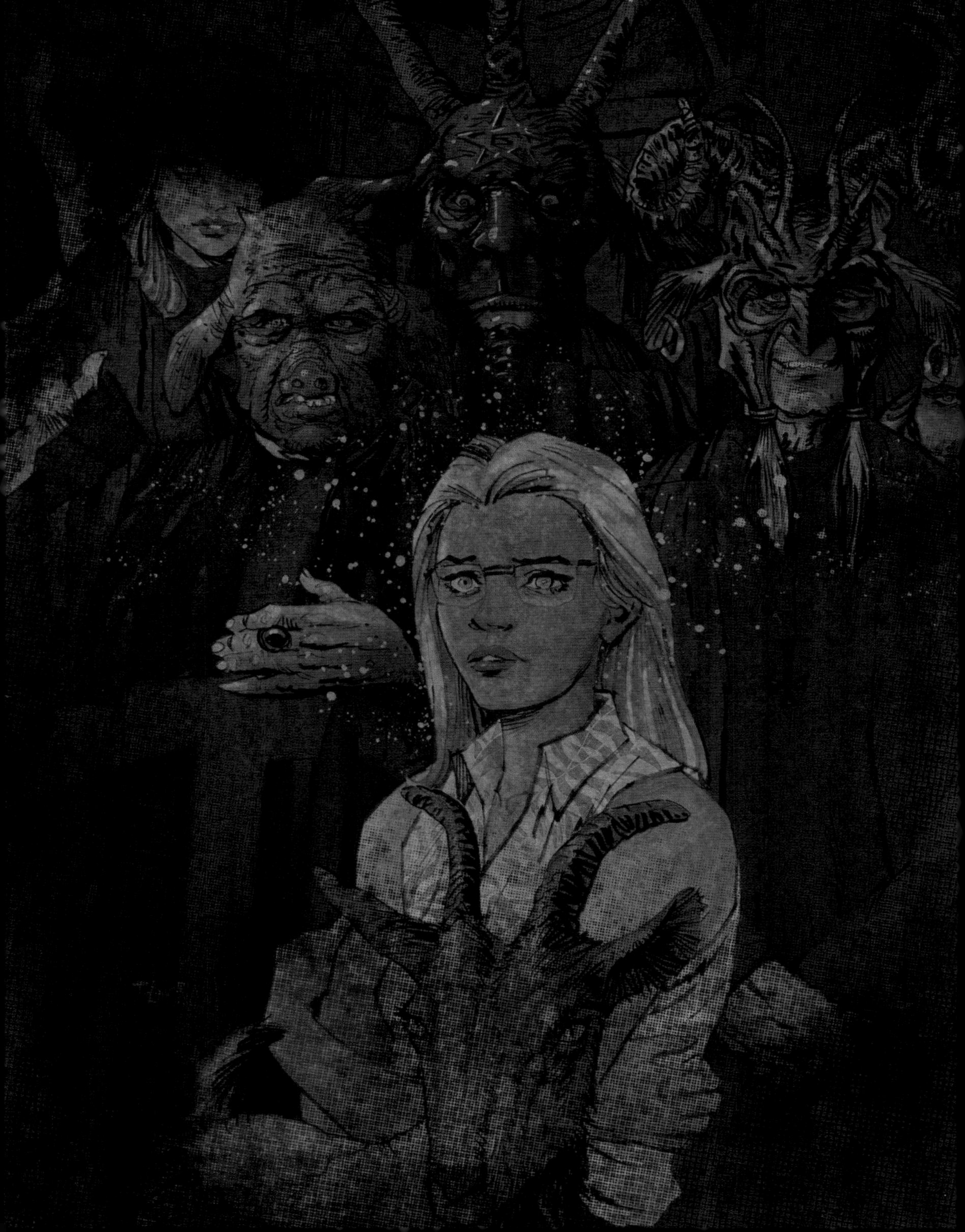

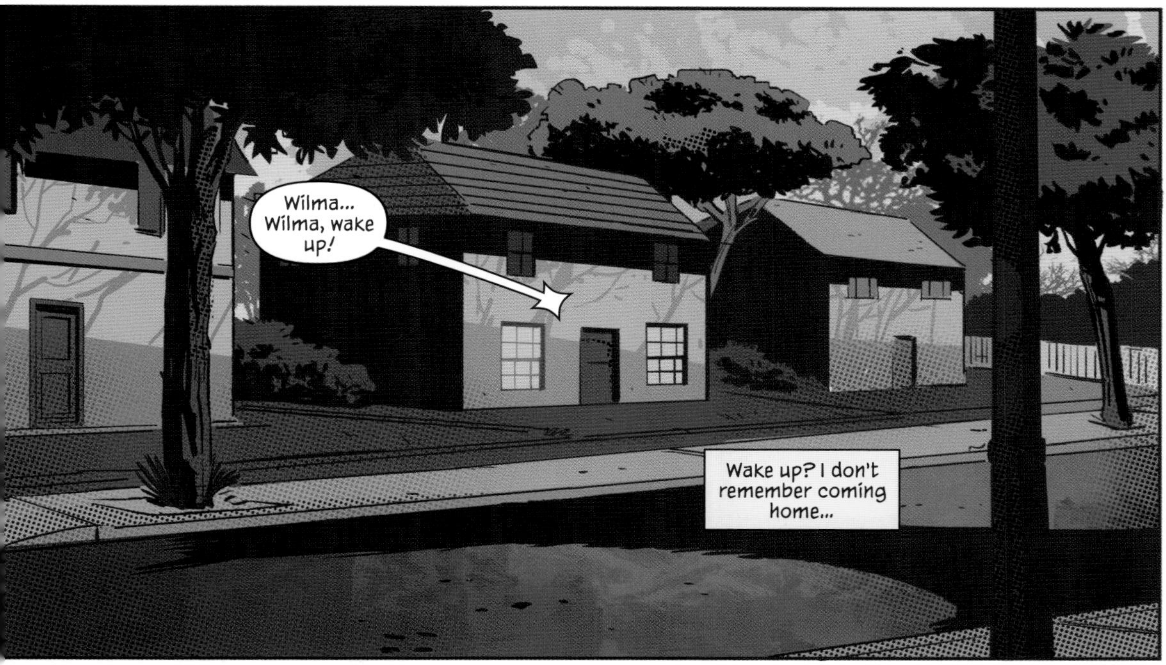
Wilma... Wilma, wake up!
Wake up? I don't remember coming home...

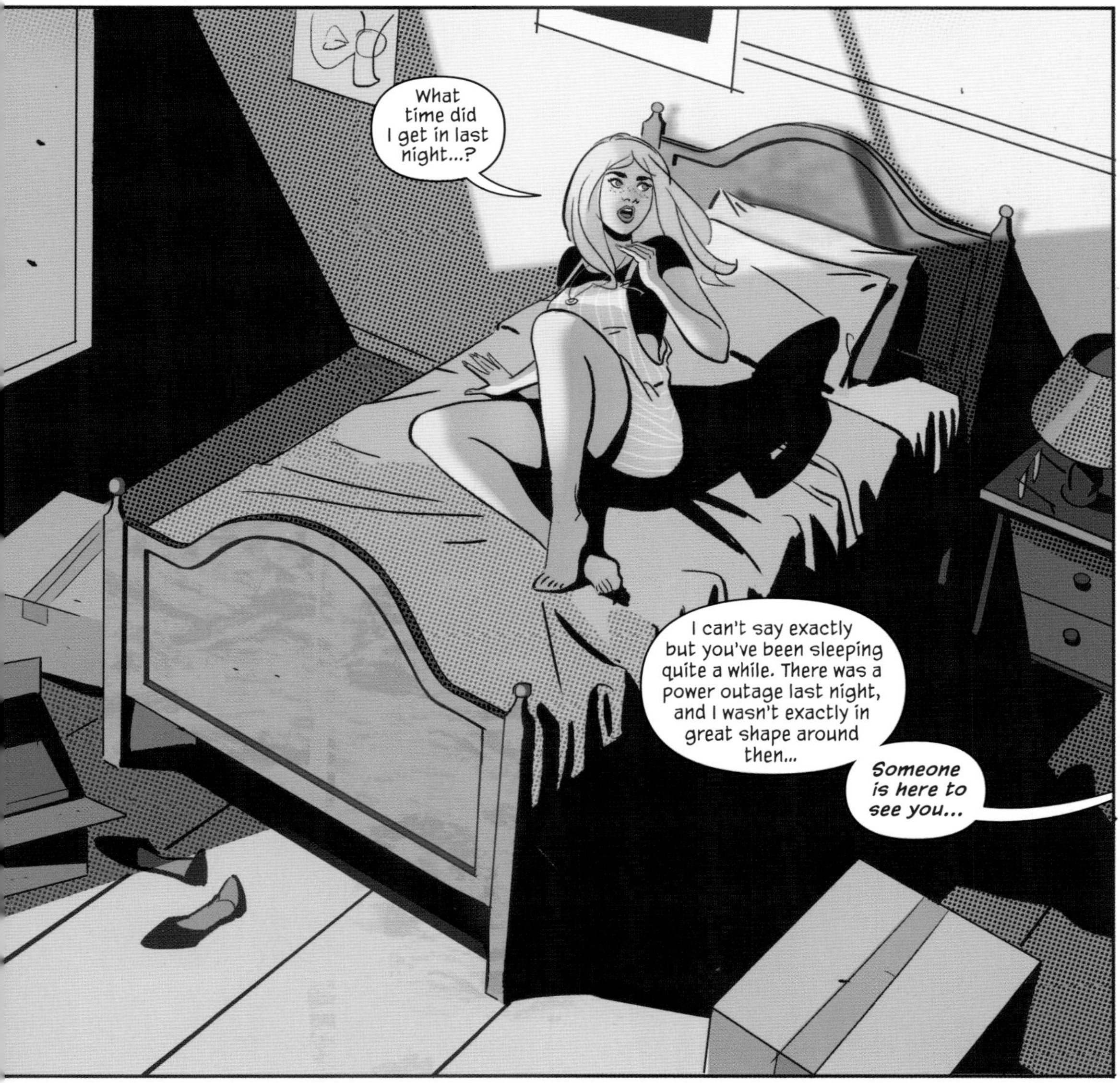
What time did I get in last night...?
I can't say exactly but you've been sleeping quite a while. There was a power outage last night, and I wasn't exactly in great shape around then...
Someone is here to see you...

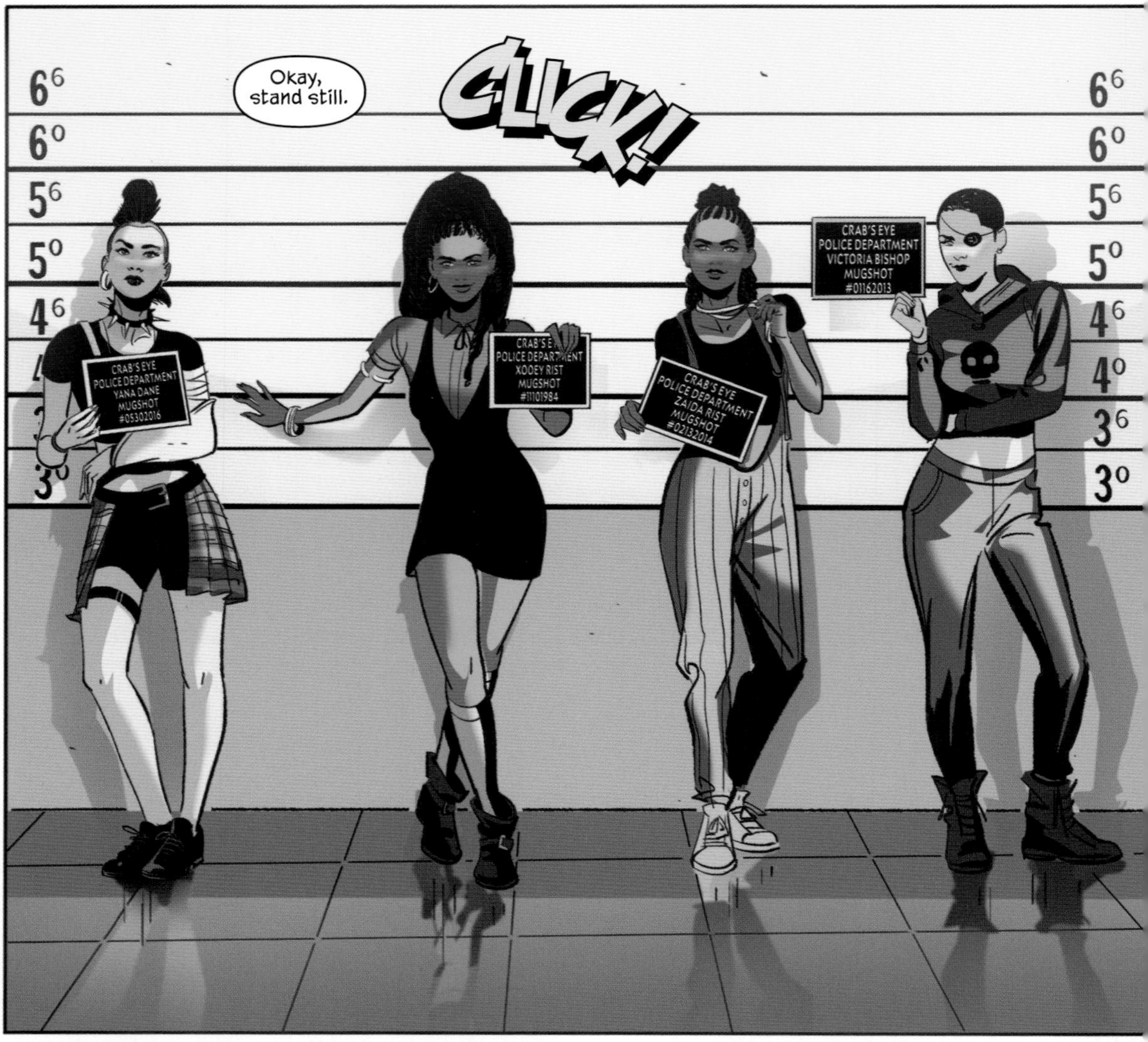
6⁶
6⁰
5⁶
5⁰
4⁶
4⁰
3⁶
3⁰
Okay, stand still.
CLICK!
CRAB'S EYE POLICE DEPARTMENT YANA DANE MUGSHOT #05302016
CRAB'S EYE POLICE DEPARTMENT XODEY RIST MUGSHOT #11101984
CRAB'S EYE POLICE DEPARTMENT ZAIDA RIST MUGSHOT #02132014
CRAB'S EYE POLICE DEPARTMENT VICTORIA BISHOP MUGSHOT #01162013

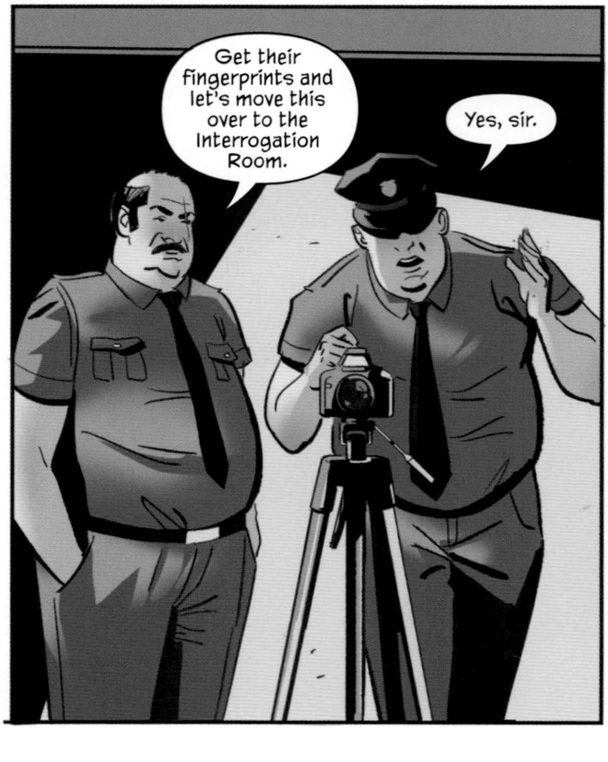
Get their fingerprints and let's move this over to the Interrogation Room.
Yes, sir.

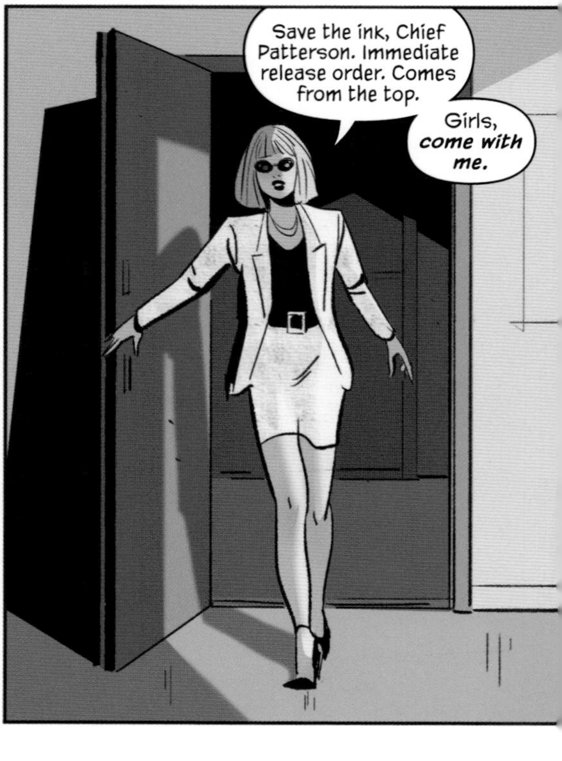
Save the ink, Chief Patterson. Immediate release order. Comes from the top.
Girls, *come with me.*

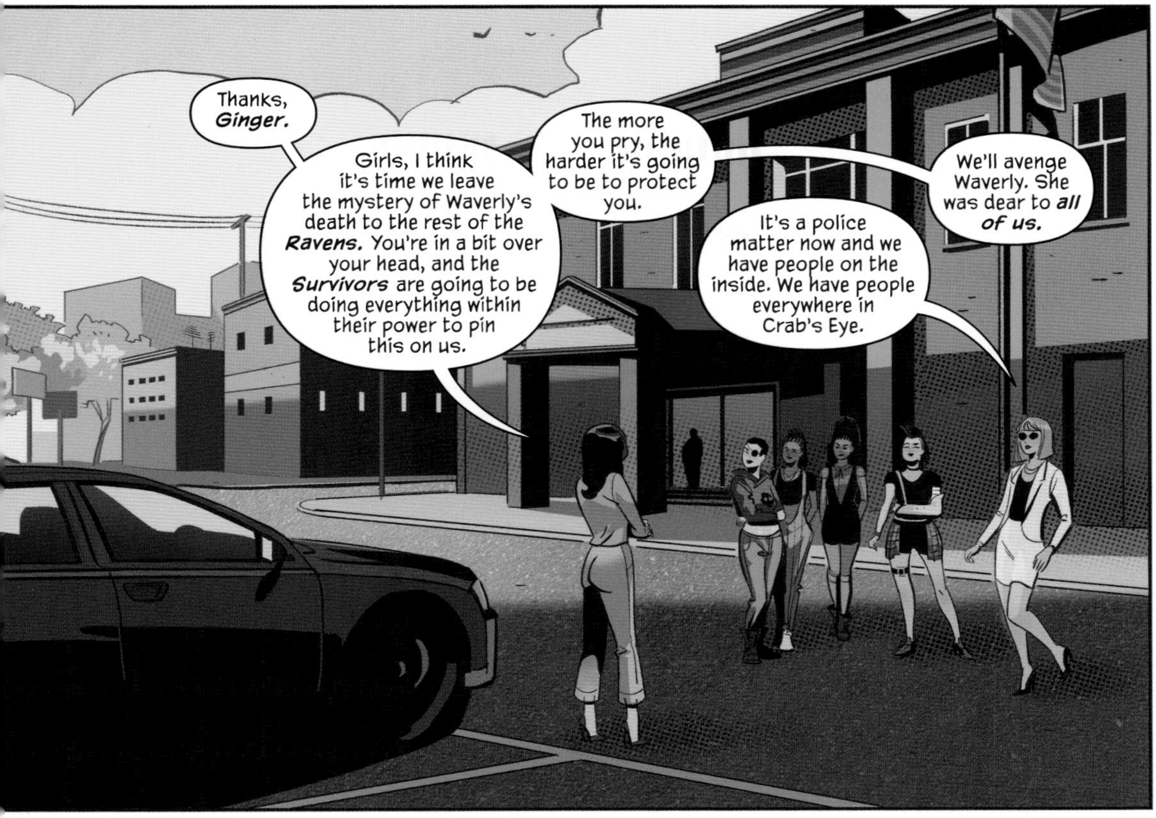
Thanks, *Ginger.*
Girls, I think it's time we leave the mystery of Waverly's death to the rest of the *Ravens.* You're in a bit over your head, and the *Survivors* are going to be doing everything within their power to pin this on us.
The more you pry, the harder it's going to be to protect you.
We'll avenge Waverly. She was dear to *all of us.*
It's a police matter now and we have people on the inside. We have people everywhere in Crab's Eye.

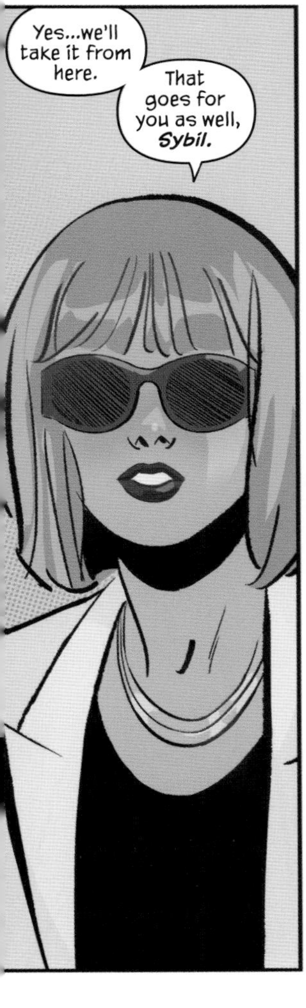
Yes...we'll take it from here.
That goes for you as well, *Sybil.*

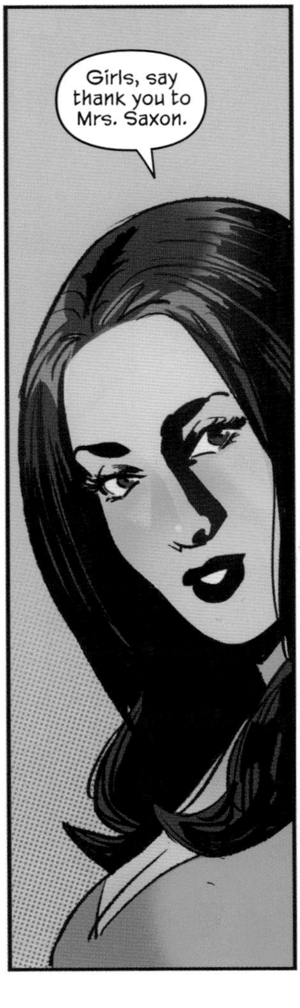
Girls, say thank you to Mrs. Saxon.

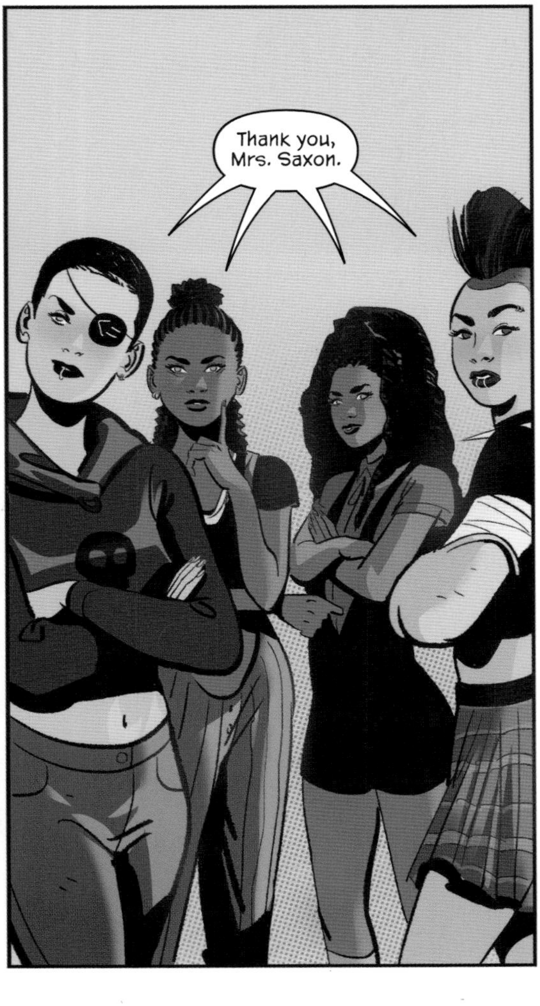
Thank you, Mrs. Saxon.

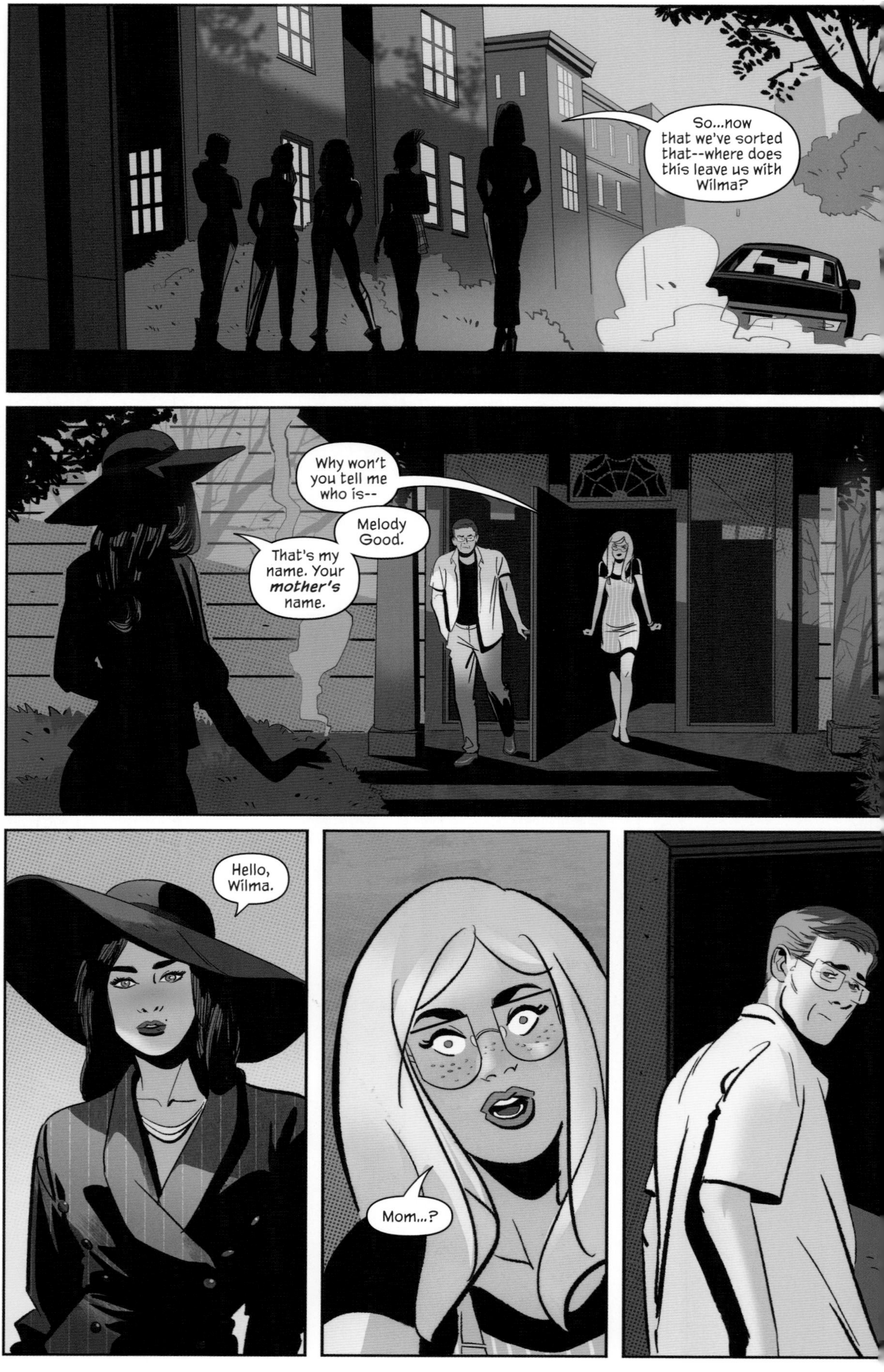
So...now that we've sorted that--where does this leave us with Wilma?
Why won't you tell me who is--
Melody Good.
That's my name. Your *mother's* name.
Hello, Wilma.
Mom...?

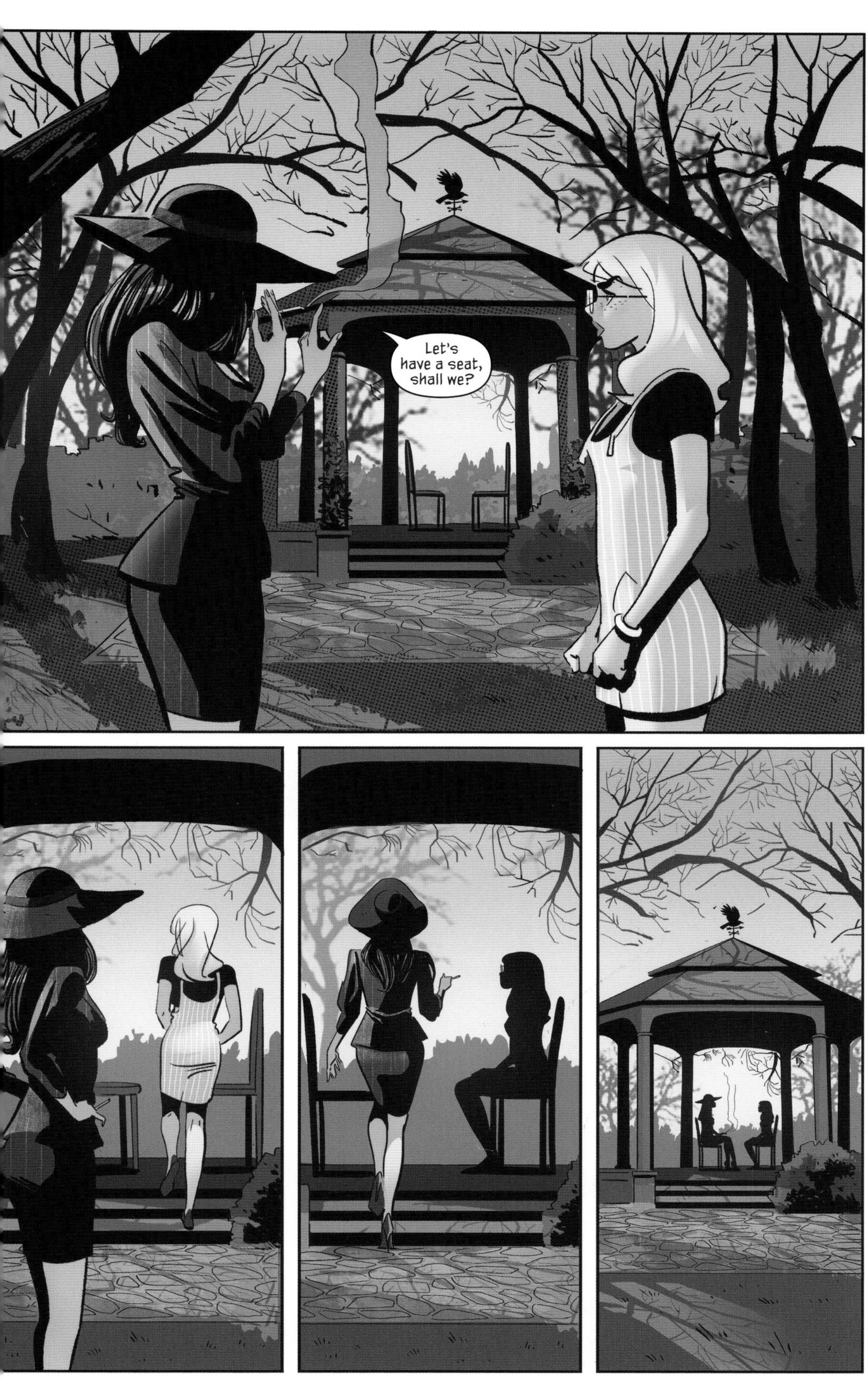
Let's have a seat, shall we?

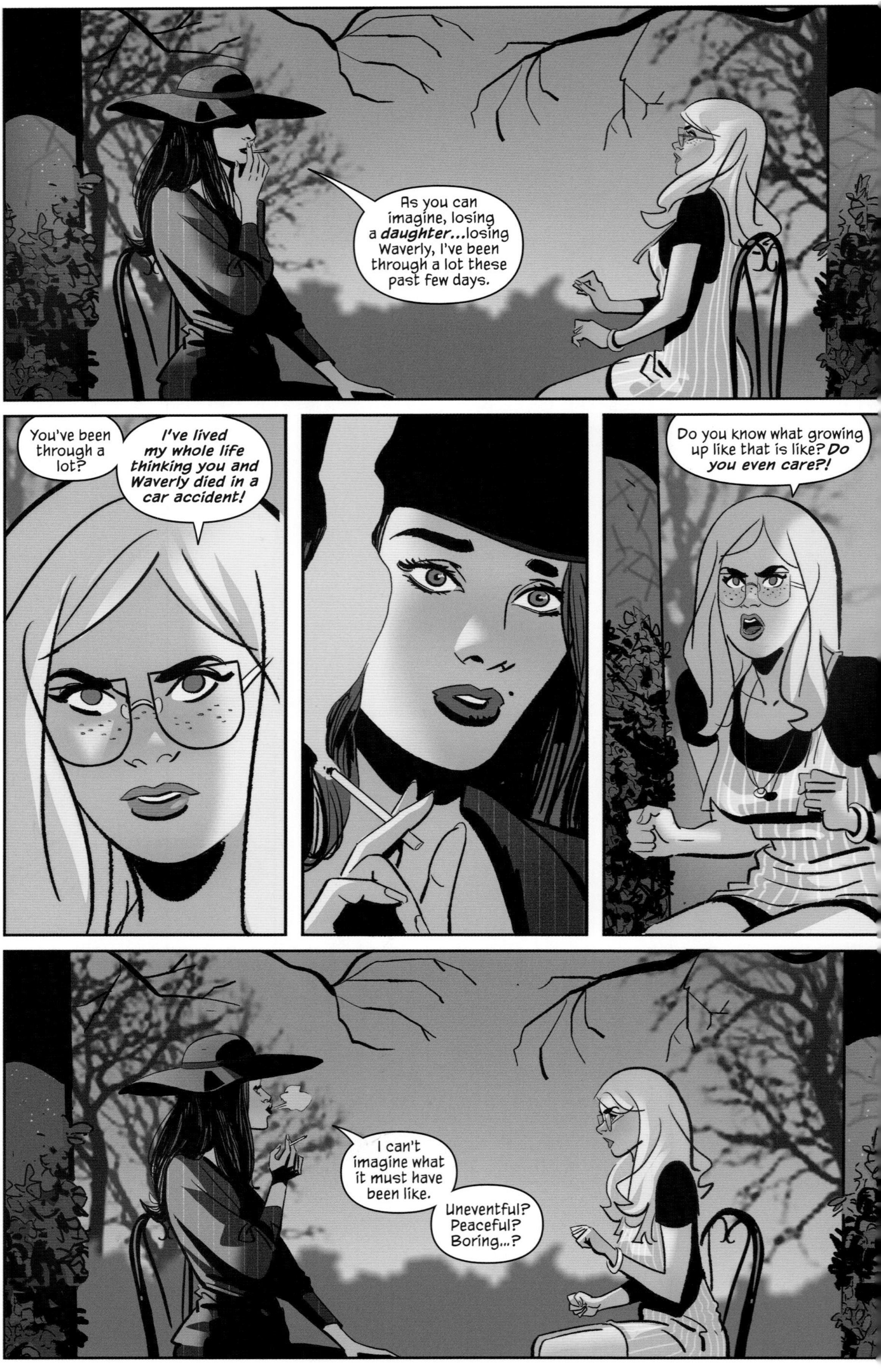
As you can imagine, losing a ***daughter...*** losing Waverly, I've been through a lot these past few days.
You've been through a lot?
I've lived my whole life thinking you and Waverly died in a car accident!
Do you know what growing up like that is like? ***Do you even care?!***
I can't imagine what it must have been like.
Uneventful? Peaceful? Boring...?

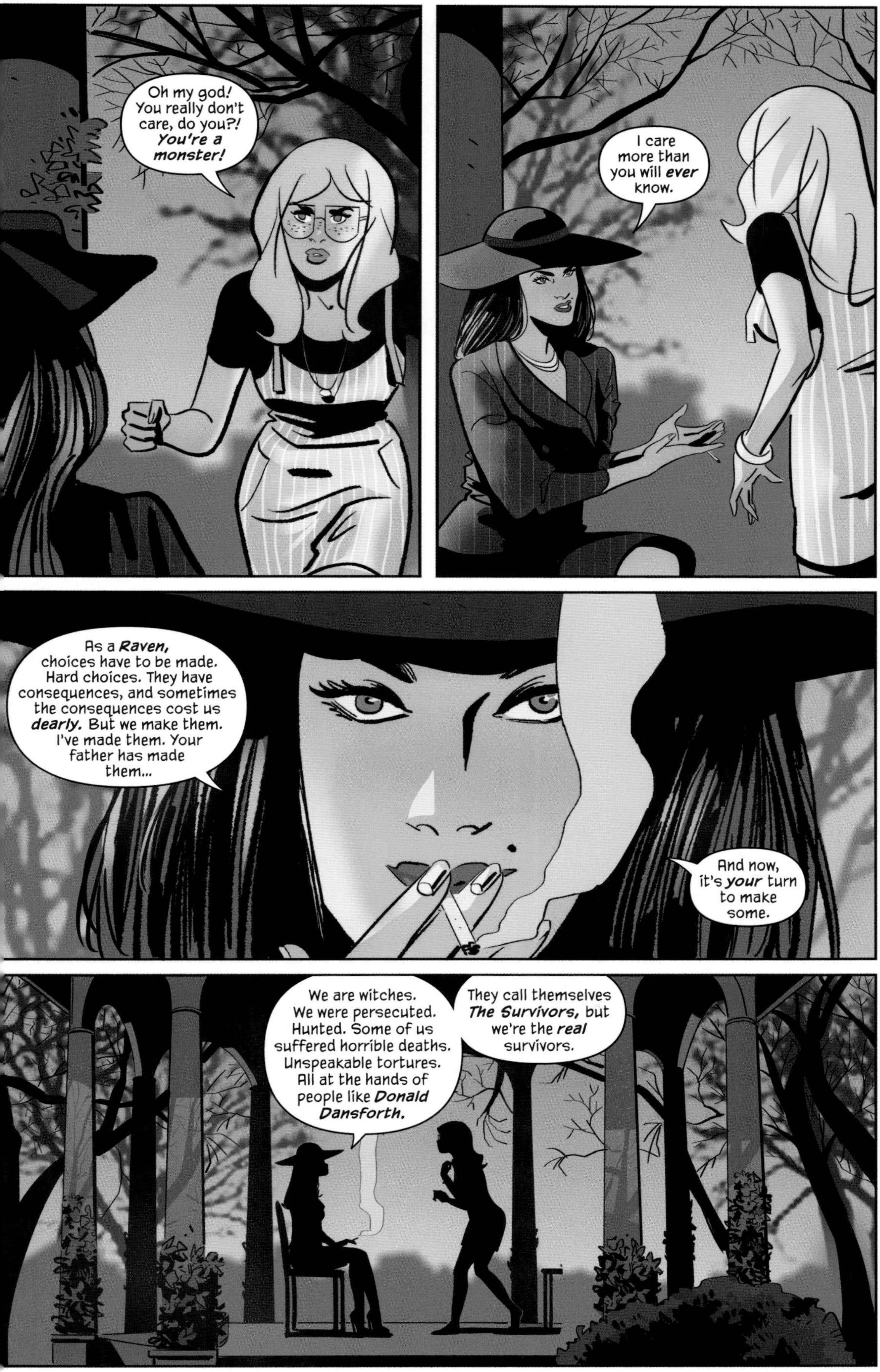
Oh my god! You really don't care, do you?! You're a monster!
I care more than you will ever know.
As a Raven, choices have to be made. Hard choices. They have consequences, and sometimes the consequences cost us dearly. But we make them. I've made them. Your father has made them...
And now, it's your turn to make some.
We are witches. We were persecuted. Hunted. Some of us suffered horrible deaths. Unspeakable tortures. All at the hands of people like Donald Dansforth.
They call themselves The Survivors, but we're the real survivors.

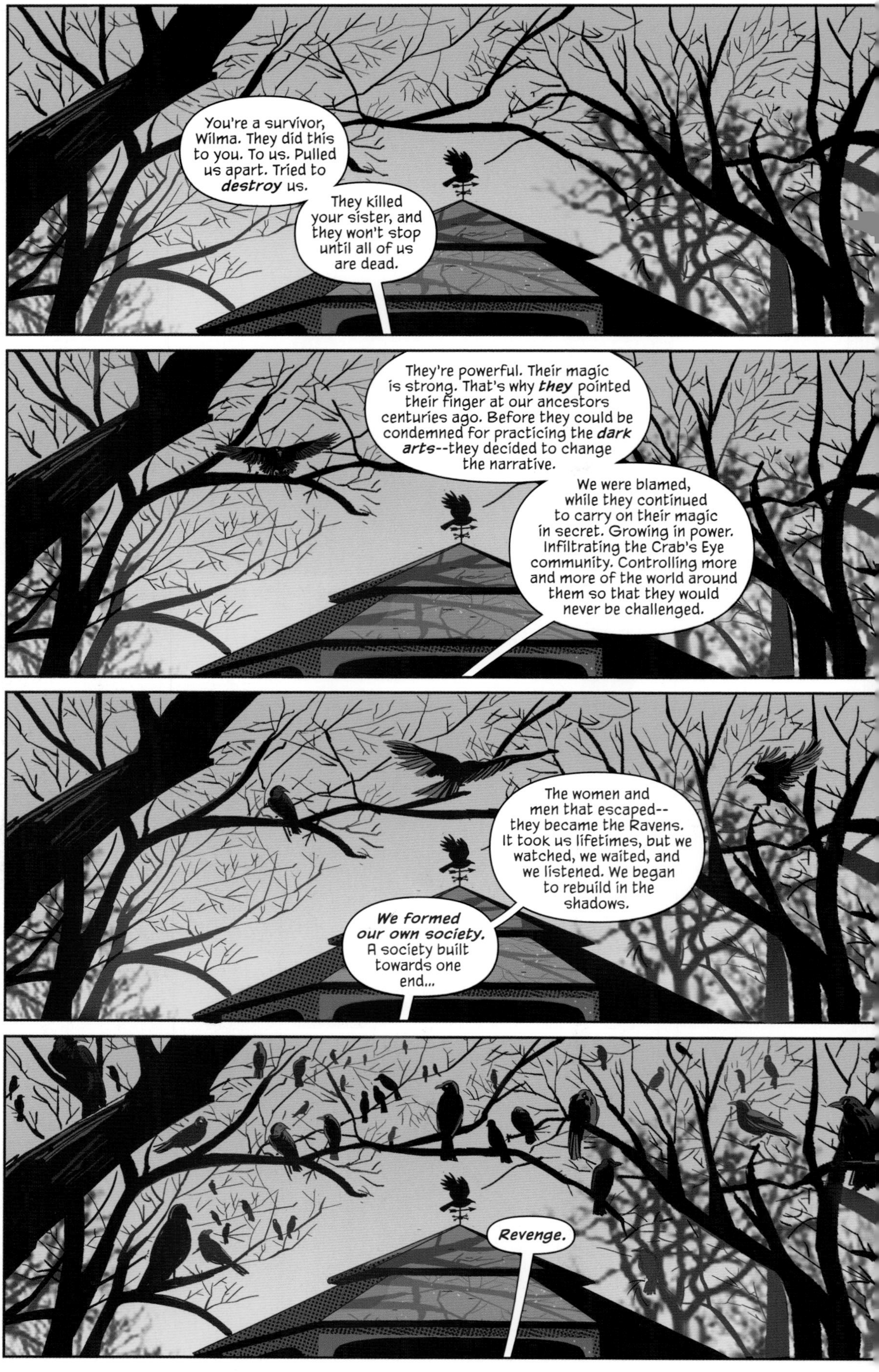
You're a survivor, Wilma. They did this to you. To us. Pulled us apart. Tried to *destroy* us.
They killed your sister, and they won't stop until all of us are dead.
They're powerful. Their magic is strong. That's why *they* pointed their finger at our ancestors centuries ago. Before they could be condemned for practicing the *dark arts*--they decided to change the narrative.
We were blamed, while they continued to carry on their magic in secret. Growing in power. Infiltrating the Crab's Eye community. Controlling more and more of the world around them so that they would never be challenged.
The women and men that escaped--they became the Ravens. It took us lifetimes, but we watched, we waited, and we listened. We began to rebuild in the shadows.
We formed our own society. A society built towards one end...
Revenge.

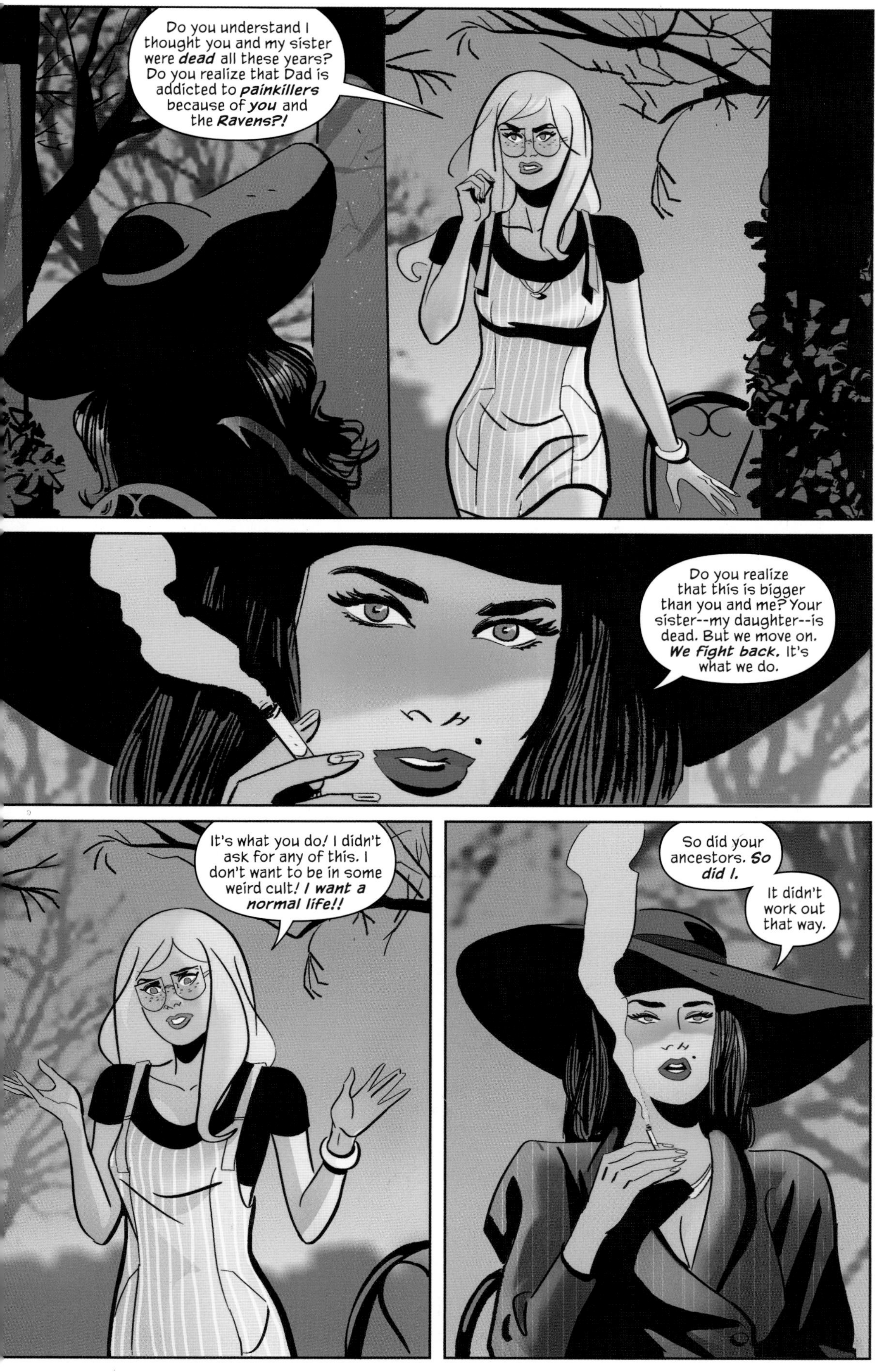
Do you understand I thought you and my sister were *dead* all these years? Do you realize that Dad is addicted to *painkillers* because of *you* and the *Ravens?!*
Do you realize that this is bigger than you and me? Your sister--my daughter--is dead. But we move on. *We fight back.* It's what we do.
It's what you do! I didn't ask for any of this. I don't want to be in some weird cult! *I want a normal life!!*
So did your ancestors. *So did I.*
It didn't work out that way.

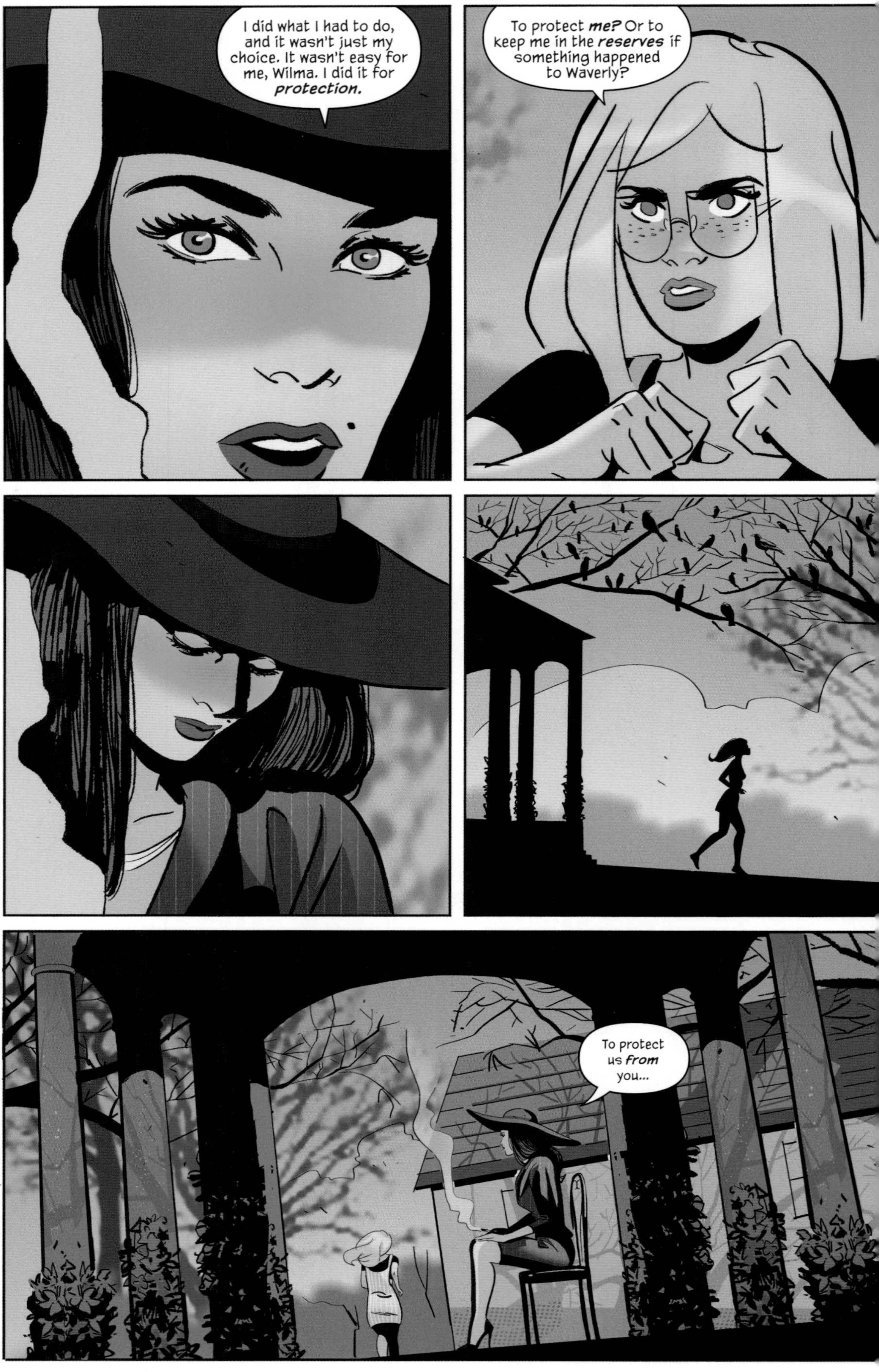
I did what I had to do, and it wasn't just my choice. It wasn't easy for me, Wilma. I did it for protection.
To protect me? Or to keep me in the reserves if something happened to Waverly?
To protect us from you...

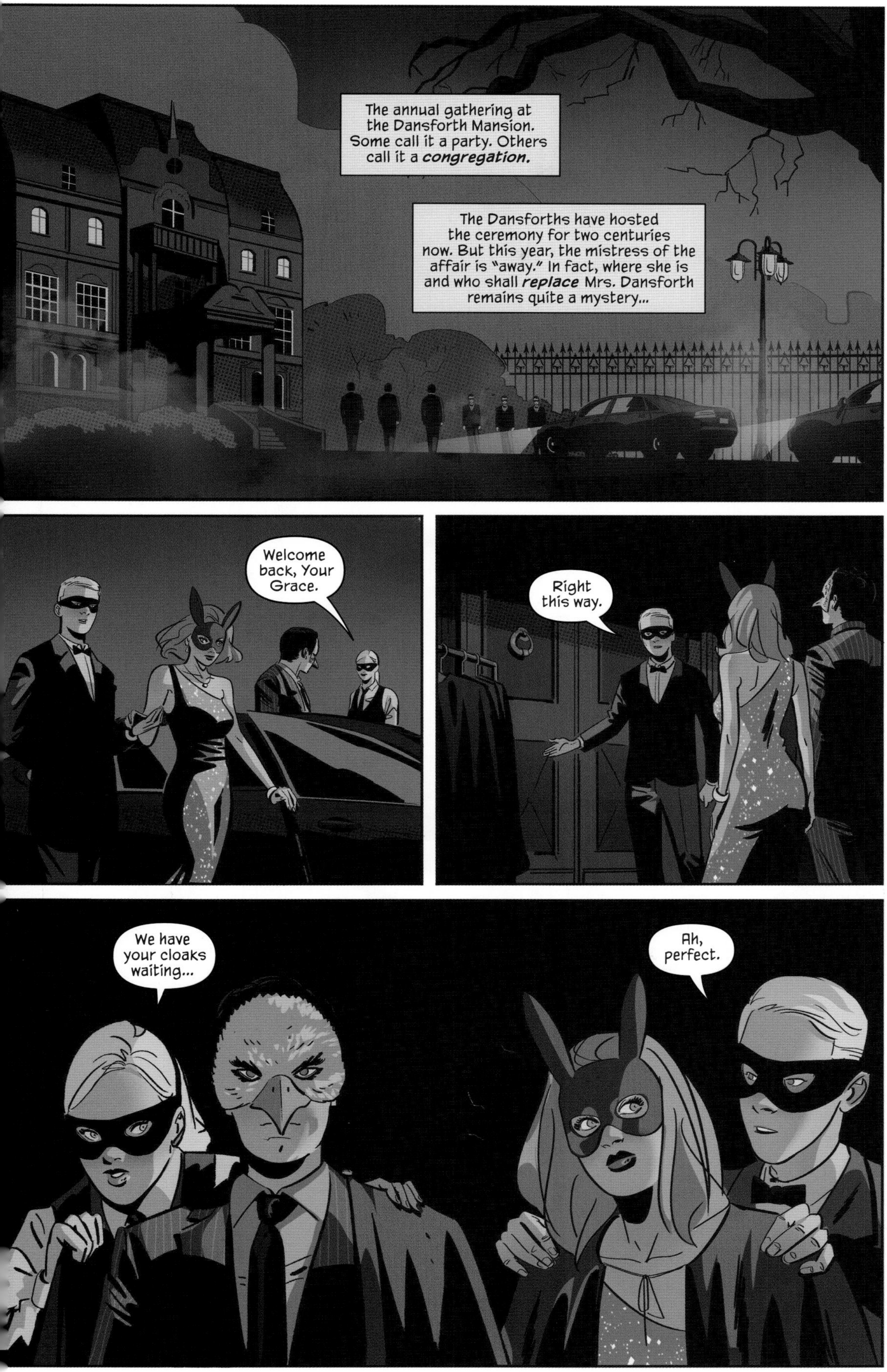
The annual gathering at the Dansforth Mansion. Some call it a party. Others call it a *congregation.*
The Dansforths have hosted the ceremony for two centuries now. But this year, the mistress of the affair is "away." In fact, where she is and who shall *replace* Mrs. Dansforth remains quite a mystery...
Welcome back, Your Grace.
Right this way.
We have your cloaks waiting...
Ah, perfect.

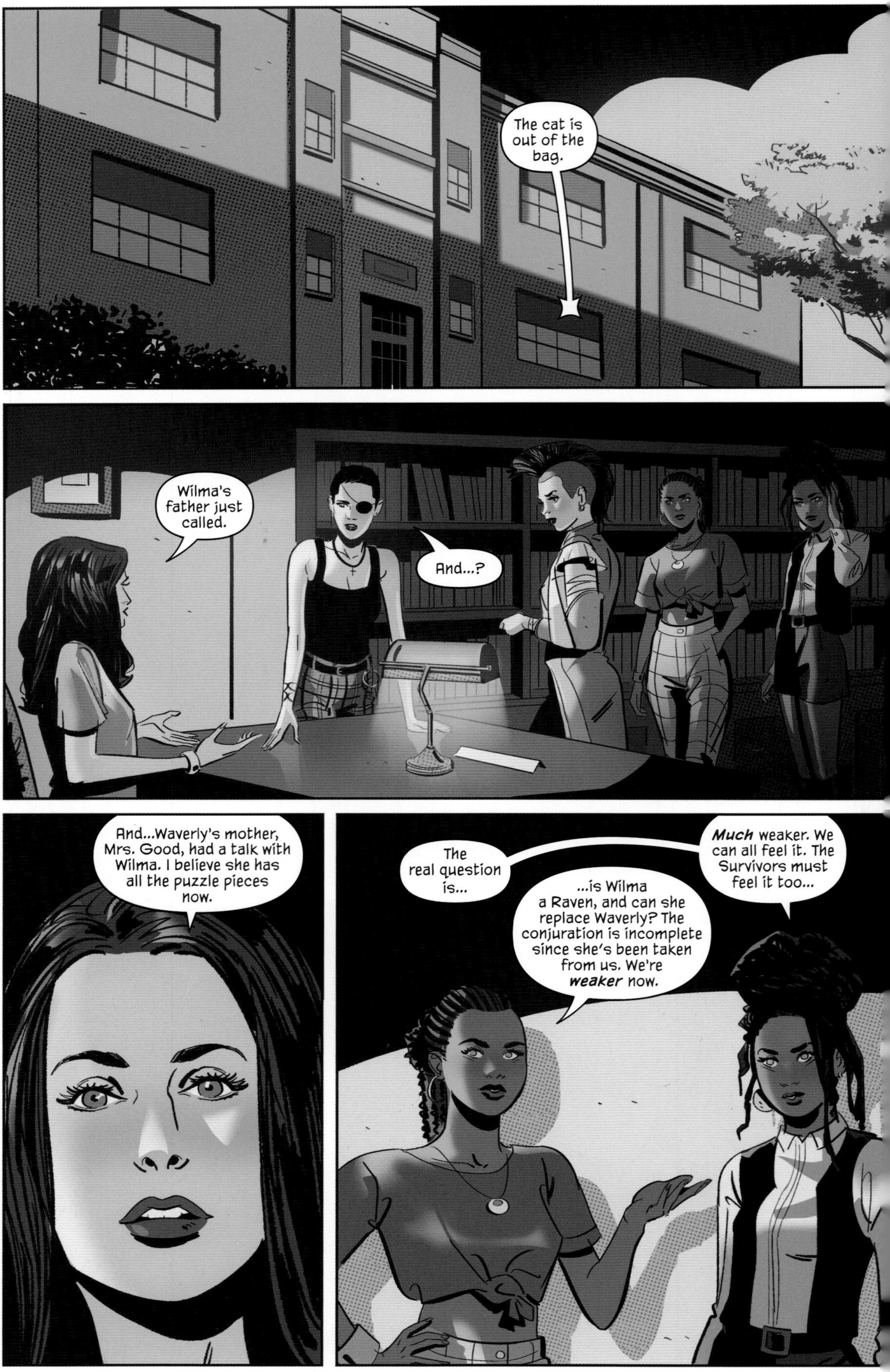
The cat is out of the bag.
Wilma's father just called.
And...?
And...Waverly's mother, Mrs. Good, had a talk with Wilma. I believe she has all the puzzle pieces now.
The real question is...
...is Wilma a Raven, and can she replace Waverly? The conjuration is incomplete since she's been taken from us. We're *weaker* now.
Much weaker. We can all feel it. The Survivors must feel it too...

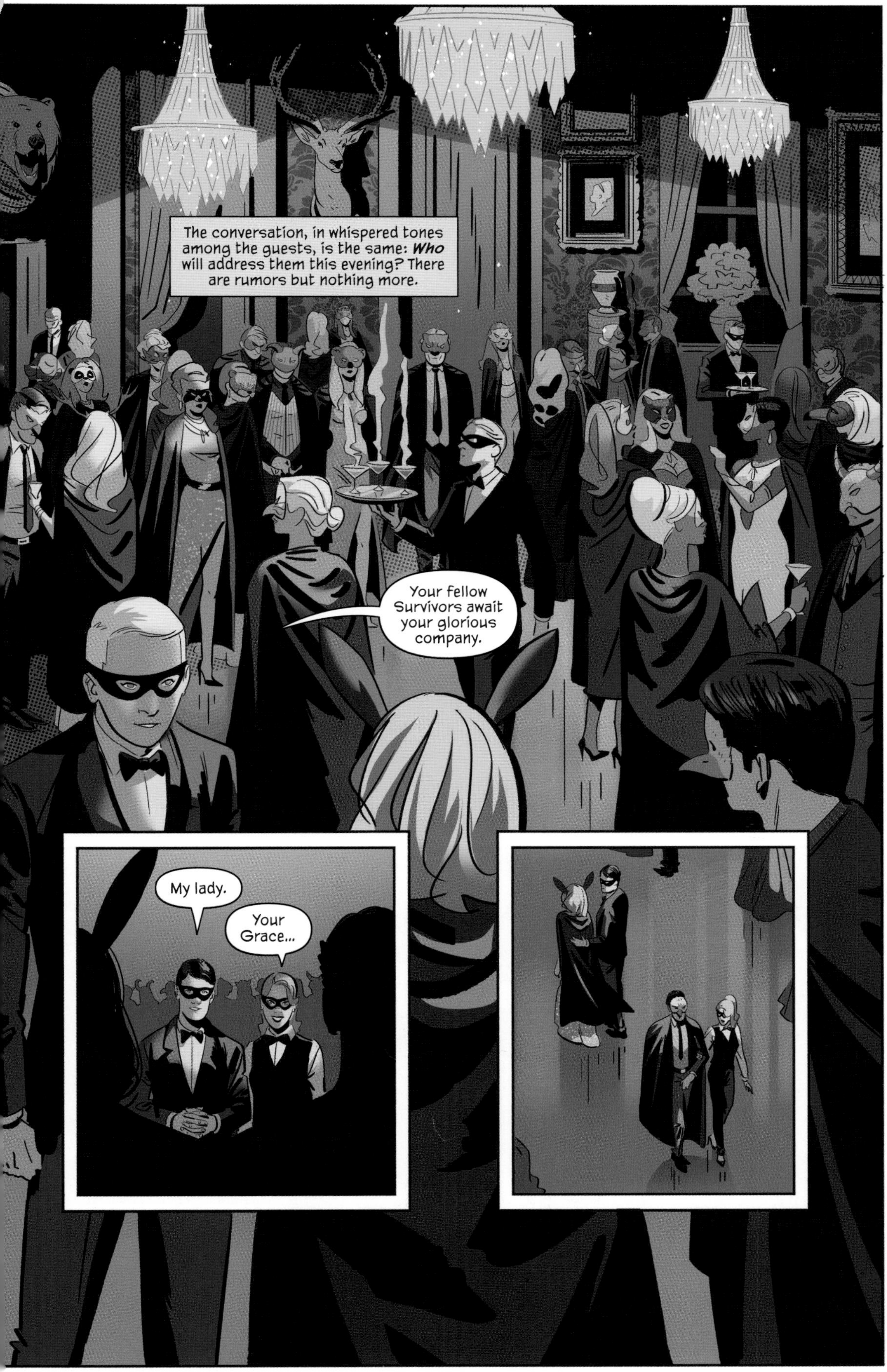
The conversation, in whispered tones among the guests, is the same: ***Who*** will address them this evening? There are rumors but nothing more.
Your fellow Survivors await your glorious company.
My lady.
Your Grace...

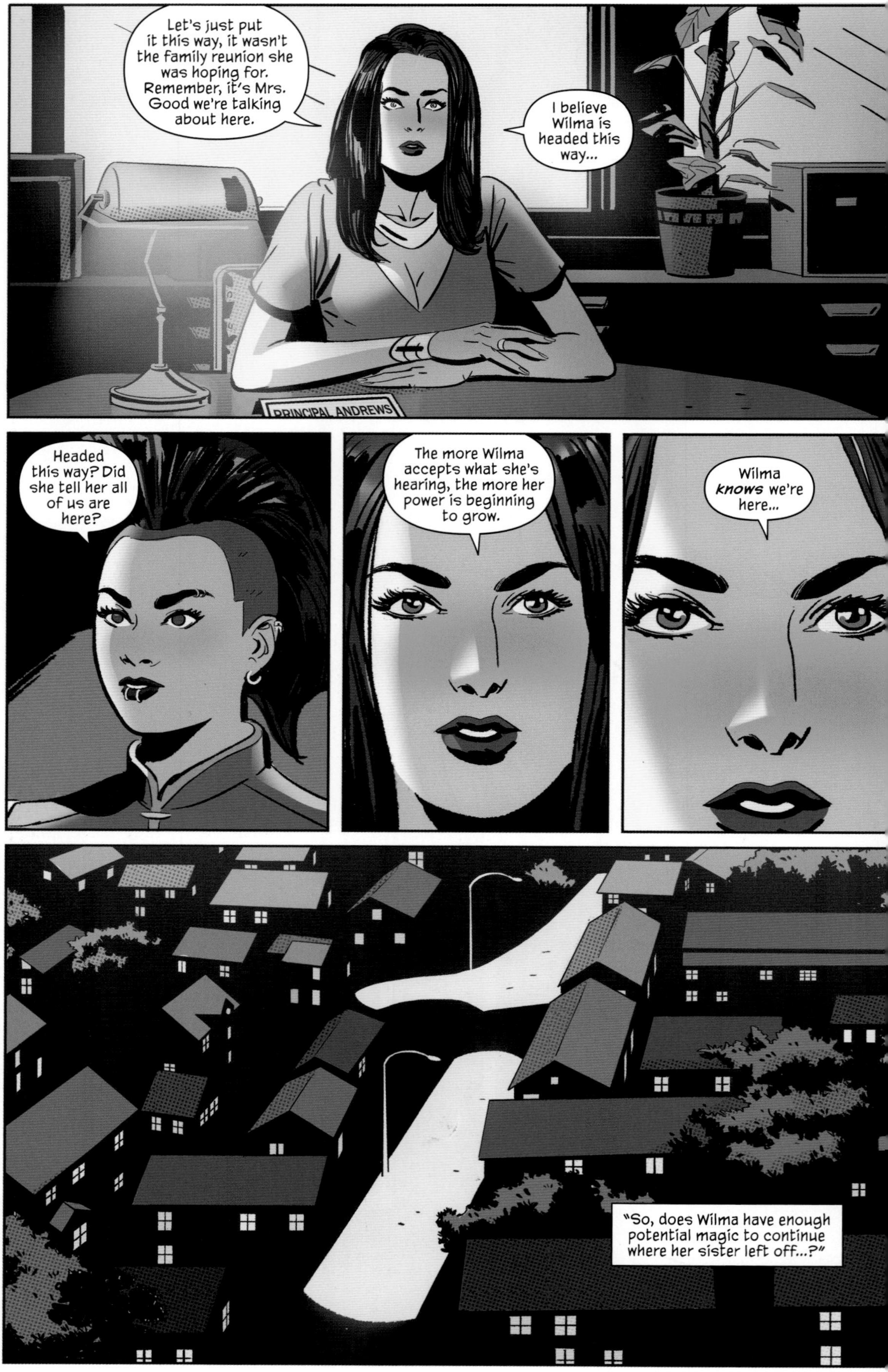
Let's just put it this way, it wasn't the family reunion she was hoping for. Remember, it's Mrs. Good we're talking about here.
I believe Wilma is headed this way...
PRINCIPAL ANDREWS
Headed this way? Did she tell her all of us are here?
The more Wilma accepts what she's hearing, the more her power is beginning to grow.
Wilma ***knows*** we're here...
"So, does Wilma have enough potential magic to continue where her sister left off...?"

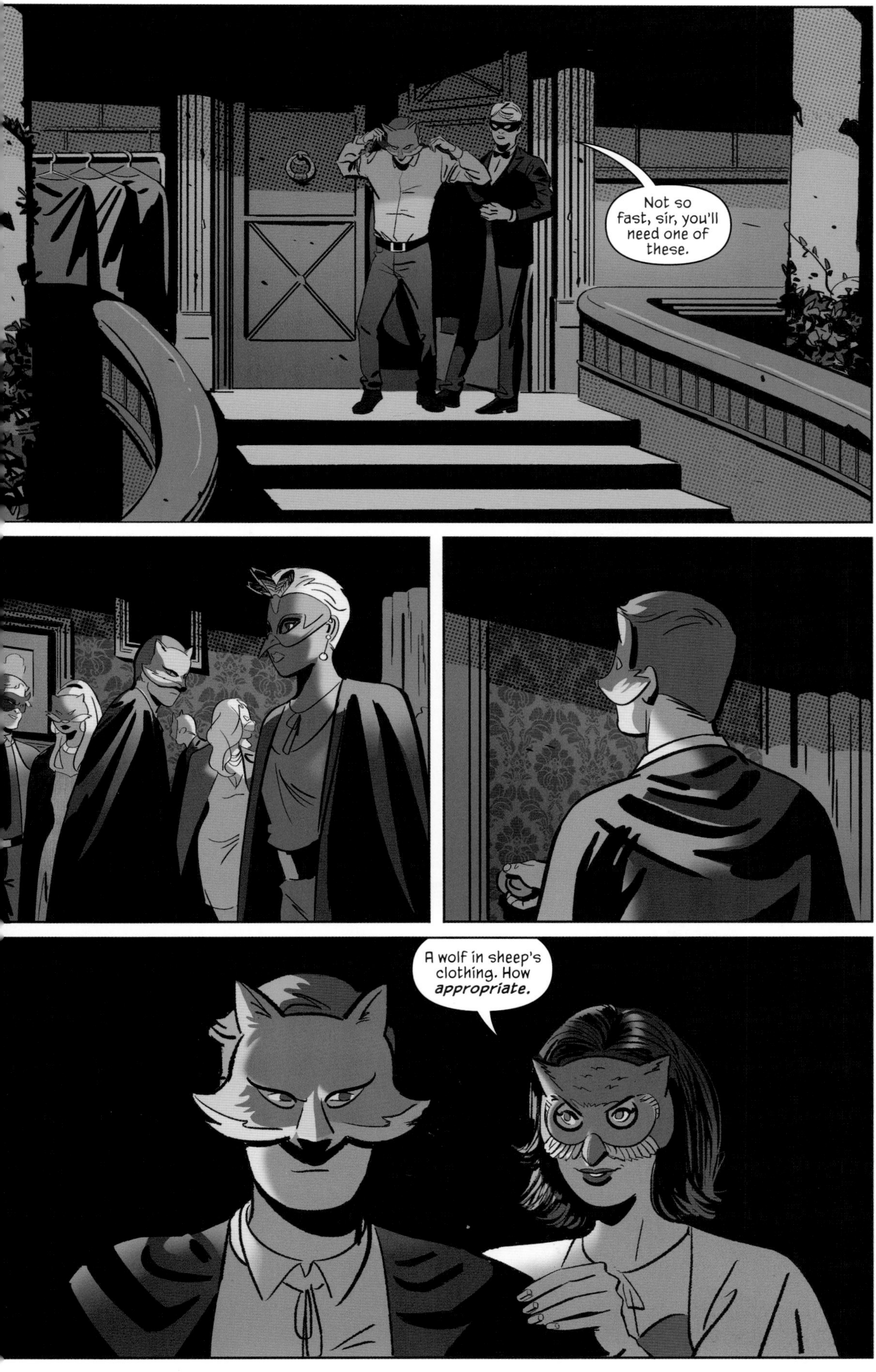
Not so fast, sir, you'll need one of these.
A wolf in sheep's clothing. How *appropriate.*

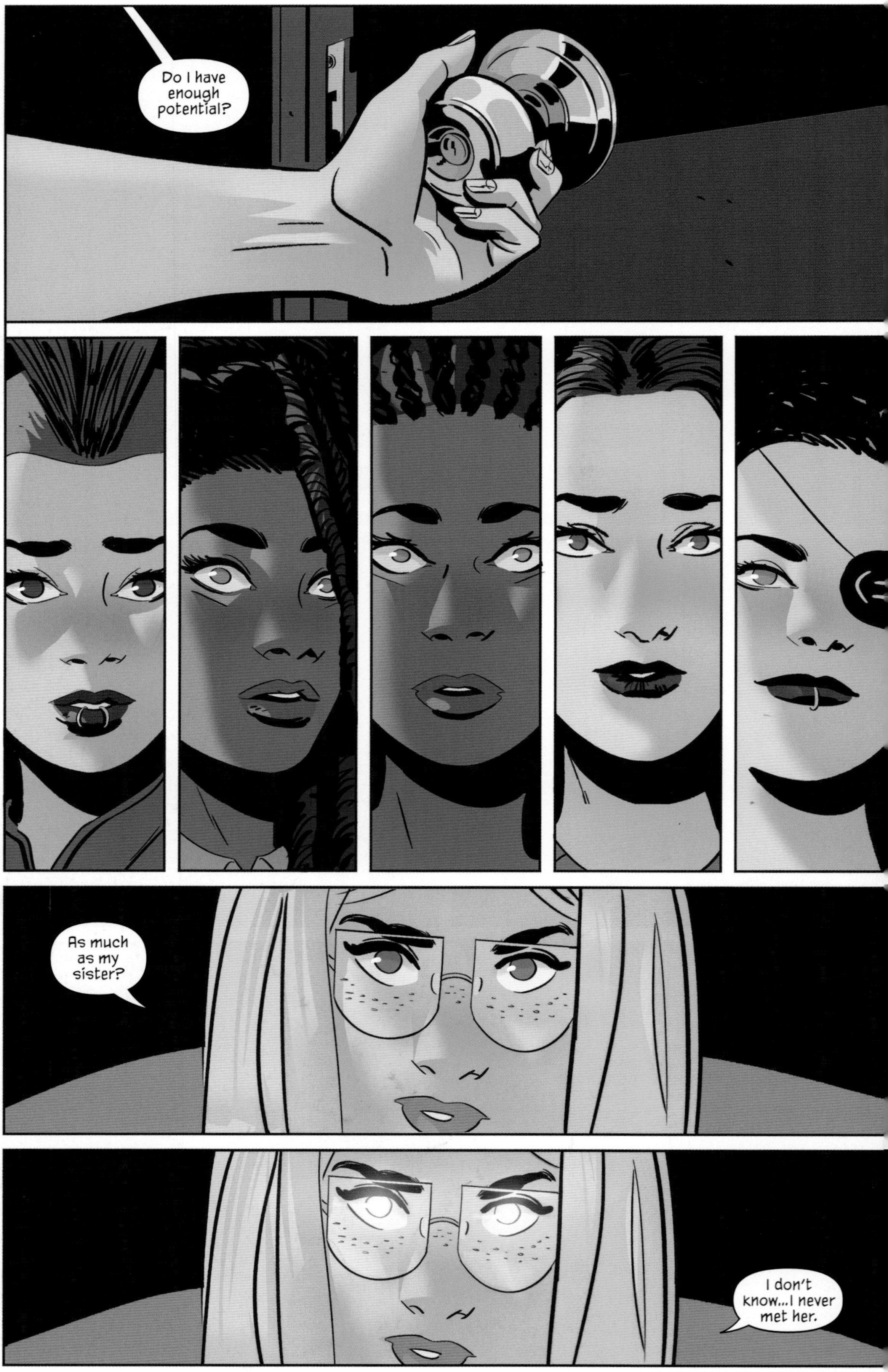
Do I have enough potential?
As much as my sister?
I don't know...I never met her.

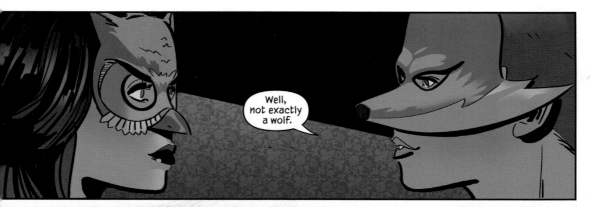

Well, not exactly a wolf.

I'm a fox.

Of course you are. So, is our little friend with you somewhere?

She's with her mother. I suspect heads are going to start rolling soon.

Ah...well, we expected that would happen sooner or later, and with a mother like Melody Good, who needs enemies?

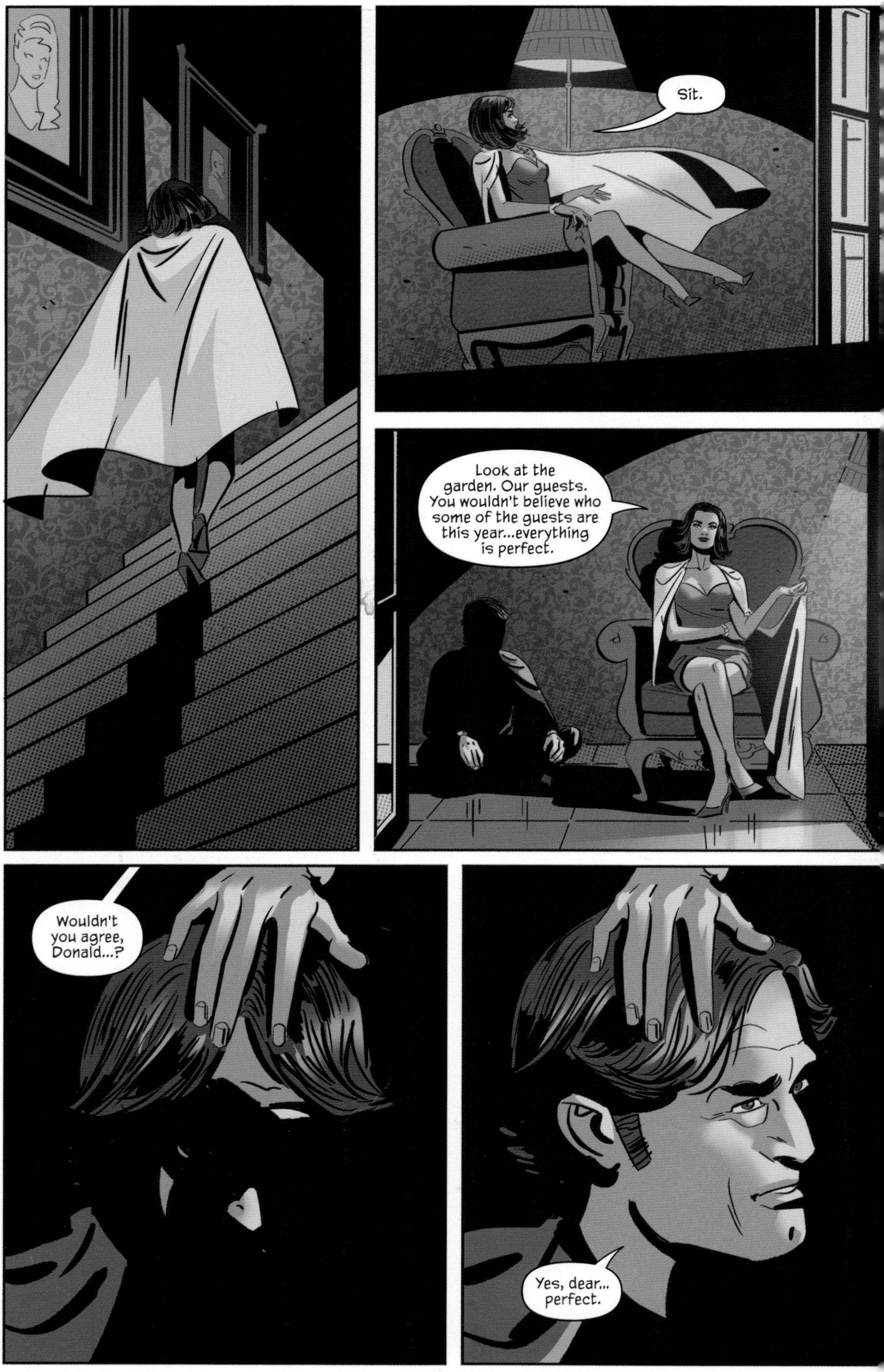
Sit.
Look at the garden. Our guests. You wouldn't believe who some of the guests are this year...everything is perfect.
Wouldn't you agree, Donald...?
Yes, dear... perfect.

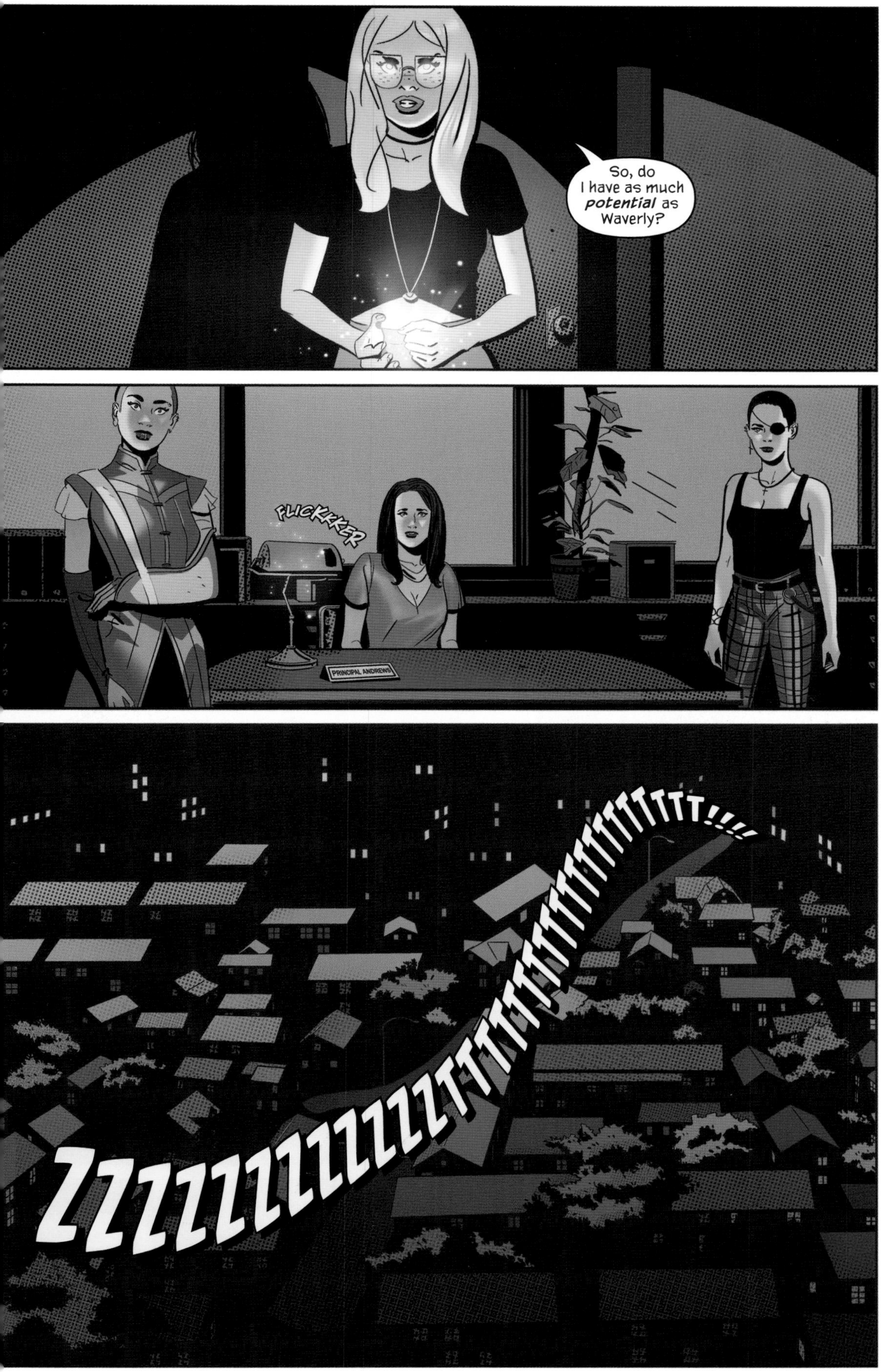
So, do I have as much *potential* as Waverly?
FLICKKKER
PRINCIPAL ANDREWS
ZZZZZZZZZZZZZZTTTTTTTTTTTTTTTTTTTTTTTTTTT!!!!

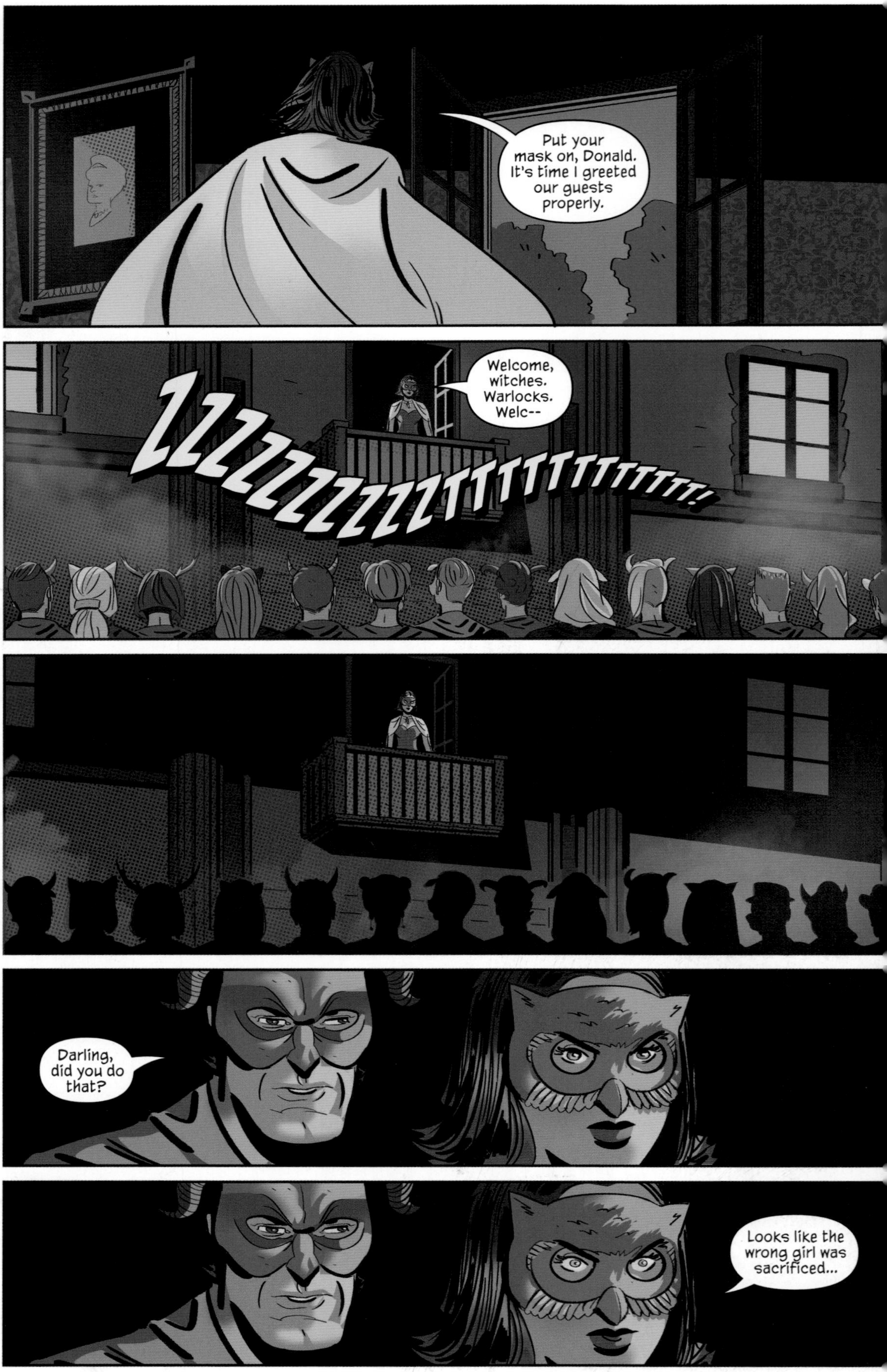
Put your mask on, Donald. It's time I greeted our guests properly.
Welcome, witches. Warlocks. Welc--
ZZZZZZZZZZZZZZZTTTTTTTTTTTTTT!
Darling, did you do that?
Looks like the wrong girl was sacrificed...

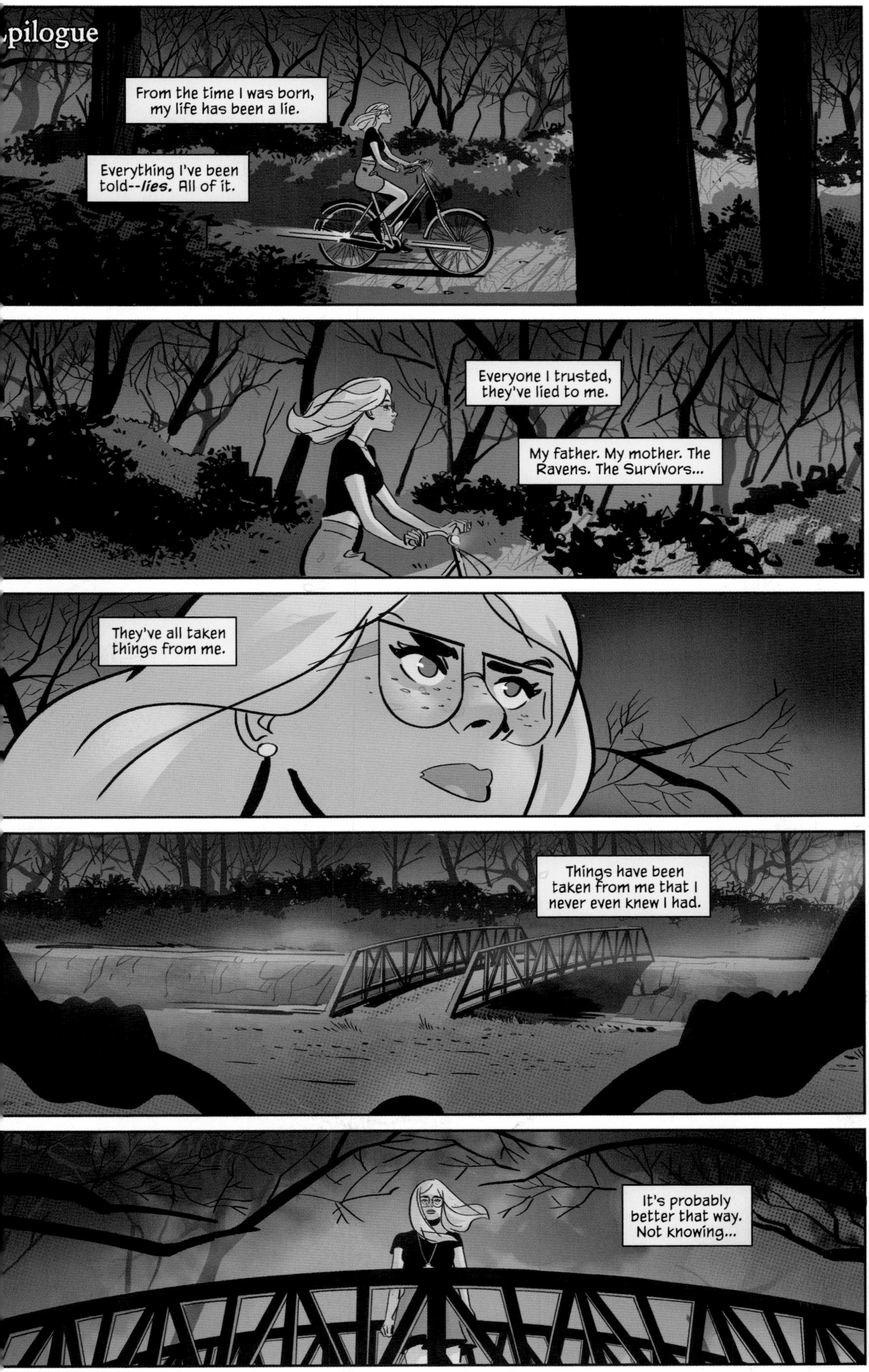
Epilogue
From the time I was born, my life has been a lie.
Everything I've been told--*lies.* All of it.
Everyone I trusted, they've lied to me.
My father. My mother. The Ravens. The Survivors...
They've all taken things from me.
Things have been taken from me that I never even knew I had.
It's probably better that way. Not knowing...

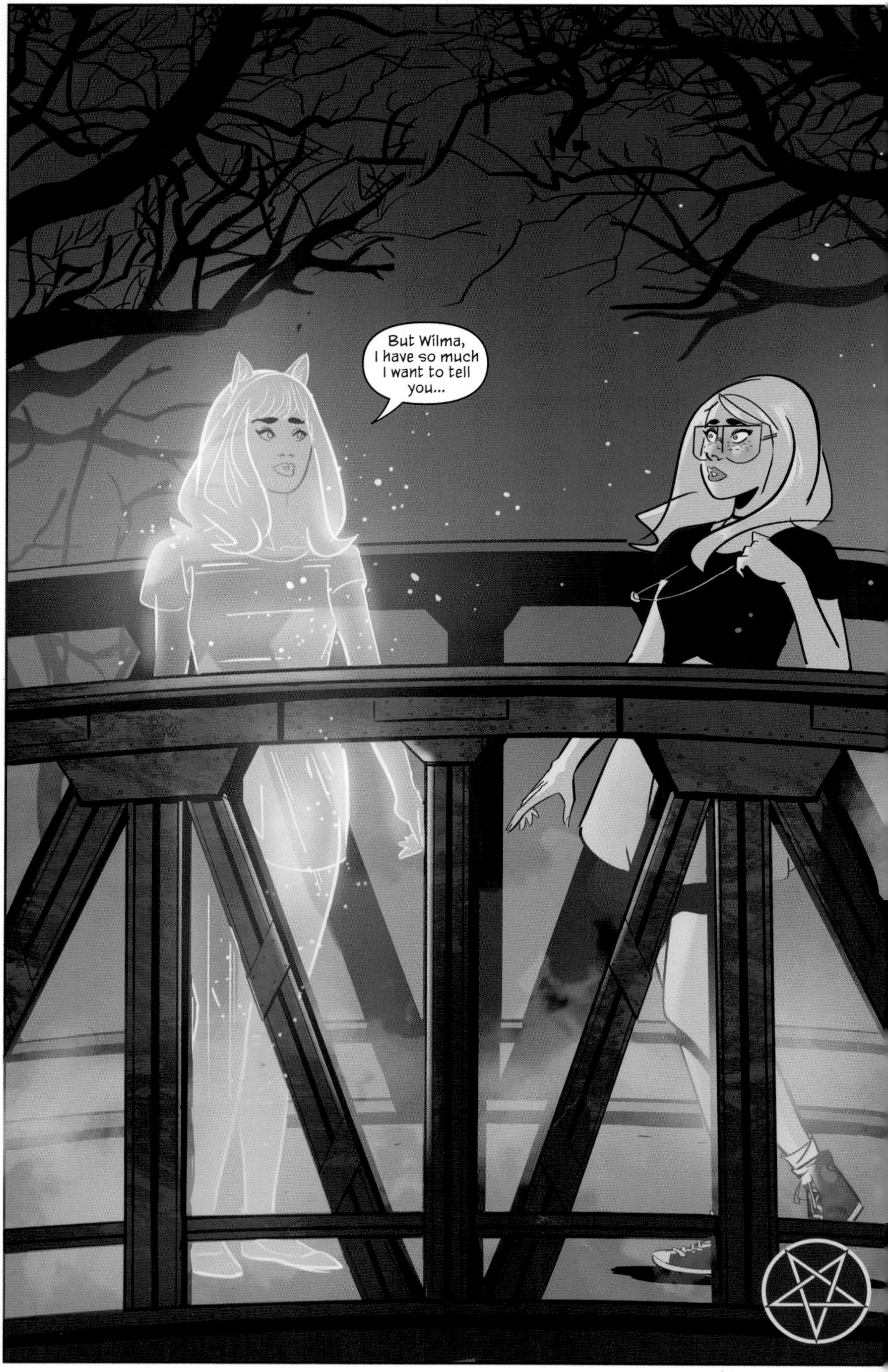
But Wilma, I have so much I want to tell you...

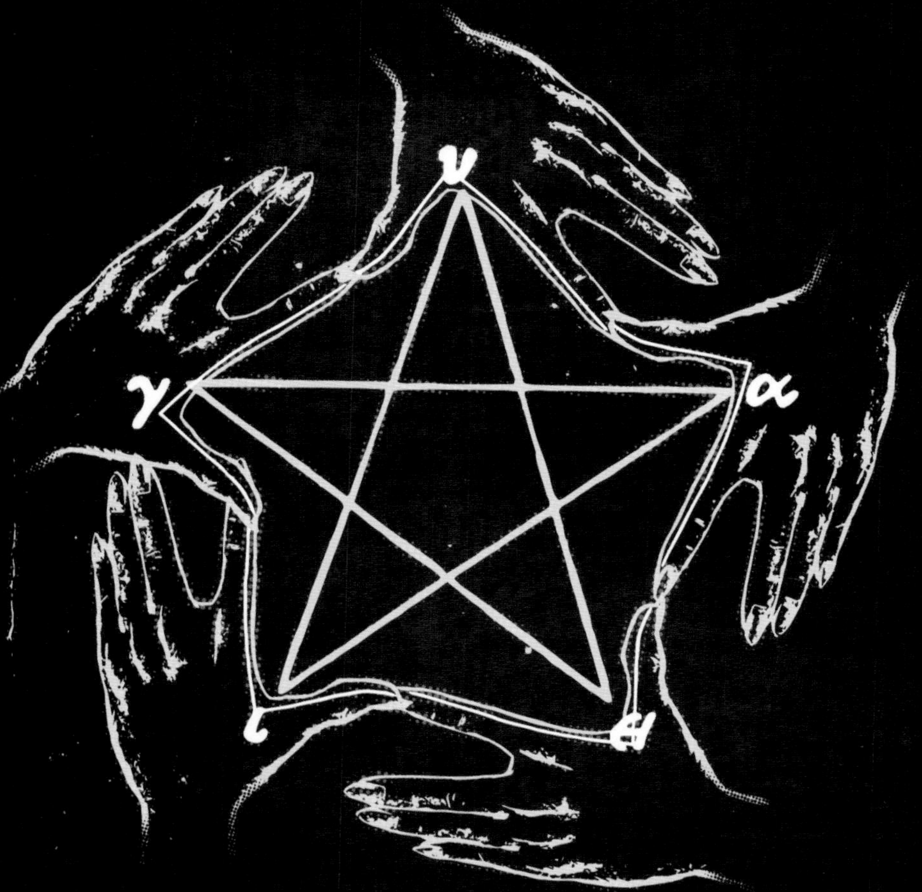
υ
α
ι
γ

Character Designs by
DAN PANOSIAN

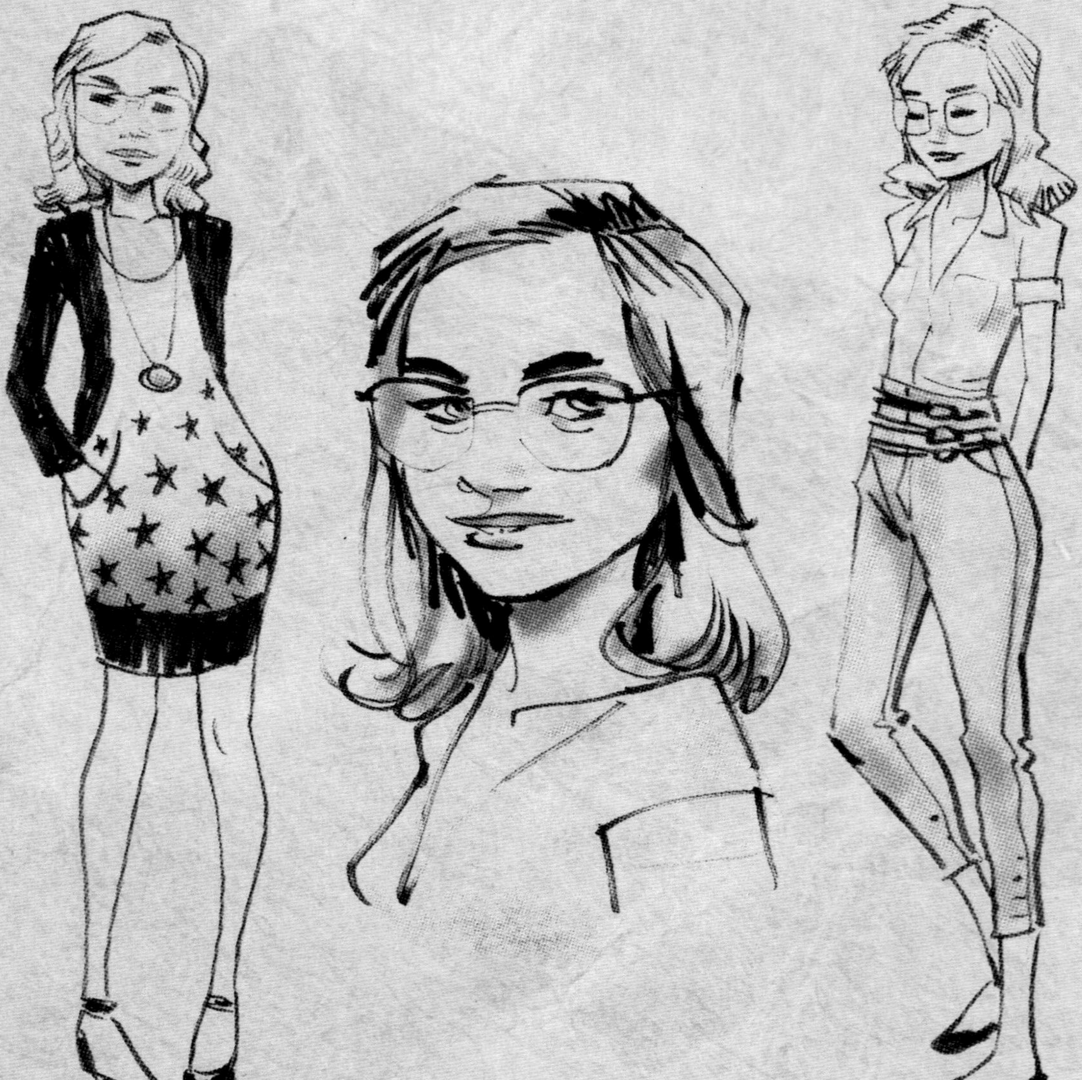

Wilma Farrington

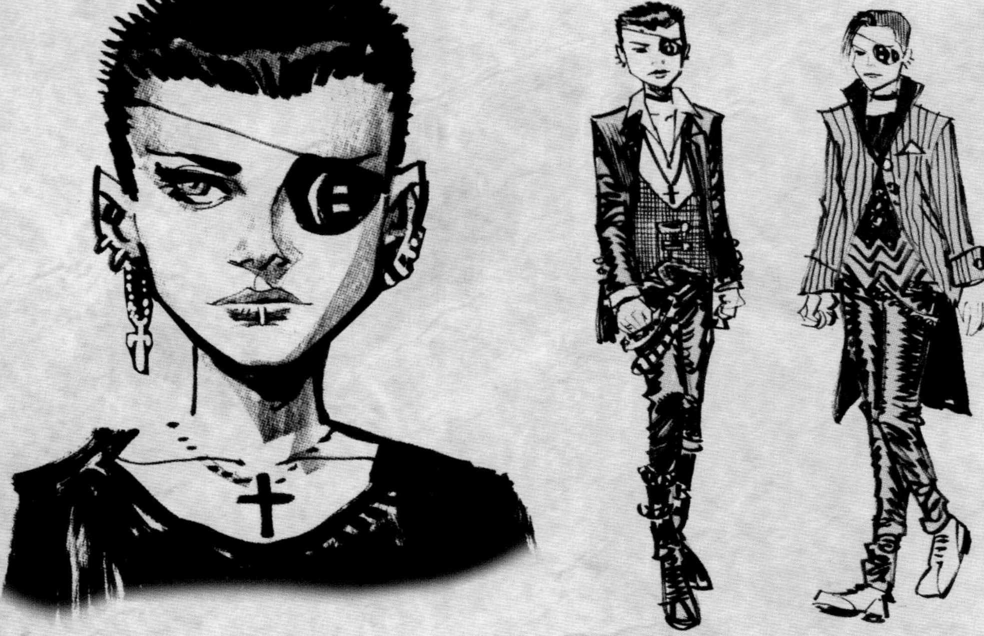

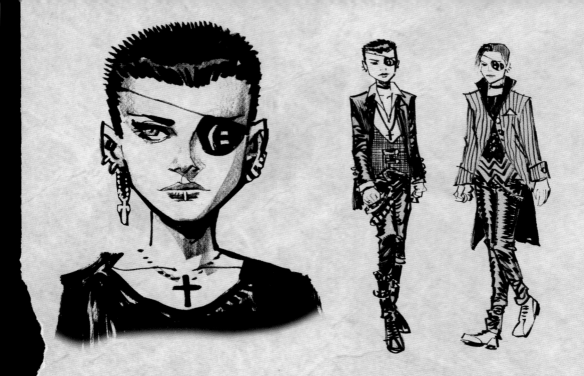

Victoria "Vikki" Bishop

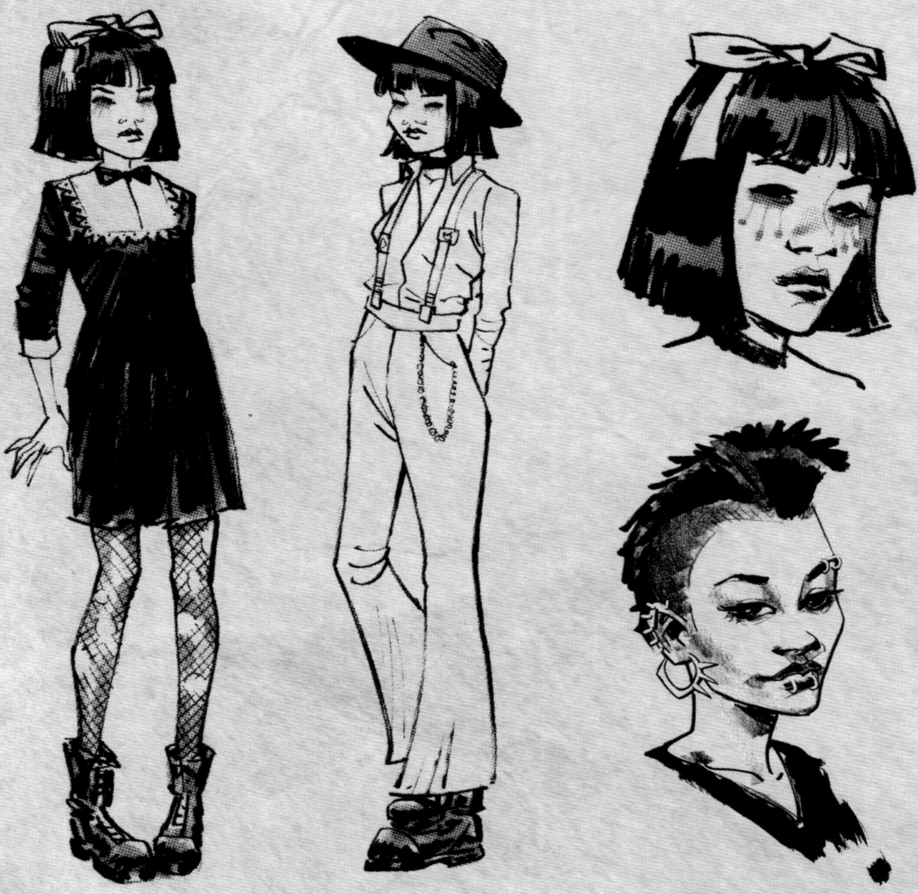

Yana Dane

Xooey and Zaida Rist

Scarlett Dansforth

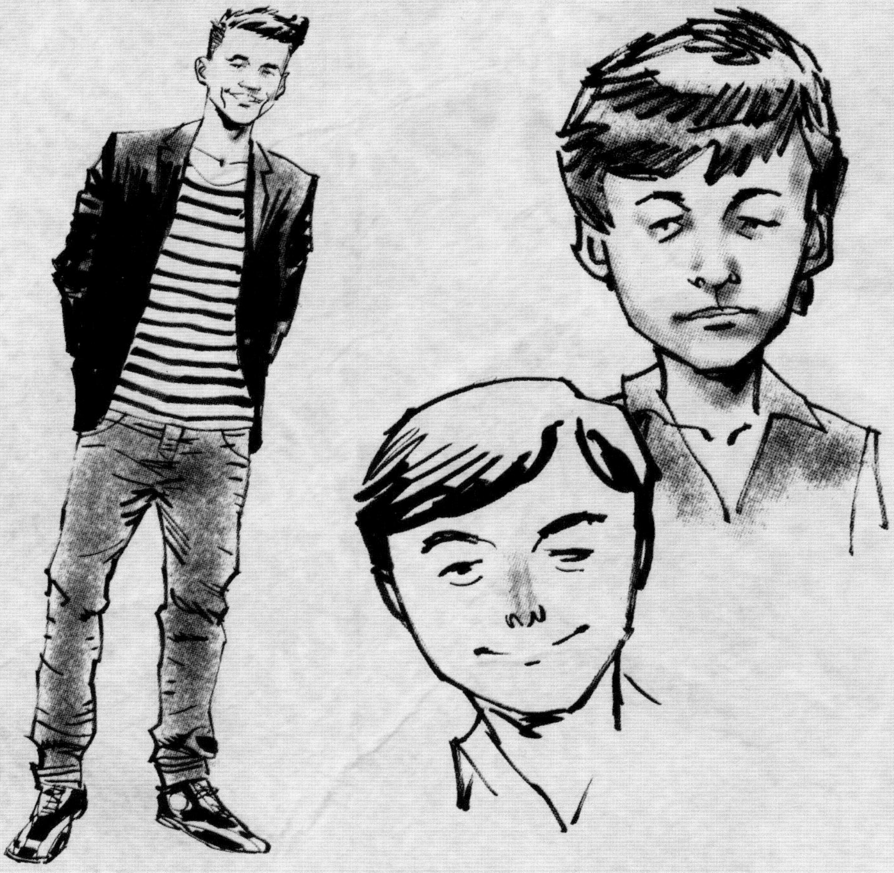

Ansel Friend

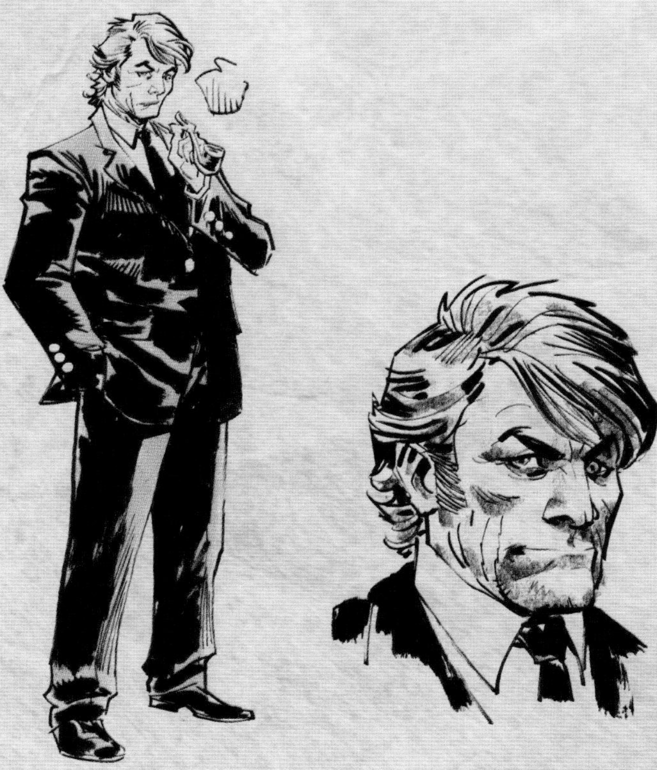

Donald "The Don" Dansforth

Waverly Good